Praise for *The Truthful Art*

"Alberto Cairo is widely acknowledged as journalism's preeminent visualization wiz. He is also journalism's preeminent data scholar. As newsrooms rush to embrace data journalism as a new tool—and toy—Cairo sets the standard for how data should be understood, analyzed, and presented. *The Truthful Art* is both a manifesto and a manual for how to use data to accurately, clearly, engagingly, imaginatively, beautifully, and reliably inform the public."

> —Jeff Jarvis, professor at CUNY Graduate School of Journalism and author of
> *Geeks Bearing Gifts: Imagining New Futures for News*

"A feast for both the eyes and mind, Alberto Cairo's *The Truthful Art* deftly explores the science—and art—of data visualization. The book is a must-read for scientists, educators, journalists, and just about anyone who cares about how to communicate effectively in the information age."

> —Michael E. Mann, Distinguished Professor, Penn State University and author of
> *The Hockey Stick and the Climate Wars*

"Alberto Cairo is a great educator and an engaging storyteller. In *The Truthful Art* he takes us on a rich, informed, and well-visualized journey that depicts the process by which one scrutinizes data and represents information. The book synthesizes a lot of knowledge and carefully explains how to create effective visualizations with a focus on statistical principles. *The Truthful Art* will be incredibly useful to both practitioners and students, especially within the arts and humanities, such as those involved in data journalism and information design."

> —Isabel Meirelles, professor at OCAD University (Canada) and author of
> *Design for Information*

"As soon as I started immersing myself in *The Truthful Art*, I was horrified (and somewhat ashamed) to realize how much I didn't know about data visualization. I've spent most of my career pursuing a more illustrative way to present data, but Alberto Cairo's clarifying prose superbly explained the finer points of data viz. Since Alberto warns us that "[data is] always noisy, dirty, and uncertain," everyone in this business had better read his book to find out how to properly construct visualizations that not only tell the truth, but also allow us to interact meaningfully with them."

> —Nigel Holmes, founder of Explanation Graphics

"To communicate data clearly, you have to think about it clearly. *The Truthful Art* dives deep and provides an enlightened introduction to the 'power tools' of data experts: science, statistics, and visualization."

—Fernanda Viégas and Martin Wattenberg, Google

"*The Truthful Art* is essential reading for my visual communication students and for anyone (at any level) who cares about telling a story visually. Get this book, read it, act on it. If you're looking for help to put your data visualization on the right track, this is it."

—John Grimwade, School of Visual Communication, Ohio University

"If I were smarter, had more patience with academia, and was more focused, I might turn out to be more like Alberto, closer to the brilliance that he applies to the nature of information architecture. His title explains a lot: truth represents a most fundamental of attitudes, in questions asked, answers given, and journeys taken. This [book] is a must on your thoughtful shelf of understanding."

—Richard Saul Wurman, founder of the TED Conference

the truthful art

data, charts, and maps for communication

alberto cairo

"Cairo sets the standard for how data should be understood, analyzed, and presented. *The Truthful Art* is both a manifesto and a manual for how to use data to accurately, clearly, engagingly, imaginatively, beautifully, and reliably inform the public."

Jeff Jarvis, professor, CUNY Graduate School of Journalism, and author of *Geeks Bearing Gifts: Imagining New Futures for News*

The Truthful Art:
Data, Charts, and Maps for Communication

Alberto Cairo

New Riders

100772748 5

Find us on the Web at www.newriders.com
New Riders is an imprint of Peachpit, a division of Pearson Education.
To report errors, please send a note to errata@peachpit.com

Acquisitions Editor: Nikki Echler McDonald
Production Editor: Tracey Croom
Development Editor: Cathy Lane
Copy Editor: Cathy Lane
Proofers: Patricia Pane, Kim Wimpsett
Compositor: Kim Scott, Bumpy Design
Indexer: James Minkin
Cover and Interior Designer: Mimi Heft
Cover Illustration: Moritz Stefaner

ISBN 13: 9780321934079
ISBN 10: 0321934075

9 8 7 6 5 4 3 2 1

Printed and bound in the United States of America

To my father

Acknowledgments

I always chuckle when someone calls me an "expert" on visualization or infographics. As a journalist, I've made a profession of being an amateur, in the two senses of the word: someone who doesn't have a deep understanding of anything, but also someone who does what he does due to unabashed love for the craft.

This book is a tribute to that second kind of amateur, folks who bring good data to the world in a time when society is drowning in tsunamis of spin and misinformation. They know that it is possible to change the world for the better if we repeat the truth often and loud enough.

I'd like to first thank my University of Miami (UM) colleague Rich Beckman. It's not an exaggeration to say that I wouldn't be where I am today without his help, advice, and mentorship.

Seth Hamblin, a friend at *The Wall Street Journal*, passed away while I was writing this book. Seth was in love with infographics and visualization. When I told him about *The Truthful Art*, he got as excited as a kid. He was a beautiful human being, and he'll be missed.

To Greg Shepherd, dean of UM's School of Communication; Nick Tsinoremas, director of UM's Center for Computational Science (CCS); Sawsan Khuri, also from CCS, a great colleague and better friend; Sam Terilli, head of our department of journalism; and Kim Grinfeder, who leads our Interactive Media program. Also at UM, I'd like to thank my colleagues in the departments of Journalism and Interactive Media, and at the Center for Communication, Culture, and Change.

To Phil Meyer, whose book *Precision Journalism* inspired me many years ago. In fact, I wrote *The Truthful Art* with the goal of being a *Precision Journalism* for the new century.

To my past colleagues at *La Voz de Galicia*, *Diario16*, DPI Comunicación, *El Mundo*, and Editora Globo. Among them, Helio Gurovitz, the former managing editor at Globo's *Época* magazine, who combines a deep knowledge of journalism with an unusual sensibility of how to use numbers and graphics.

Also, to my clients and partners worldwide, particularly Jim Friedland, for all his support in the past two years.

Many people read this book while it was in the works. My editor, Nikki McDonald, and my copyeditor, Cathy Lane, kept an eye on me at all times, and did their best to make me meet deadlines (they failed).

Stephen Few sent me detailed notes about each chapter. Steve is both a friend and arguably my most severe critic. I've done my best to incorporate as much from his feedback as possible, but not all. I know that Steve will still disagree with some of my musings, but those disagreements can be great topics to ponder while enjoying some fine wine and cheese.

Erik Jacobsen also provided detailed feedback. His notes have been invaluable.

Three statisticians, Diego Kuonen, Heather Krause, and Jerzy Wieczorek, read the most technical chapters and made sure that I was not writing anything particularly silly. Others who commented on the book are: Andy Cotgreage, Kenneth Field, Jeff Jarvis, Scott Klein, Michael E. Mann, Isabel Meirelles, Fernanda Viégas, Martin Wattenberg, and Sisi Wei. Thank you all.

Thanks also to all the individuals and organizations who let me showcase their work in *The Truthful Art*. You're too numerous to mention, but you'll see your names in pages to come.

Some of my followers on Twitter volunteered for the last round of proofreading. They are: Mohit Chawla, Fernando Cucchietti, Stijn Debrouwere, Alex Lea, Neil Richards, Frédéric Schütz, and Tom Shanley.

Special thanks to Moritz Stefaner, for giving me permission to use one of his amazing graphics on the cover of this book.

To Nancy.

Finally, and above all, thanks to my family.

About the Author

Alberto Cairo is the Knight Chair in Visual Journalism at the School of Communication of the University of Miami (UM), where he heads specializations in infographics and data visualization. He's also director of the visualization program at UM's Center for Computational Science, and Visualization Innovator in Residence at Univisión.

He is the author of the books *Infografía 2.0: Visualización interactiva de información en prensa*, published just in Spain in 2008, and *The Functional Art: An Introduction to Information Graphics and Visualization* (New Riders, 2012).

In the past two decades, Cairo has been director of infographics and visualization at news organizations in Spain and Brazil, besides consulting with companies and educational institutions in more than 20 countries. He also was a professor at the University of North Carolina-Chapel Hill between 2005 and 2009.

Cairo's personal weblog is www.thefunctionalart.com. His corporate website is www.albertocairo.com.

His Twitter handle is @albertocairo.

Additional Materials

I designed many of the charts and maps you're about to see in *The Truthful Art*, but I haven't written much about the software I used to create them. If you're interested in learning about tools, please visit my weblog, www.thefunctionalart.com, and go to the **Tutorials and Resources** section on the upper menu.

There, you will find several articles and video lessons I recorded about programs and languages like R, iNzight, and Yeeron, among others.

Contents

PART III functional

PART IV practice

Preface

It All Begins with a Spark

Why is it that when one man builds a wall, the next man immediately needs to know what's on the other side?

—Tyrion Lannister in George R.R. Martin's *A Game of Thrones*

There's probably something you don't know about college professors: we tend to have peculiar hobbies.

In October 2014, I spent my entire fall recess catching up with R, a programming language for statistical analysis; ggplot2, an R library that creates nice-looking charts; and Tableau, a data visualization program.[1] Learning any software tool without using it is impossible, so I needed some data to play with, and not just any data, but data I could care about.

A few months back, my family and I had moved to a new home, so I had briefly visited the Miami-Dade County Public Schools website (DadeSchools.net) to check the quality of the elementary school, middle school, and high school in our area. Each had a grade of A. I had felt reassured at the time, but also a bit

---

1 I hope that this doesn't impress you. I am by no means an advanced user of any of these tools. All graphics in these pages were designed with very little knowledge of how to use them properly. For more information, visit http://www.r-project.org/, http://ggplot2.org/, and http://www.tableau.com.

Region	SchoolName	Reading2012	Reading2013	ReadingDifference	Math2012	Math2013	MathDifference	SchoolGrade	BoardDistrict
5	0041 AIR BASE ELEMENTAR	82	80	-2	71	75	4	A	9
7	0070 CORAL REEF MONT AC	71	73	2	64	56	-8	A	9
4	0071 EUGENIA B THOMAS K	69	69	0	66	64	-2	A	5
7	0072 SUMMERVILLE ADVANT	57	50	-7	50	54	4	B	9
6	0073 MANDARIN LAKES K-8	34	32	-2	38	39	1	C	9
6	0081 LENORA BRAYNON SMI	28	29	1	26	47	21	F	2
1	0091 BOB GRAHAM EDUCATI	68	70	2	68	66	-2	A	4
1	0092 NORMAN S EDELCUP	73	72	-1	78	77	-1	A	3
7	0100 MATER ACADEMY	68	68	0	73	76	3	A	4
4	0101 ARCOLA LAKE ELEMEN	39	32	-7	41	39	-2	C	2
7	0102 MIAMI COMMUNITY CH	38	41	3	43	47	4	D	9
4	0111 MAYA ANGELOU ELEME	45	35	-10	59	50	-9	B	5
4	0121 AUBURNDALE ELEMENT	53	51	-2	56	55	-1	A	6
4	0122 DR ROLANDO ESPINOS	65	64	-1	66	63	-3	A	5
5	0125 NORMA BUTLER BOSSA	70	67	-3	74	70	-4	A	7
5	0161 AVOCADO ELEMENTARY	45	33	-12	45	45	0		9
4	0201 BANYAN ELEMENTARY	73	74	1	72	70	-2	A	8
5	0211 DR MANUEL C BARREI	71	71	0	74	68	-6	A	7
1	0231 AVENTURA WATERWAYS	68	68	0	67	67	0	A	3
1	0241 R K BROAD/BAY HARB	76	75	-1	81	77	-4	A	3
5	0251 ETHEL KOGER BECKHA	85	80	-5	89	90	1	A	8
6	0261 BEL-AIRE ELEMENTAR	32	32	0	36	48	12	D	9
5	0271 BENT TREE ELEMENTA	70	61	-9	69	60	-9	A	8
5	0311 GOULDS ELEMENTARY	36	40	4	51	52	1	B	9
7	0312 MATER GARDENS ACAD	75	76	1	84	85	1	A	4
1	0321 BISCAYNE ELEMENTAR	45	42	-3	52	50	-2	B	3
7	0332 SOMERSET ACAD -SIL	62	66	4	54	64	10	A	9
7	0339 SOMERSET ACAD -SO	67	57	-10	60	54	-6	B	9
1	0341 ARCH CREEK ELEMENT	47	48	1	47	48	1	B	1
7	0342 PINECREST ACADEMY	72	75	3	78	76	-2	A	7
6	0361 BISCAYNE GARDENS E	37	35	-2	39	37	-2	D	1
7	0400 RENAISSANCE ELEM C	80	82	2	76	82	6	A	5

Figure P.1 The top portion of a spreadsheet with data from public schools in Miami-Dade County.

uneasy, as I hadn't done any comparison with schools in other neighborhoods. Perhaps my learning R and Tableau could be the perfect opportunity to do so.

DadeSchools.net has a neat data section, so I visited it and downloaded a spreadsheet of performance scores from all schools in the county. You can see a small portion of it—the spreadsheet is 461 rows tall—in **Figure P.1**. The figures in the Reading2012 and Reading2013 columns are the percentage of students from each school who attained a reading level considered as satisfactory in those two consecutive years. Math2012 and Math2013 correspond to the percentage of students who were deemed reasonably numerate for their age.

While learning how to write childishly simple scripts in R, I created rankings and bar charts to compare all schools. I didn't get any striking insight out of this exercise, although I ascertained that the three public schools in our neighborhood are decent indeed. My job was done, but I didn't stop there. I played a bit more.

I made R generate a scatter plot (**Figure P.2**). Each dot is one school. The position on the X-axis is the percentage of students who read at their proper level in 2013. The Y-axis is the same percentage for math proficiency. Both variables

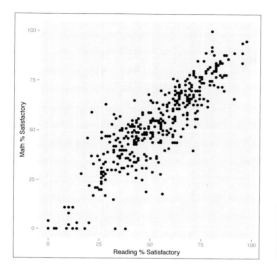

Figure P.2 Each dot on the chart is a school. Reading and math skills are strongly related.

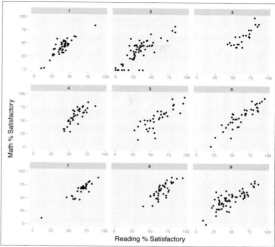

Figure P.3 The same data, divided by school board.

are clearly linked: the larger one gets, the larger the other one tends to become.[2] This makes sense. There is nothing very surprising other than a few outliers, and the fact that there are some schools in which no student is considered proficient in reading and/or math. This could be due to mistakes in the data set, of course.

After that, I learned how to write a short script to design not just one but several scatter plots, one for each of the nine school board districts in Miami-Dade County. It was then that I became really intrigued. See the results in **Figure P.3**.

There are quite a few interesting facts in that array. For instance, most schools in Districts 3, 7, and 8 are fine. Students in Districts 1 and 2, on the other hand, perform rather poorly.

At the time I was not familiar with the geography of the Miami-Dade school system, so I went online to find a map of it. I also visited the Census Bureau website to get a map of income data. I redesigned and overlaid them. (See **Figure P.4**. Warning: I didn't make any adjustment to these maps, so the overlap isn't perfect.) I got what I foresaw: the worst-performing districts, 1 and 2, encompass low-income neighborhoods, like Liberty City, Little Haiti, and Overtown.

---

2 In statistics, we may call this a "strong positive correlation." But I'm getting a bit ahead of myself.

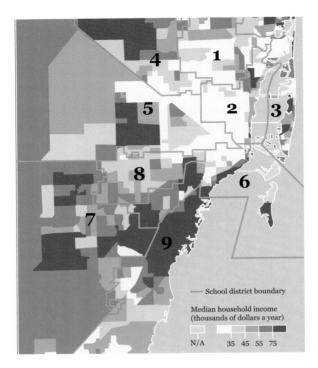

Figure P.4 Median household income in the nine school board districts of Miami-Dade County.

Immediately, questions started piling up in my head. Is the relationship between bad schools and low household income direct? Does a bad education lead to reduced wages? Or do kids coming from low-income families go to school being already disadvantaged, and that worsens the scores of the schools they attend? Am I getting causality right? What are other possible variables that affect both school performance and income?

What about the outliers in those charts, those schools in Districts 1 and 7, for instance, that are so far from their flocks? Or that school in District 3 that got a perfect score in math? And what about District 6? Schools in that plot are much more spread out than in the others. Is that related to the sharp divide between a richer strip on the east (Coconut Grove) and poorer blocks on the west within that school district?

And more: have all these percentages and grades changed substantially in the past few years? If so, is it due to real variation in the quality of our public education or because of changes in the methods researchers use to measure attainment? So many questions.

And so the seeds for many potential stories got planted. I didn't have an idea of what they might be at that point or if any of them would be worth telling. I just got a glimpse, an enticing clue. As most visualization designers and data journalists I know will tell you, sometimes it is not you who finds good ideas when you're seeking them. Instead, good ideas find you in the most unexpected circumstances.

Good ideas are fleeting things, so I feverishly scribbled notes in a computer application called Stickies, short messages for my future self, musings of a mind in a state of joyous flow. I added, "Find some education experts.[3] Ask them. Contact the folks running dadeschools.net. You'll likely need more data from the U.S. Census Bureau's website." And so on and so forth.

As the saying goes, every great story begins with a spark. Fun ensues.

---

3 Here's Robert B. Reich—who isn't an expert on education but was Secretary of Labor under President Bill Clinton—in his book *Saving Capitalism* (2015): "A large portion of the money to support public schools comes from local property taxes. The federal government provides only about 10 percent of all funding, and the states provide 45 percent, on average. The rest is raised locally (...) Real estate markets in lower-income communities remain weak, so local tax revenues are down. As we segregate by income into different communities, schools in lower-income areas have fewer resources than ever. The result is widening disparities in funding per pupil, to the direct disadvantage of poor kids." Another possible clue to follow.

Introduction

The Island of Knowledge and the Shoreline of Wonder

Never before have we had so many tools to learn and to communicate. Yet the art of talking, listening, and ascertaining the truth seems more elusive than ever in this Internet and cable age, lost in a bitter stream of blather and misinformation.

—Maureen Dowd, "Toilet-Paper Barricades,"
The New York Times (August 11, 2009)

It's a fact of life that kids put their parents to the test with their boundless and unpredictable curiosity. I have three small children, ages 4, 8, and 10. Here are some of the questions that I got from them while writing these lines, followed by my thoughts and the actual answers I gave them.

Ten-year-old boy: "Daddy, how can I build a hobbit house in the Minecraft video game?"

My thought: "That's a damn good question. Would it be possible to build J.R.R. Tolkien's Middle Earth in Minecraft?" (Sorry, I'm a nerd.)

My answer: "No idea, kiddo. I don't even know how to play Minecraft. Why don't you watch *The Lord of the Rings* movies again? I will be happy to watch them with you."

Four-year-old girl: "Daddy, do you have a baby in your tummy?"

Thought: "Man, kids can be brutally honest."

Answer: "No, sweetie. Only mommies can carry babies in their tummies. Daddy just has big muscles."

Eight-year-old girl: "Daddy, why do planets never stop spinning?"

Thought: "Huh…"

Answer: "Why don't you Google it, honey?" (Just kidding, although I believe that many parents in my position would go for that one.)

My actual answer was: "Can you give me a few hours? Then I'll be able to explain it to you."

My daughter's question forced me to take my fingers off the keyboard and think for a minute. My memory of Newtonian physics was a bit rusty, but I was sure that the fact that planets keep rotating is related to the laws of motion. I dusted a couple of popular science books from my shelves and also looked for some articles on the Internet. Then I grabbed a pencil, a pen, and some crayons: I think more clearly when I draw. I ended up with a series of sketches that I'm going to call an "infographic," a graphical display intended to convey information.

Here's the story I told my daughter.

Our First Infographic

Let's begin here, on planet Earth. When you throw a ball (**Figure I.1**), it tends to move forward and spin around its own center. The faster we throw the ball and the heavier it is, the more momentum, or impetus, it carries. There are two kinds of momentum in this case: linear (forward motion) and angular (spinning.)

It is obvious that the ball will not move forever. Eventually, it will stop. Why? First of all, the ground, as well as the air, provides friction (**Figure I.2**). Air is a

Figure I.I The first sketch that I made for my daughter. When you throw a ball to the floor, it tends to move forward (linear momentum) and to rotate around its own axis (angular momentum).

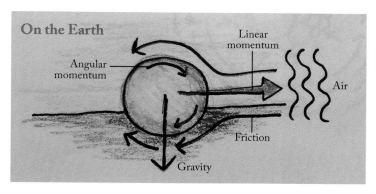

Figure I.2 Gravity and friction with the air and with the ground will make the ball stop moving.

fluid, like water. Imagine that you jump into a swimming pool. When you enter the water, your speed decreases, right? That's friction at work. Friction is a word we use to describe an interesting phenomenon: the air and the ground absorb the momentum that the ball carries.

Now, imagine that you're an astronaut floating in deep space (**Figure I.3**). (My daughter pointed out that this illustration is inaccurate; the person in it should be wearing a spacesuit! Extra credit for her.) There's no air in space. Therefore, there's almost no friction. If we throw our imaginary green ball, it is likely that

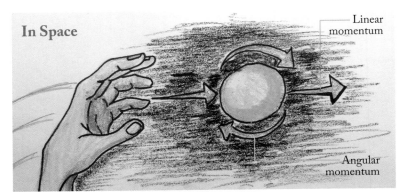

Figure 1.3 No visual explanation is perfect, and this one isn't an exception. Notice that the drawing isn't accurate, and not just because the person in it isn't wearing a space suit. If the hand adopts that position when throwing, the ball won't spin that way, or at all.

it will take millions and millions of years to stop moving forward. It won't stop spinning until then either. We call this **conservation of momentum**: if there's nothing to interfere with the ball, it won't stop moving.

Next, let's go back in time zillions of years, to the era when none of the planets in the solar system existed. Just the sun was there, surrounded by large clouds of dust particles. These clouds spun at a very, veeeery slow speed.[1] The particles were held together and bound to the sun by gravity (**Figure 1.4**).

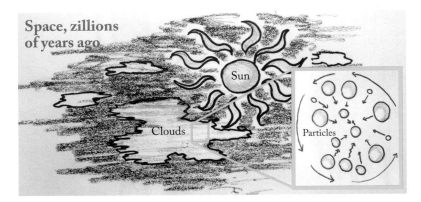

Figure 1.4 Our solar system, zillions of years ago.

1 Where did this initial momentum come from? There's some homework for you!

Something interesting happened then: little by little, gravity made these little particles move closer and closer to each other. And the closer they were, the faster they spun. The reason why that happened is a bit complicated to explain, but it isn't crucial for now, so let's leave it for another day.

The last step is the easiest to understand. The particles in the clouds moved so close to each other that they ended up merging. Earth and the other planets were born from collapsing dust clouds (**Figure I.5**), and they keep spinning, at least for now, because there's very little in space to stop them from doing so.

I must confess that my daughter didn't get all this at first. It was just a bit too much information to digest. So I went over the entire sequence of drawings with her again. While doing it, I realized that this exercise embodied a few points that I make in all my courses, namely:

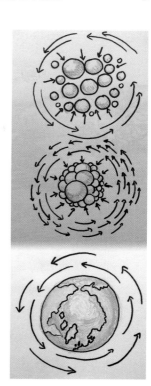

Figure I.5 The particles collapse and form the planets in the solar system.

- **When you design a graphic to explain something, getting the information right comes first.** No good infographic or data visualization—we'll learn the difference between the two soon—can be based on deficient data and analysis. The quality of your graphics depends fundamentally on the quality of your reporting or research, not just on how good a graphic designer you are.

- **Being concise and clear doesn't imply oversimplifying.** Any act of communication involves a controlled reduction of complexity, up to the point when reducing matters further would hurt the integrity of the information. I adapted the message to my audience by getting rid of jargon and equations, but I respected the essence of the facts and my daughter's intelligence.

- **Good design isn't about embellishment but about structuring information to enable understanding.** That said, aesthetic appeal is a worthy goal, as it can help make our messages more attractive and, as a consequence, more effective.

- **Graphics that encode information function as cognitive aids.** If I had described the process using *just* words, it's likely that you'd feel compelled to mentally visualize little balls and arrows. My drawings are intended to do that work for your brain.

- **If words are sometimes useless by themselves, so are charts, maps, diagrams, and illustrations.** It is in the *combination* of words (spoken or written) and visuals that the magic of understanding often happens.

Quite good for such a simple exercise, right? And there's more.

The Island of Knowledge

I got another insight from this tale about spinning planets. After I finished the explanation for the second time, my daughter remained silent for a few seconds. Then she asked, "OK, I get it. But Earth spins very fast. Why aren't we thrown into space, then?"

Understanding never quenches the thirst for *more* understanding, does it? Quite the contrary is true: the more we learn, the more aware we become of the gaps in our knowledge. As physicist **Marcelo Gleiser** wrote, "The knowledge that we have defines the knowledge that we can have… As knowledge shifts, we ask new kinds of questions that we couldn't have anticipated."[2]

Gleiser's book is titled after the most evocative metaphor I know about the human quest for understanding: the island of knowledge. It seems that the first person to refer to it was New York Methodist pastor **Ralph W. Sockman**, who is believed to have said: **"The larger the island of knowledge, the longer the shoreline of wonder."**[3]

Chet Raymo (1998) expanded the metaphor beautifully:

> All scientific knowledge that we have of this world, or will ever have, is as an island in the sea of mystery. We live in our partial knowledge as the Dutch live on polders claimed from the sea. We dike and fill. We dredge up soil from the bed of mystery and build ourselves room to grow.

Of course, being a visualization designer, I couldn't resist making a little illustration of what happened inside my daughter's brain (**Figure I.6**): the island of knowledge expanded for her, but so did the shoreline of wonder, draining new land out of the sea of mystery.

---

2   In his book *The Island of Knowledge*, (2014).

3   I haven't been able to track the source of this quote, so take this with a grain of salt.

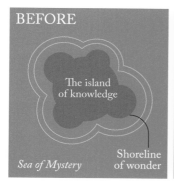 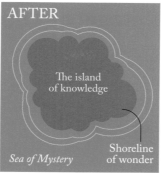

Figure I.6 The island of knowledge and the shoreline of wonder.

Finding the right answers to good questions makes us capable of posing even better and more profound ones. We can all enjoy this process. If you allow me a brief digression, this is the reason why I believe that we should teach our kids to love not knowledge per se, but *learning*. They should be encouraged to cherish the very quests they undertake, not just their products.

Good data visualizations and explanation infographics **communicate information** and, as a result, they can increase our understanding. That's their first role, and it's what I was focusing on when I made the drawings for my daughter.

But **graphics may also prompt exploration**. They reveal as much as much as they lead to new questions. A graphic may tell you a compelling story, but it can also invite you to expand the shoreline of wonder in ways that its creators didn't predict. Here's famous visualization designer **Moritz Stefaner** in a manifesto titled "Worlds, not stories."[4]

> Data visualization can help us both to understand complex issues a bit better, but also to provide images to debate about, to refer back to, and sometimes just to meditate over... I want [people] to use the visualizations I provide as starting points for their own explorations... Consequently, any serious visualization of a sufficiently complex topic should always aim at exposing the complexity, the inner contradictions, the manifold nature of the underlying phenomenon. I like to provide users with a structured way to explore a complex phenomenon on their own terms, in a sensually rich mosaic of media and facts rather than a pre-digested narrative with a surprise at the end. To me, interesting topics rarely boil down to a single story.

4   Moritz Stefaner: http://well-formed-data.net/archives/1027/worlds-not-stories

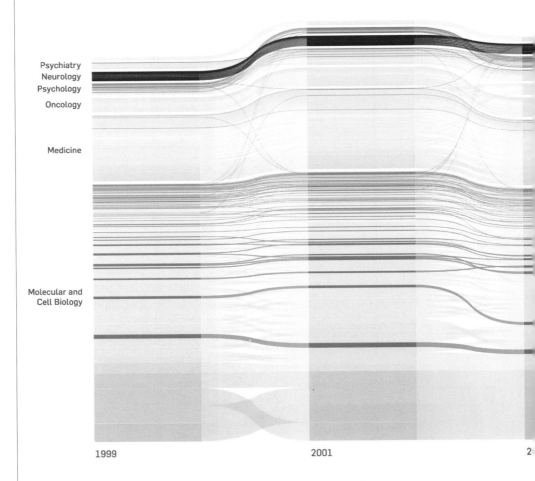

The emergence of neuroscience

Psychiatry
Neurology
Psychology

Oncology

Medicine

Molecular and
Cell Biology

1999   2001   2

This visualization documents the formation of neuroscience as a field of its own right over the last decade. Originally scattered across related disciplines (such as medicine, molecular and cell biology or neurology), the neuroscientific journals start to define a niche of their own, reflected in the dense cluster emerging in 2005.

First, almost 8000 scientific journals are clust citation patterns, and using the map equation, into groups, the map equation specifies the the can describe a trajectory of a random walker c ing the map equation over all possible network information flow across directed and weightec ture of how citations flow through science.

Second, using the Eigenfactor™ Score, the jou portance – much as Google's PageRank algori pages. The Eigenfactor™ Score measures the would spend with the respective journal, if the by randomly following citations in the journals

Figure 1.7 Visualization by Moritz Stefaner (http://moritz.stefaner.eu), in collaboration with Martin Rosvall, Jevin West, and Carl Bergstrom at the Bergstrom Lab, University of Washington.

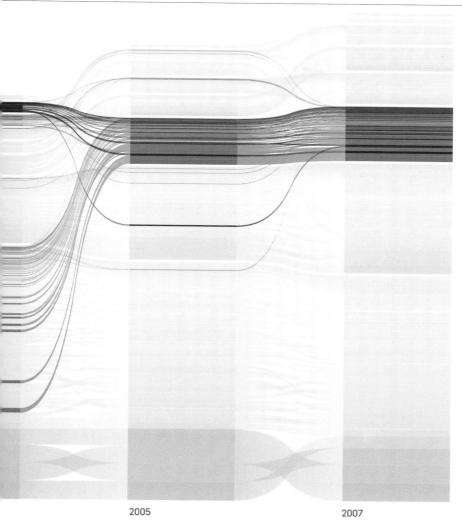

Neuroscience

2005   2007

This process is repeated in two-year chunks from 1999–2007, in order to capture changes in clustering and shifts in importance over the years. For this diagram, we picked only the clusters relevant to the formation of neuroscience.

In the visualization, each cluster occupies a vertical column block in the respective year's column, further subdivided into a block for each journal. Each journal is connected with a horizontal band over the years. The height of each journal reflects the Eigenfactor Score. All journals in the cluster that corresponds to the field of neuroscience in year 2007 are highlighted to tell the story of the formation of this field of science. The coloring is based on the cluster assignments in the first year, 1999.

Visualization: Moritz Stefaner (http://moritz.stefaner.eu)
Data analysis: Eigenfactor team (http://eigenfactor.org)

http://well-formed.eigenfactor.org

Stefaner doesn't reject traditional linear narrative techniques outright, but he prefers to build interactive displays that enable discovery. His work embodies this approach. In 2009, he partnered up with the Bergstrom lab in the biology department at the University of Washington to create **Eigenfactor**,[5] a project that visualizes citation patterns between scientific journals.

Some of those visualizations are illuminating. Take a look at **Figure I.7** (on the previous pages). What do you notice? To me, besides the striking beauty of this Sankey diagram,[6] its central message is clear: modern neuroscience is the result of the confluence of several disciplines.

That's the main story I extract. Yours can be different than mine. What you'll get from this graphic depends on the knowledge that you had before facing it. As a journalist, I can be standing on a different place of the shoreline of wonder than a scientist. Stefaner's visualization may expand the shoreline in slightly different directions for each of us (**Figure I.8**) and, therefore, it will lead us to stare at two increasingly disparate patches of the horizon above the sea of mystery.

A few weeks ago, I stumbled upon a graphic designed by data scientist **Gilad Lotan** (**Figure I.9**) that further illustrates how the communication and exploration

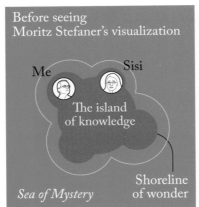

Figure I.8 The island of knowledge expands in different directions, depending on your previous knowledge. The role of scientist in this illustration is played by my friend Sisi Wei, who works for the nonprofit investigative journalism organization ProPublica.

---

5   Visualizing information flow in science:
http://truth-and-beauty.net/projects/well-formed-eigenfactor/

6   There's some jargon for you! We'll learn about Sankey diagrams soon.

Figure 1.9 Visualization by Gilad Lotan (http://giladlotan.com/). Lotan writes, "This is a network graph representation of my Twitter followers after I acquired the bots. The top cluster represents my 'real' followers, who are intertwined: many follow each other, clearly a community of users. The bottom purple region represents the fake accounts, who are completely separate—structurally they're clearly not a real community, with very little connectivity between the accounts."

dimensions of visualization design complement each other. In an article published in the *Los Angeles Times* and on the website Medium.com,[7] Lotan described a particularly quirky experiment.

In the past few years, services that promise to increase your standing on social media are thriving. For a few bucks, you can be followed by thousands of fake Twitter accounts. Lotan wanted to answer two questions: first, does buying fake followers lead to more real followers? And second, how are fake followers

7   Gilad Lotan: '(Fake) friends with (Real) benefits':
https://medium.com/i-data/fake-friends-with-real-benefits-eec8c4693bd3

connected to accounts created by actual people? The short answer to the first question is *yes*. To understand why, you should read Lotan's article.

The answer to the second question is in the visualization that Lotan designed with the data he collected. The multi-colored blob on top represents his 2,600 followers before the experiment. Being part of a virtual community, the nodes are strongly connected and close to each other. The purple cloud at the bottom corresponds to the 4,000 faux followers Lotan paid for. Notice how scattered and sparsely linked they are. No community exists here. This is the main message revealed by transforming thousands of data points into a visual shape.

Many more insights could hide in this intricate display, though. To discover them, we'd need to scrutinize it attentively. Again, communication and exploration go hand in hand. We can tell stories with graphics, but we can also let people build their own stories with them.

To rephrase all this a bit, let's say that a good visualization is:

1. reliable information,

2. visually encoded so relevant patterns become noticeable,

3. organized in a way that enables at least some exploration, when it's appropriate,

4. and presented in an attractive manner, but always remembering that honesty, clarity, and depth come first.

This, in a nutshell, is what half of this book is about.

The other half is about what *precedes* design. There are obstacles that hinder the expansion of the island of knowledge. It's not possible to become a professional visualization designer without learning how to overcome them.

Some of these obstacles arise from the territoriality of academic disciplines and the lack of communication between them. I still remember the first time that I read an introduction to cartography textbook, for instance, and my surprise at realizing that many of the design principles that I had learned in journalism school were almost identical to the ones that makers of data maps follow. Academically speaking, I'm one of the least territorial people you'll ever meet, so in this book I will shamelessly borrow from graphic design, journalism, the philosophy of science, statistics, cartography, and many other areas.

Other obstacles to the expansion of the island of knowledge are much more insidious.

Candid Versus
Strategic Communication

This is a book not just about how to design information graphics but about how to design *candid* information graphics. At its core lies a simple idea: **The purpose of infographics and data visualizations is to enlighten people—not to entertain them, not to sell them products, services, or ideas, but to *inform* them**. It's as simple—and as complicated—as that.

What I call candid communication is practiced by professionals whose main goal is (or *should* be) to increase society's collective knowledge. They usually come from disciplines like the sciences, statistics, journalism, cartography, information design, and so on. Their importance in a world increasingly brimming with nonsense and propaganda is paramount.

This is no trivial challenge. See **Figure I.10**. It compares the number of public relations specialists with the number of journalists in the United States. It

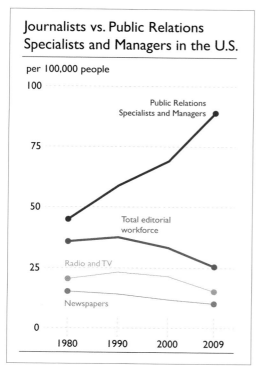

Figure I.10 The number of professionals working in public relations has expanded greatly in the past three decades, while the number of journalists has dropped. (Graph based on McChesney and Nichols, 2011.)

reminds me of a problem I've written about elsewhere:[8] in the past few years, strategic communication—the world of advertisement, PR, marketing, etc.—has hijacked the very word "infographics." This word used to define data-rich graphical displays intended to spread newsworthy information. It has a long and noble history in the journalism industry.[9]

Today, the word "infographics" generally means puerile posters used as clickbait. Search for the word on the Internet and you'll see what I mean. No candid communication here, in general. You'll mostly find bland, simplistic, and tendentious visuals based on shaky data, designed mainly to draw Web traffic, not to inform.

Needless to say, journalists can and do lie to the public, and most strategic communicators may be honest, but it's also fair to acknowledge that "convey your best understanding of what the truth is" is the core mandate for journalists, while "never deceive the public [but] present the facts in a way that sheds as much positive light [on your cause or company] as possible"[10] is the central position for specialists in strategic communication. The second portion of that sentence is crucial, as it renders the whole statement contradictory.

One of the most intriguing books I've read recently is *All Marketers Are Liars* (2005). The title is a joke—in part. Its author, **Seth Godin**, writes that marketing is about creating compelling stories. He explains, "A great story is true. Not true because it's factual but true because it's consistent and authentic."

Godin excuses himself saying that marketers "are just storytellers. It's the consumers who are liars. As consumers, we lie to ourselves every day... Successful marketers are just the providers of stories that consumers choose to believe."

As a good marketer, Godin enjoys toying with words. I'll have some things to say in this book about storytelling in visualization, but I can give you a heads-up: the stories I'm interested in are not the ones that are shiny simulacra of truth, no matter how "authentic" and "consistent" they are. In fact, reality is rarely

---

8 Reclaiming the word "infographics,"
http://www.thefunctionalart.com/2012/12/claiming-word-infographics-back.html

9 The most venerable news graphics conference is called the "Malofiej Infographics Summit" for a reason: http://www.malofiejgraphics.com/.

10 Principles of Public Relations:
http://smallbusiness.chron.com/10-principles-public-relations-10661.html. A classic definition of PR: "Public relations is a strategic communication process that builds mutually beneficial relationships between organizations and their publics" (1982, Public Relations Association of America's National Assembly). This is as vague as it gets. That "mutually" doesn't mean that the relationship is *equally* beneficial for the organizations and for the public.

consistent, but messy and nuanced. Therefore, messiness and nuance should be part of any candid act of graphics communication.

Second, there's a substantial difference between *lying* and *deceiving* (ourselves or others). Lying is always a conscious action. You know what the reality is, but you choose to frame it in a way that advances your agenda. Deceit, though, isn't necessarily conscious. You can simply be oblivious of reality and, as a consequence, you may mislead yourself or others.

Third, it's true that human beings can't be completely factual or objective. Our brain is a flawed meat machine chiseled by evolution, not a computer. We all have cognitive, cultural, and ideological biases, but that doesn't mean that we can't strive to be factual. *Truth* is unattainable, but **trying to be truthful is a realistic and worthy goal**, and there are certain techniques that can help us pursue it.

There's a deep difference between those who surrender to their own biases, or willingly embrace them, and those who work hard to identify and curb them, even if they'll never completely succeed. This book is a tribute to this second group.

Continuing with Godin: In another part of his bestseller he writes, "Maybe who is lying to whom isn't all that important, in the end, as long as the connection has been made and the story has been successfully told." In other words, what really matters is if consumers buy your product, service, or idea, not if any of them has any substance.

Godin points out that marketing techniques can be used to advance good causes. No doubt about that. But I'd like to add something right away: **in strategic communication, you may begin with a message and then look for information to support it. In candid communication, you begin with the information, and *then* you thoroughly analyze it to discover the messages worth spreading are.** Or you begin with a message, but then you collect your information in a way that it could lead you to refute that very message.

If our quest for truthfulness leads us to conclude that the stories we wish to tell or the graphics we are so eager to design are inaccurate or plainly untrue—well, we'll need to be ready to drop them outright. We must never distort our data so they fit into our preconceived narratives, no matter how much we love them.

You may think that this is just a platitude. Twisting reality a bit to get your story across effectively isn't that inappropriate, is it? After all, we all do it every day, and nobody gets hurt. Nobody? It's all a matter of degree.

Let's think of an extreme case. The **Discovery Institute**, a non-profit organization based in Seattle, is dedicated to misinforming people about science. This is not really how the folks who work there describe themselves, of course, but it's exactly what they do. Numerous books by scientists, like Donald R. Prothero's *Evolution: What the Fossils Say and Why it Matters* (2007), include long sections describing Discovery's misdeeds in detail.

Discovery's main activity is to popularize creationism, although the organization prefers to call it "intelligent design." This is the fallacy that Darwinian evolution cannot account for the appearance of new species in our planet.

Discovery has a budget of millions of dollars. Most of it seems to be devoted to promotion, as the organization doesn't conduct any proper research. Its websites, graphics, books, and lectures are sleek and lavishly produced. Discovery does fantastic marketing and PR—according to Godin's definitions—but its marketing and PR hurt society by distorting data and spreading baloney.

Excellent strategic communication, which is what Discovery excels at, isn't always backed up by excellent information. If you think that this doesn't have harmful consequences, think again. According to the Pew Research Center, 33 percent of U.S. adults are incorrectly convinced that "humans existed in present form since the beginning of time."[11]

It's rare to find a case that is as clear-cut as this one. Truth and untruth aren't absolutes but stand at the end points of a fuzzy continuum. Still, a warning is worthwhile: **there are people out there who aren't in the business of expanding the island of knowledge by navigating beyond the shoreline of wonder. They are in the business of transforming that shoreline into a dark, impassable marsh**.

In the kind of visualizations I'm interested in, the quality of the information precedes the quality and visual appeal of the graphics themselves. It's impossible to have one without the other. Many pundits, marketers, and activists of all ideological stripes are willfully ignorant of this precept. This endangers us all by muddling our public discourse.

This is why the chart in Figure I.10 concerns me so much. I feel uncomfortable with the world it announces.

---

11 www.pewforum.org/2013/12/30/publics-views-on-human-evolution/

In the Good Ol' Days…

Before the advent of the World Wide Web, in the early 1990s, we used to get our information mainly from newspapers, radio, and TV. If you are my age, you probably remember the pre-WWW days, waiting for the morning paper or the evening news to learn what had happened in your community, your country, or around the world.

News organizations, and the journalists who worked for them, acted as gate-keepers: they decided what information was worth publishing. They chose their sources—sometimes unwisely—and they filtered and shaped our view of reality.

It was far from an ideal world. I'm no romantic. Journalists are as prone to error and bias as anyone else. We can be tricked by spin doctors, and we often miss the most relevant stories of our time.

Not to mention that news organizations have carelessly helped promote bad ideas, such as climate change denialism and unproven alternative medical therapies, just to name a couple.[12]

It's hardly surprising that trust in news media and professional journalists is low today. But robust journalism serves us well. Here is **Charles Lewis**, a famous investigative reporter:

> In a society increasingly beset by public relations, advertising, and other artificial sweeteners manufactured by message consultants and communications flacks, how does an ordinary citizen decipher truth…?[13]

Helping people tell bullshit from facts should certainly be a duty for all journalists and information designers. Whenever we get information from anyone, we have to make sure that it's reliable, to the extent of our knowledge and analytical skills. We need to ask our sources: **how do you know?** And moreover: **how do you know *that you know*?**, as that will force them to disclose the methods and data used to reach their conclusions.

---

12 Supporters of these causes have traditionally been very fond of professional marketing, by the way. Do read Ben Goldacre's *Bad Science: Quacks, Hacks, and Big Pharma Flacks* (2010) when you have three or four hours to spare. You're welcome.

13 See "To Learn More" at the end of this chapter.

Journalists also do original reporting about relevant matters. Here by my side I have the August 24, 2014, edition of the *Miami Herald*. One long story in this issue explains how Haitian Americans in Florida are being preyed upon by Ponzi scheme crooks who advertise in Creole-language radio. Another one is a well-balanced study of a violent Liberty City neighborhood in Miami.

The *Herald* has a long tradition of heavy-hitting investigative reporting. In August 1992, category 5 Hurricane Andrew leveled much of south Miami-Dade county. In December that year, the *Herald* published a special 16-page supplement titled "What Went Wrong" that revealed that houses built between the 1980s and the 1990s were more likely to have suffered serious damage than older ones, due to lax inspection of building quality and zoning in the decade that preceded the hurricane. The supplement was supported by plenty of graphics (**Figure I.11**), and it won a Pulitzer Prize for public service in 1993.

When I see stories like these, I wonder: aren't we in danger of losing a central pillar of a democratic society, now that so many traditional news organizations are at risk of crumbling? If the *Miami Herald* and other publications like it disappear, who is going to expose wrongdoing in a systematic manner so the public can be aware of it?

You could argue that plenty of startups populate the current media landscape: Vox.com, Mic.com, FiveThirtyEight, The Huffington Post, Gawker, Quartz, Buzzfeed, and so on. Aren't they protecting their readers against the roaring tides of noise and spin? Even if they try to, not all of them have been very effective so far. According to what **Ryan Holiday** says in his scathing jeremiad ***Trust Me, I'm Lying: Confessions of a Media Manipulator*** (2012), many online news organizations don't fact-check their sources, don't do proper editing, and don't produce much original reporting.

Figure I.11 (opposite) A sample of the graphics published by the *Miami Herald* on December 20, 1992. Here's how the *Herald* described the project: "IN TODAY'S *Herald* is a 16-page report titled 'What Went Wrong.' Investigative reporters working with engineers and other experts examine why so many homes that shouldn't have suffered heavy destruction during Hurricane Andrew did (…) The first comprehensive analysis of Andrew's havoc concludes that shoddy construction helped turn a devastating storm into the most costly disaster in U.S. history. During a four-month investigation, the *Herald* analyzed damage reports on 60,000 houses and matched these by computer with millions of property and building records." (Reporting, charts, maps, and illustrations by Stephen K. Doig, Jacquee Petchel, Dan Clifford, Lisa Getter, Patterson Clark, Jeff Leen, Luis Soto, and Don Finefrock.)

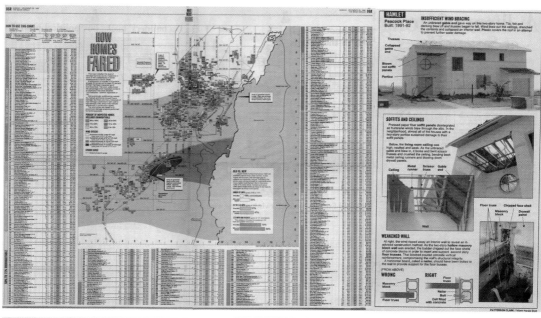

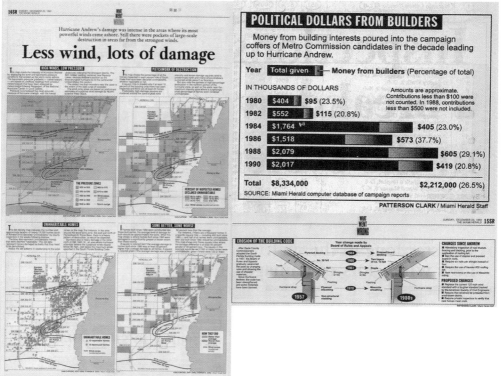

There are exceptions, of course. Vice News, for example, is deservedly famous for its excellent and edgy video documentaries. And, to be fair, the companies mentioned before are investing more resources every year in improving their journalism.

In the meantime, **what's left for regular citizens to do?** Now that anyone can reach hundreds, thousands, or even millions of people through personal websites, blogs, and social media, who is going to make sure that information that goes viral on Twitter, Facebook, or on any other platform is accurate? And who's going to create original visualizations that help people stay informed on important matters, and conduct better lives?

Perhaps the answer is me. And you. Any and all of us.

Your Inner Skeptic, Your Inner Journalist

Here's a little secret: most of the maps, charts, and diagrams that I'll praise in this book are "journalistic" in the sense that the designers who created them first did their best to make sure that their information was relevant, factual, and accurate, and only then did they present it in a way that was accessible and engaging.

However, not all of those designers call themselves journalists.

What Is a Journalist, Anyway?

When I was in college, I remember that one of my professors said that a journalist is someone in charge of producing the news. And what is "the news"? Here we can borrow from **Jack Fuller**, ex-president and publisher of the *Chicago Tribune*: "News is a report of what a news organization has recently learned about matters of some significance or interest to the specific community that news organization serves."

Got it. But here's a story: back in 2010, when I was the director of infographics and multimedia at the Brazilian weekly news magazine *Época*, I heard of a young computer scientist called **Maurício Maia**. Maurício lives in São Paulo, a city that suffers from heavy rains during the summer. Many streets in the city flood periodically, so he decided to create an interactive map and database of past floods, to identify the best and the worst areas. He downloaded publicly available datasets from government websites, and he transformed them into a tool that he made available for free.[14] What would you call what Maurício did? I call it journalism.

I'm not the only one. **Jeff Jarvis**, a professor at City University of New York, once wrote that "there are no journalists, there is only the service of journalism."[15] Maybe this is a bit too extreme, but it rings true. If you are a designer, you may have recalled **Laszlo Moholy-Nagy**'s famous saying, **"Designing is not a profession but an attitude."** We are all designers, in the sense that we're creatures who have a taste for organizing matter and ideas into objects and patterns. Perhaps we all are—or can become—journalists, too, every once in a while at least.

The Elements of Journalism, a classic introduction to the practice, says that "the purpose of journalism is to provide people with the information they need to be free and self-governing." It then lists what is needed to fulfill this task:

1. Journalism's first obligation is to the truth.

2. Its first loyalty is to citizens.

3. Its essence is a discipline of verification.

4. Its practitioners must maintain an independence from those they cover.

5. It must serve as an independent monitor of power.

6. It must provide a forum for public criticism and compromise.

7. It must strive to make the significant interesting and relevant.

8. It must keep the news comprehensive and proportional.

9. Its practitioners must be allowed to exercise their personal conscience.

I'd like to argue that these shouldn't be the exclusive values of a specific professional group. Society as a whole will be better off if they become civic values that the entire population embraces. The world will turn into a much nicer place if more of us learn about what data and evidence are and

---

14 Maurício was puzzled when I phoned him to say that I wanted to hire him to work on my team. He said, "I am not a journalist!" I didn't succeed; he was making too much money as a freelancer. His website, in which he discusses his projects, is http://mmaia.tumblr.com/

15 Jeff Jarvis: "There are no journalists" http://buzzmachine.com/2013/06/30/there-are-no-journalists-there-is-only-journalism/

become more critical as a result. And it'll be even nicer if we also learn how to convey that evidence in a clear, compelling, and useful manner through data visualizations, infographics, or interactive and searchable tables.

Maurício Maia committed an act of journalism. He spent time devising a visual tool that citizens of São Paulo could take advantage of. I believe that acts of candid, evidence-based communication and of useful design like Maia's aren't frequent enough, while marketing, PR, and advocacy are pervasive. Nothing against any of the latter—they have a role in a market economy—but the former are the ones that I hold dear and will feature in this book.

Who is this book for, then? This book is written first for designers and journalists who wish to communicate effectively with data visualization and infographics. If you're in this group, this book may give you a glimpse into the worlds of science, statistics, and information design. It won't teach you everything you need to know, but it may open many doors.

I also write for anyone who isn't a professional designer or journalist, but wishes to understand and use visualization. Therefore, this book is also for scientists, data analysts, business intelligence types, etc.

If you are in this second group, please take a look at another quote by **Charles Lewis**:

> Imagine a world in which individual researchers [and many other kinds of experts] and journalists are sometimes looking for truth in all the same places, using the same exciting new data technologies and analytics, exchanging ideas and information, and sometimes working and writing together, whether side by side or across borders and genres. These collaborative fact-finders, fact-checkers, truth-seekers, and truth-tellers will all come from different perspectives.... but all will share the deep curiosity, patience, determination, and mettle that have always characterized the investigative reporter.[16]

Let me suggest something similar: we live in a world where special interests spend millions of dollars pushing their agendas, promoting their ideologies, and selling their unsubstantiated claims with almost no interference. They can reach us more effectively than in any previous era thanks to the Internet and social media. They like to use data, infographics, and visualization because they believe that people trust them more than they trust mere words.

16 LEWIS (2014), page 224

Arguably, it's time to push back. Perhaps after reading this book you will consider joining the virtual alliance of people whose purpose is to expand the island of knowledge by exploring the mysteries that lie beyond the shoreline of wonder. This process is much simpler than you may think. You decide that you have something relevant to communicate; you gather data and scrutinize them thoroughly to make sure that you get everything right; and then you design your graphics.

I will be delighted if, ultimately, I am able to convince you that this is an endeavor worth pursuing.

To Learn More

Authors who claim ownership of everything they write are delusional. Therefore, at the end of each chapter you will find a section like this that will lead you to the readings that inspired most of my thoughts. There's also a complete bibliography in the last pages.

Here are some books to expand on the content of this introduction, besides the ones mentioned in the text itself:

- Gleiser, Marcelo. *The Island of Knowledge: The Limits of Science and the Search for Meaning.* New York: Basic Books, 2014.

- Goldacre, Ben. *Bad Science: Quacks, Hacks, and Big Pharma Flacks.* New York: Faber and Faber, 2010.

- Lewis, Charles. *935 Lies: The Future of Truth and the Decline of America's Moral Integrity.* New York: PublicAffairs, 2014.

- McChesney, Robert Waterman, and John Nichols. *The Death and Life of American Journalism: The Media Revolution that Will Begin the World Again.* Philadelphia, PA: Nation, 2010.

- Raymo, Chet. *Skeptics and True Believers: The Exhilarating Connection between Science and Religion.* New York: Walker, 1998.

- Starkman, Dean. *The Watchdog That Didn't Bark: The Financial Crisis and the Disappearance of Investigative Journalism.* New York: Columbia University Press, 2014.

PART I

foundations

I

What We Talk About When We Talk About Visualization

No matter how clever the choice of the information, and no matter how technologically impressive the encoding, a visualization fails if the decoding fails. Some display methods lead to efficient, accurate decoding, and others lead to inefficient, inaccurate decoding. It is only through scientific study of visual perception that informed judgments can be made about display methods.

—William S. Cleveland, *The Elements of Graphing Data*

In the introduction, I threw around terms such as "visualization," "infographics," "information graphics," and so on, without defining them. Each book about visual communication on my shelves uses these terms with a slightly different meaning. So, for consistency and to avoid confusion later, let me set down some definitions—while not claiming that my definitions are better than anybody else's.

"Visualization" is my umbrella term. **A visualization is any kind of visual representation of information designed to enable communication, analysis, discovery, exploration, etc**. Almost every picture I'll show is, therefore, a visualization. In this book I don't cover all branches of visualization, just those intended to communicate effectively with the general public. I will barely mention visualizations created exclusively with artistic purposes, for instance, which belong to the realm of data art.

A chart is a display in which data are encoded with symbols that have different shapes, colors, or proportions. In many cases, these symbols are placed within a Cartesian coordinate system. The word "plot" is a synonym of "chart" in this book, as it's commonly used to refer to a few specific charts in the professional literature ("scatter plot" sounds more familiar than "scatter chart").

See **Figure 1.1** for a few examples of charts. Yes, I know—*lollipop* chart. You read that right. I think that it was Tableau's visualization designer and data analyst **Andy Cotgreave** who came up with this term. Who said that designers and statisticians don't have a sense of humor?

In some cases, visualization designers prefer "diagram" to "chart." For instance, in the introduction you read about a Sankey diagram[1] designed by Moritz Stefaner. If I were 100 percent consistent, I should call that example a "Sankey chart," but I acknowledge that Sankey diagram is a popular name. I'd be fine with calling this a "flow chart," too.

A side note for scientists and statisticians: I know that many of you prefer "graph" when you refer to charts built on a Cartesian coordinate system, but some mathematicians might claim that they own that word in reference to connection and network graphics—that is, "graph theory," which is a branch of mathematics. I'm not willing to unleash a turf war, so I'll just say that you're both right and that we can all get along, even after considering that this author is a journalist.[2]

---

1 Sankey diagrams are named after Matthew Henry Phineas Riall Sankey, an engineer who used this graphic form to display the efficiency of a steam engine. Sankey was not the first one to use Sankey diagrams, by the way. Charles Joseph Minard, a French cartographer, became famous in the middle of the nineteenth century thanks in part to the many flow charts and maps he designed. See Michael Friendly's "Visions and Re-Visions of Charles Joseph Minard" at http://www.datavis.ca/papers/jebs.pdf.

2 If you have friends who are scientists, ask them what they think about journalists. Have an umbrella (or a shield) handy.

A map is a depiction of a geographical area or a representation of data that pertains to that area (Figure 1.2). I may use the term "data map" every now and then to refer to this second kind of map.

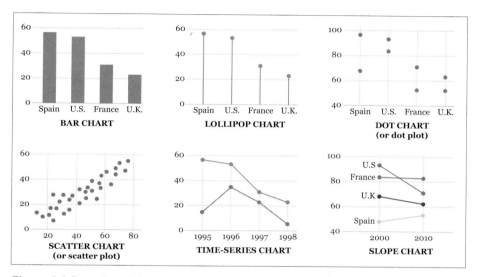

Figure 1.1 Examples of charts. Not all charts have an X-axis and a Y-axis. Pie charts, for instance, aren't based on a Cartesian coordinate system.

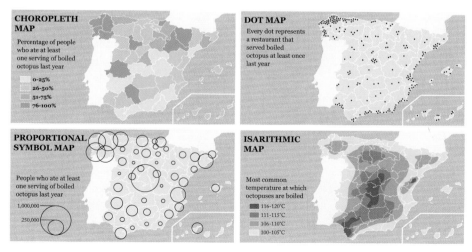

Figure 1.2 Examples of data maps. I was born in Galicia, that region in northwestern Spain where people seem to be so fond of eating boiled octopus (it's delicious, if properly cooked). All data here are fake, of course.

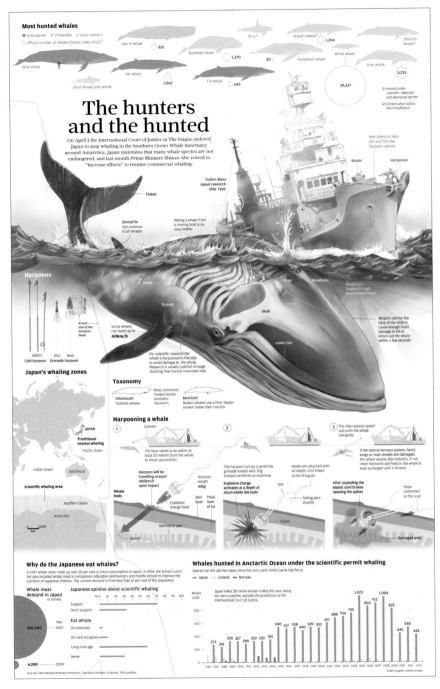

Figure 1.3 Infographic by Adolfo Arranz for the *South China Morning Post*.

An infographic is a multi-section visual representation of information intended to communicate one or more specific messages. Infographics are made of a mix of charts, maps, illustrations, and text (or sound) that provides explanation and context. They can be static or dynamic. What defines an infographic is that its designer doesn't show all information she gathered, but just the portion that is relevant for the point (or points) that she's trying to make. See **Figure 1.3**.

Infographics are sometimes, but not always, organized in a linear fashion, like narratives and step-by-step explanations. They can be rich in detail, and they usually include unobtrusive drawings, icons, and pictograms to increase the visual appeal of the display. Infographics can be lush, colorful, and fun if their designers don't forget that their fundamental goal is to make the public better informed (**Figure 1.4**). Clarity and depth are paramount in infographics. Bells and whistles are secondary and optional.

A data visualization is a display of data designed to enable analysis, exploration, and discovery. Data visualizations aren't intended mainly to convey messages that are predefined by their designers. Instead, they are often conceived as tools that let people extract their own conclusions from the data.

Figure 1.5 is an example of data visualization. This is an image of an interactive graphic created by the design firm **Periscopic**, showing terrorist groups and attacks since 1970. The display can be rearranged at will: by name of group, by most victims, by how recent the activities of the groups are, and so on. A reader on the Web can also hover over any of the groups and see specific figures. In my case, as I was born in Spain, my point of entry to this data visualization was ETA, the Basque terrorist group that killed more than 800 people between 1968 and 2010. If you live in the United States, you probably focused first on the Taliban or al-Qaeda (or al-Qa'ida, as it's spelled in this project). A good data visualization may yield different insights to each person.

Finally, I'll be using the term "news application," which I've borrowed from the nonprofit investigative journalism organization ProPublica. **A news application is a special kind of visualization that lets people relate the data being presented to their own lives**. Its main goal is to be useful by being customizable according to each person's needs.

Figure 1.4 Infographic by Francesco Franchi and Alessandro Giberti. Illustration by Danilo Agutoli. Published by *Il Sole 24 ORE* (Italy).

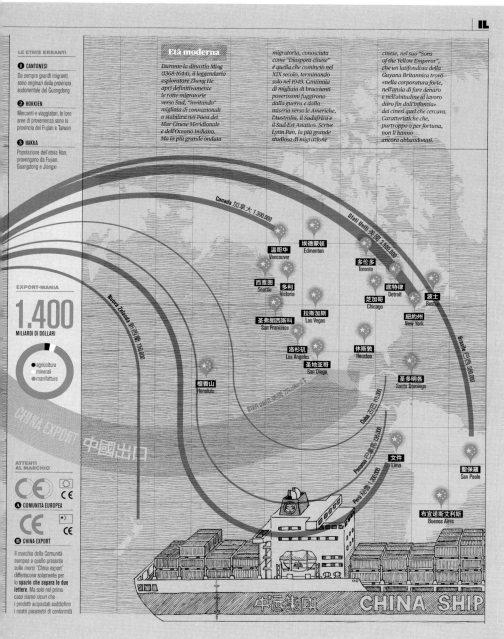

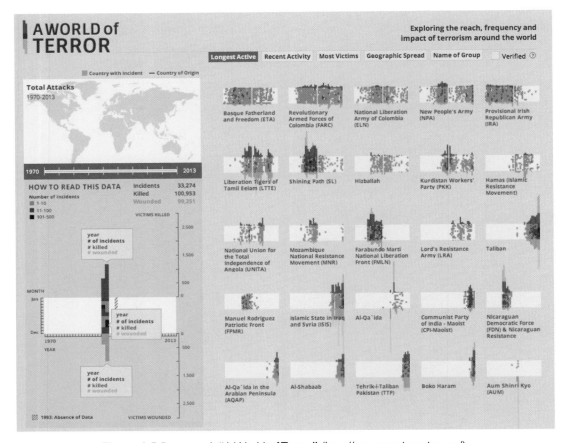

Figure 1.5 Periscopic's "A World of Terror" (http://terror.periscopic.com/).

A news application can be a simulator, a calculator, or an interactive visual database like "Treatment Tracker" (**Figure 1.6**), a project that lets *you*, the consumer, see—and I'm quoting here—"payments to individual doctors and other health professionals serving the 46 million seniors and disabled in (Medicare's) Part B program." You can find and compare any individual or set of providers with this application.

Another example of a news application is *The Wall Street Journal*'s "Health Care Explorer" (**Figure 1.7**). It was launched before President Barack Obama's Affordable Care Act went into effect to help U.S. citizens navigate myriad healthcare options. Input *your* own age, choose *your* state and county, and pick the kind of

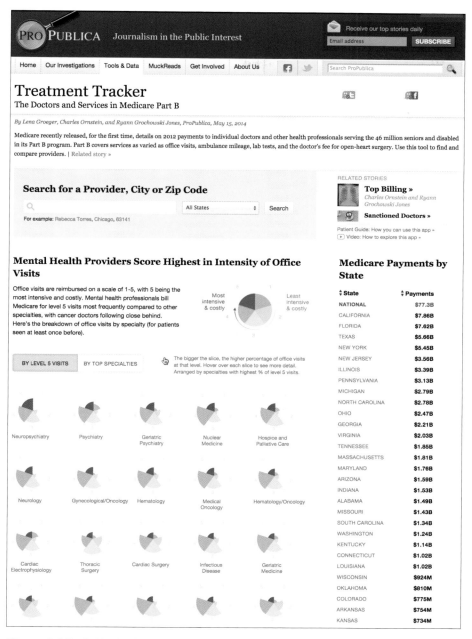

Figure 1.6 ProPublica's "Treatment Tracker" (http://projects.propublica.org/treatment/).

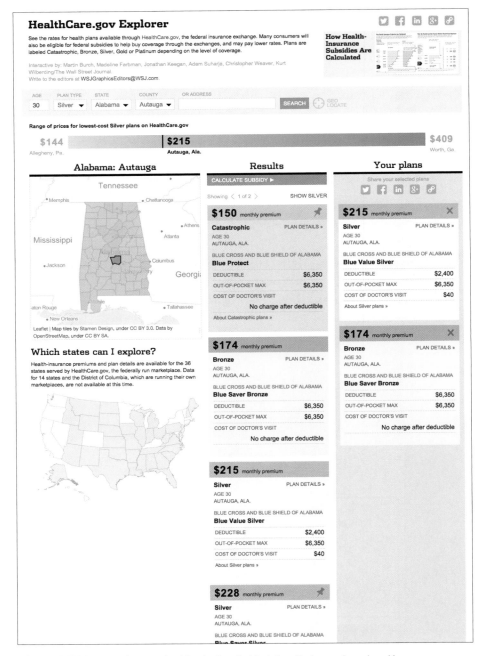

Figure 1.7 News application by Martin Burch, Madeline Farbman, Jonathan Keegan, Adam Suharja, Christopher Weaver, Kurt Wilberding/*The Wall Street Journal* (http://graphics.wsj.com/health-care-explorer).

plan that *you're* more interested in. Click Search, and *you'll* be able to compare plans in your area. Then, *you* can pin the ones that look more promising. To *you*.

You may have already realized that the boundaries that separate all these kinds of visualizations are blurry. Some visualizations are designed to spread a message or to tell a story based on a subset of the information available to the designer. We can use the word "infographics" to refer to these visualizations. Other graphics are designed mainly, but not exclusively, to enable exploration, and so we may want to call them "data visualizations."

But what do you call a project like "Beyond the Border," by *The Guardian* (**Figure 1.8**)? This image belongs to one of the many graphics integrated within a multimedia package that also showcases photos, video, and abundant text.

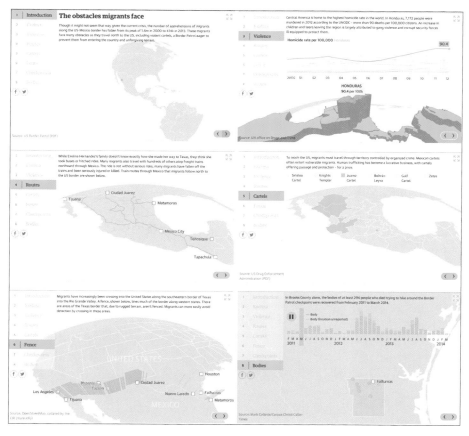

Figure 1.8 Visualization by Feilding Cage for *The Guardian* (http://www.theguardian.com/world/ng-interactive/2014/aug/06/-sp-texas-border-deadliest-state-undocumented-migrants).

This *Guardian* graphic is, in part, an infographic, as it's a step-by-step narration that walks you through the key obstacles that undocumented migrants face in the United States. But according to my own definition, it's also a data visualization, as some of the charts and maps can be explored at will. Besides, most scenes in this hybrid product show a link to the sources of the data: the U.S. Border Patrol, the U.S. Drug Enforcement Administration, the United Nations, etc.

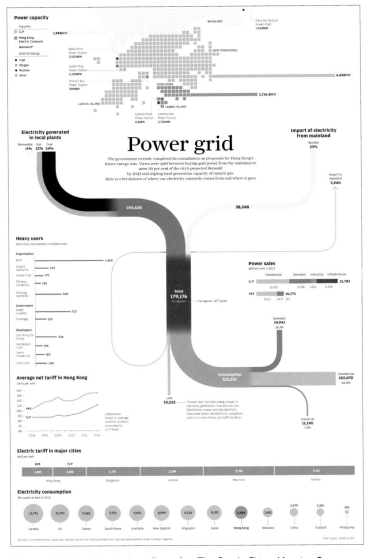

Figure 1.9 Graphic by Jane Pong for *The South China Morning Post.*

The boundaries aren't very clear even when we talk about static graphics. **Figures 1.9** and **1.10** are two visualizations by the *South China Morning Post*. Are they infographics? Well, yes. But aren't they also data visualizations? Don't you feel compelled to spend time poring over them, digging for curious facts and connections?

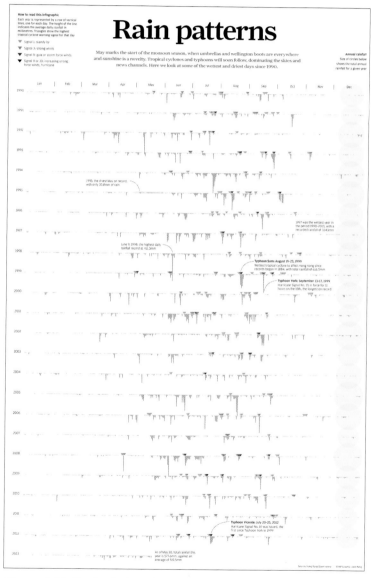

Figure 1.10 Graphic by Jane Pong for *The South China Morning Post*.

In my previous book, *The Functional Art*, I explained that terms like "infographics" and "data visualization" or dichotomies like "explanation" versus "exploration" and "presentation" versus "analysis" aren't absolutes.

Any visualization presents information and allows at least a limited amount of exploration or even customization, so it may be hard to tell for sure if a graphic is really an infographic, a data visualization, or a news application. You may be able to say, though, that it leans more toward one of those realms, depending on what the main intentions of the designer are.

To be honest, I don't care much about strict taxonomy. What really matters to me is if a visualization is illuminating. For that, the designers need to keep certain important features and principles in mind. We turn to them in the following chapter.

To Learn More

- Harris, Robert L. *Information Graphics: A Comprehensive Illustrated Reference.* New York: Oxford UP, 1999. This one is a must if you want to learn what most kinds of charts, maps, and diagrams are usually called.

- Rendgen, Sandra (editor). *Information Graphics.* Köln: Taschen, 2012. This massive volume—it weights eight pounds!—will open your eyes to what I like to call "the varieties of the visualization experience."

2

The Five Qualities of Great Visualizations

The greatest value of a picture is when it forces us to notice what we never expected to see.

—John W. Tukey, *Exploratory Data Analysis*

In April 2013, **Enrico Bertini**, a professor of visualization at the NYU Polytechnic School of Engineering, posed a challenge to his community. In a blog post titled "Where are the data visualization success stories?" he wrote:

> I see a lot of visualization around me now, and I am extremely excited about it. Yet, are we making any real difference? I mean, are we having any real impact on people's lives other than telling them beautiful stories? Yes, I know, impact could be defined in a million different ways, and it may be hard to capture. But why do I never stumble on to an article or blog post showing, I don't know, for instance, how a visualization helped a group of doctors do something remarkable? Is it just because this stuff does not get reported or what?[1]

---

1 http://fellinlovewithdata.com/reflections/visualization-success-stories

On Twitter I replied that success happens every time that a statistician, an economist, a scientist—or any citizen, for that matter—discovers something useful thanks to a simple chart or map. But Enrico was making a very good point: we, designers, journalists, programmers, and computer scientists who do visualization for a living don't think often enough about the triumphs in our disciplines.

For decades, we have taken certain cherished notions for granted: that visualization *works*; that learning how to do it properly can make anybody better not only at communicating relevant facts about the world, but also at exploring them; and that it is a craft based not on artistic predispositions, but on embracing certain principles and heuristics derived from experience and scientific inquiry. I believe those ideas are right. But they are far from being self-evident.

Therefore, I felt prompted to come up with examples of graphics that changed public understanding. There are quite a few, but my favorite among the ones that I remembered immediately is the **hockey stick chart (Figure 2.1)**, designed by professors Michael E. Mann, Raymond S. Bradley, and Malcolm K. Hughes. Let me first explain what this chart is and how it came about, and then I'll tell you how **it demonstrates the values that lie at the core of this book**.

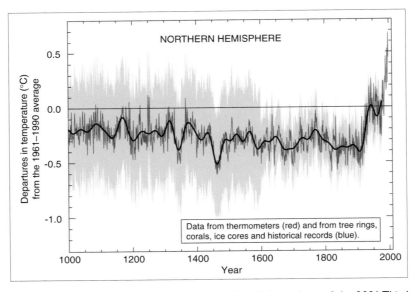

Figure 2.1 The hockey stick chart. Summary For Policymakers of the 2001 Third Assessment Report of the Intergovernmental Panel on Climate Change.

The Hockey Stick Chart

The fact that Earth has warmed in the past century, that it continues doing so at an alarming pace, and that humans have a key role in that warming isn't controversial today outside of fringe—but very well-financed—partisan dens. I'm writing these words on the day that the Intergovernmental Panel on Climate Change (IPCC) is releasing its latest assessment report, the fifth since 1990.[2] Its conclusion: climate change is "unequivocal." Disagreements exist on the details, as is normal in science, and a lot of research remains to be done, but most of the scientific community agrees that climate change is a worrisome reality.[3]

The situation was different in 2001. That year, the IPCC published its third report. It was, arguably, the most controversial up to that point mainly because it prominently showcased the bomb of a chart in Figure 2.1. That graphic shows temperature variation measured in degrees Celsius in comparison to the 1981 to 1990 average, the zero line in the middle of the Y-axis.

What later came to be known as the "hockey stick chart" had already appeared, in slightly different forms, in scientific papers published in 1998 and 1999.[4] One of them explained that the 1990s had been the warmest decade on record and that 1998, the latest year included in the chart, had been the hottest ever.

As the systematic record of temperatures began only in the seventeenth century, the researchers had to look into multiple sources of paleoclimate data to draw a complete picture of temperatures in the past millennium. They used **proxy variables**[5] such as tree-ring growth rates and changes in varved sediments, ice cores, and corals.

---

2 For a summary, read http://www.theguardian.com/environment/2013/sep/27/ipcc-climate-report-digested-read.

3 Thousands of scientists from all over the world work on the IPCC reports, which strive to accurately reflect the consensus and disagreements within the scientific community. If you are among those who still believe that the IPCC is a conspiracy of radical scientists to get lavish government funding, it's probably because you've never been close to a real scientist. Nothing brings more pleasure to researchers than to cruelly debunk their colleagues' results.

4 Mann, Michael E., Bradley, Raymond S., and Hughes, Malcolm K. "Northern Hemisphere Temperatures During the Past Millennium: Inferences, Uncertainties, and Limitations." Geophysical Research Letters, Vol. 26, No. 6, pages 759-762, March 15, 1999.

5 A proxy variable is a measurable unit or entity that can be used to study something that is hard, or even impossible, to observe directly. As an analogy, think of HIV, the virus that causes AIDS. Most tests that detect its presence in the human body don't look for the virus. They try to find other clues of its presence, such as antibodies, which fight against infections. The entity "antibodies-against-HIV," in this case, is a proxy of the entity "HIV virus."

No statistical estimate is fully accurate, so the authors were careful to display uncertainty in their chart: notice the gray strip that surrounds the lines. With a very high degree of confidence, scientists can claim that the temperature of each year was within the range defined by the uppermost and the bottom tips of that gray strip.

The gray band grows thinner the closer we get to the present. Here's why: as measurement tools and techniques improved, the data available to calculate average temperatures became much more precise and reliable. As a consequence, uncertainty became smaller.

The message of the chart is unambiguous: in the first years of the twentieth century, temperatures experienced a sharp rise. This was a time when emissions of human-made greenhouse gases, like carbon dioxide from fossil fuels, increased rapidly.

The hockey stick chart went unnoticed, except in scientific circles, until it was picked up by the IPCC for the 2001 report. After that, it became one of the most famous, influential, and disputed graphics ever. Michael E. Mann, his colleagues, and many climate scientists who had participated in the IPCC reports throughout the years began to receive vicious attacks—character assassination attempts, really—from individuals, political groups, and other organizations that have a vested interest in denying the reality of global warming, no matter how solid the evidence is.[6]

As Mann himself wrote in 2012, "The controversy that the hockey stick would ultimately generate had little to do with the depicted temperature rise in and of itself. Rather, it was a result of the perceived threat this simple graph represented to those who are opposed to governmental regulations or other social restraints aimed at protecting our environment and the long-term prospects for the health of our planet."[7]

---

6   It's actually rock-solid. A couple of short summaries that can lead you to other readings: http://www.theatlantic.com/technology/archive/2013/05/the-hockey-stick-the-most-controversial-chart-in-science-explained/275753/ and http://www.scientificamerican.com/article/behind-the-hockey-stick/. See also Naomi Oreskes's and Erik M. Conway's book *Merchants of Doubt* (2010). The authors reveal that the tactics used by climate change deniers today are identical to the ones the tobacco industry used decades ago to cast doubt over the evidence linking cigarette consumption and lung cancer.

7   Mann, Michael E. *The Hockey Stick and the Climate Wars: Dispatches from the Front Lines* (2012).

The hockey stick chart is one of the most iconic and persuasive visualizations ever created. It's a success story, in Enrico Bertini's words, because it has certain qualities:

1. **It is truthful**, as it's based on thorough and honest research.

2. **It is functional**, as it constitutes an accurate depiction of the data, and it's built in a way that lets people do meaningful operations based on it (seeing change in time).

3. **It is beautiful**, in the sense of being attractive, intriguing, and even aesthetically pleasing for its intended audience—scientists, in the first place, but the general public, too.

4. **It is insightful**, as it reveals evidence that we would have a hard time seeing otherwise.

5. **It is enlightening** because if we grasp and accept the evidence it depicts, it will change our minds for the better.

These five qualities constitute the framework this book is built upon. All of them are dangerously polysemic, so let me briefly explain them.

Truthful

If you randomly pick a book about visualization from your local bookstore or library, I have the hunch that one of the words you will find more often in it is "clarity."[8] We designers and journalists obsess over presenting things concisely, simply, clearly, and elegantly. Otherwise, people would be confused and upset when reading our graphics.

Information designer **Richard Saul Wurman** calls himself an "information architect" and has explained why in several books, like his delightful fable 33: *Understanding Change & the Change in Understanding* (the boldface here is mine):

> I mean architect as in the creating of systemic, structural, and orderly principles to make something work—the thoughtful making of either artifact, or idea, or policy that **informs because it is clear**.[9]

8 Now that so many books are available in digital format, I'd love to see an analysis of the words that are most often used. Perhaps my hunch is completely wrong!

9 This quote also appears in Wurman's classic *Information Architects* (1997).

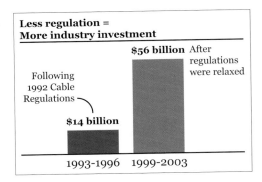

Figure 2.2 In 10 seconds, tell me everything that looks fishy in this chart.

But do those things really inform *because they are clear*? Or is clarity just a means? Should clarity be the prime value of visualization design? Hold those questions in mind for just one minute while looking at **Figure 2.2**.

The original chart, which was similar to mine, was published on the home page of the website of the National Cable & Telecommunications Association. The NCTA is a trade organization that does very effective public relations and lobbying for U.S. cable companies.[10]

Here's what the chart suggests: As a consequence of U.S. government regulations in 1992, cable companies invested little money in infrastructure. After regulations were relaxed, investment boomed. There you go. You see this chart on Twitter, as I did, and if you don't inspect it closely or if you're absentminded, you may walk away convinced of what the headline says: less regulation = more industry investment.

Let's scrutinize the chart for a bit, though. **Get used to not just *seeing* or looking at visualizations but to *reading* them.** Marketers are very aware of the fact that most people don't pay a lot of attention to what they see and that charts and data maps can be very persuasive, as they look so sciencey.[11]

---

10 Visit https://www.ncta.com.

11 In 2014, Aner Tal and Brian Wansink, two researchers at Cornell University, published a study in the journal *Public Understanding of Science* titled "Blinded with science: Trivial graphs and formulas increase ad persuasiveness and belief in product efficacy." The results of their experiments were revealing: "The mere presentation of elements associated with science alongside claims about medication efficacy increases persuasion. People who were given graphs or formulas along with claims regarding medication efficacy displayed greater belief in medication effectiveness."

First of all, assuming that these figures are adjusted for inflation (I didn't check), notice that there are years missing. What happened between 1996 and 1999? Did these companies invest nothing during those years? That's unlikely. Second, there are four years between 1993 and 1996 (first bar) and *five* between 1999 and 2003. If you want to add up the investments in those time periods, at least you should make sure that they encompass the same number of years.

Here's some advice for you: whenever a designer, journalist, PR person, advertiser, or your own sweet Auntie Julie shows you a visualization with just a few figures that are the result of adding up, rounding, or averaging tons of data, distrust him or her. In a world full of graphics devoid of nuance, crooks thrive. **If someone hides data from you, it's probably because he has something to hide**.

When the NCTA promoted this chart on Twitter, proudly announcing that it proved that government regulations are evil, my baloney alarm started screaming like crazy.[12] I tweeted back, detailing some misgivings. The person running the NCTA's account replied that anyone interested in seeing the data in more detail could navigate through their page to find an obscure blog post that's not even linked from their index page.

What I found was a chart like the one in **Figure 2.3**. It tells a completely different story. The Cable Television Protection and Competition Act—this is the evil

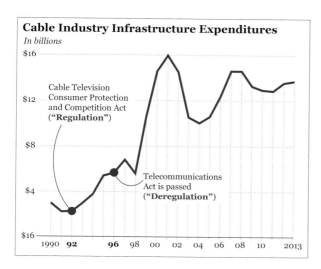

Figure 2.3 Do government regulations really hinder investment in cable infrastructure?

---

12 I also call it "bullshit alarm."

regulation that was the focus of the first chart—was passed in 1992. Investment in infrastructure didn't plunge right after but began growing healthily.

Following the deregulatory Telecommunications Act of 1996, investment fell, possibly because of the financial crisis of 1997–98, and then took off. Thanks to that piece of legislation? No idea. It could be. Or maybe not, as that increase corresponds to the rapid expansion of Internet access and the dot-com bubble between 1997 and 2000. In those years, an increasing amount of people got interested in accessing online content. Therefore, the spike in the line chart was likely just a reaction to high demand.

Even if all my conjectures above were wrong, I'm already conditioned to distrust the NCTA. This is the consequence of clear and effective, but ultimately deceitful, communication: **misleading people isn't just morally unacceptable, it also undermines your credibility**.

Note that I haven't used the word "lie." I don't think that the first graphic is a complete lie. The numbers in it are right, mathematically speaking. They are the result of adding up the investments of two periods of time, even if they are of different lengths. The first chart may be true, even if its headline isn't. But the second one is much *truer*. It provides a much more accurate and factual depiction of the topic. **Truth and untruth aren't absolutes. They are the extremes at either end of a spectrum**, an idea that I will expand upon in the next chapter.

Therefore, I don't think that clarity should be the prime goal of visualization design. Getting our information as right as possible—that's what being truthful means in the context of this book—comes first.

Being truthful involves two different but tightly connected strategies:

- **Avoid self-deception.** We humans evolved to see patterns in meaning- less noise. We jump to conclusions. We see causality where there's only correlation. Truthful graphics are created by people who do their best to prevail over their intellectual shortcomings and cognitive and ideological biases by applying certain critical thinking techniques.

- **Be honest with your audience.** Show them your best understanding of what the reality is. Or, to use the words of Carl Bernstein, one of the reporters who broke the Watergate story in the 1970s, we should strive to pursue and deliver "the best obtainable version of the truth."

I can envision what some of you are thinking: "Oh, but we humans can't be objec- tive and truthful!" Perhaps you have read some critical theorists and sociologists of science too literally[13] or attended Journalistic Reporting 101 in college and got convinced of these two ideas: (a) that the "Truth" is never fully available to us, as we're prone to making reasoning mistakes, and (b) that *we can't strive to prevent and overcome those mistakes*. (a) makes sense; (b) doesn't.

Creating truthful graphics also involves making the right design choices. Here's the first hint that the five qualities of great visualizations aren't independent from each other but are tightly interrelated: to make a truthful graphic, you also need to pay attention to its functions or purposes.

In **Figure 2.4**, I'm presenting the production cost of two products. They clearly co-vary, don't they? Maybe not. Notice that the chart has two Y-axes and, as economist Gary Smith once said, "If you double the axes, you can double the mischief. Using two vertical axes and omitting zero from either or both opens a statistical beauty parlor with many cosmetic possibilities."[14]

As we'll soon see, not all charts need a zero baseline, but being careless with scales and axes is always dangerous. The data look quite different if we plot the lines on the same scale (**Figure 2.5**).

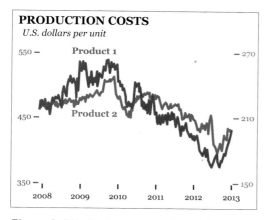

Figure 2.4 Dual-axis charts can be easily misinterpreted.

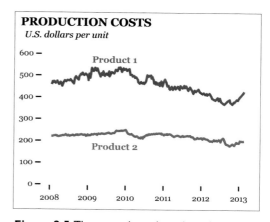

Figure 2.5 The same data, plotted on the same scale. As a general rule, avoid dual-axis charts.

---

13 Here's a quote from popular philosopher Bruno Latour: "'Reason' is applied to the work of allocating agreement and disagreement between words. It is a matter of taste and feeling, know-how and connoisseurship, class and status. We insult, pout, clench our fists, enthuse, spit, sigh, and dream. Who reasons?" I tend to think the best of people, so I'll assume that Latour's ideas are much more nuanced than what those words, and many others in his oeuvre, suggest. I can't be sure, though, as he is a notoriously ironic, obscure, and contradictory author.

14 In his book *Standard Deviations* (2014)

Functional

If getting your information right is the most important step in creating any visualization, the second one is helping the audience interpret it correctly.

In my previous book, *The Functional Art,* I explained that choosing graphic forms to encode information is not mainly a matter of personal taste but can be based on rational thinking. Later in this book I'll dig deeply into this process, which is akin to designing any object meant to be usable and useful: you begin with raw matter, you think of a purpose it can be used for, and then you shape it in a way that enables people to achieve that purpose.

This isn't such an easy task. Look at **Figure 2.6**. I am hiding the percentages in the second pie chart on purpose. The goal of these charts is to help people estimate change—that's explicit in the headline. Try to compare the popularity of hip-hop in 1994 and in 2014; tell me if reggae was more popular in 2014 than it was in 1994. And samba? It's clear that country and classic music were equally popular in 1994, but what about in 2014?

Comparing slices within a single pie chart is hard enough. Comparing two or more pie charts is even more difficult.[15] We're being forced to pay attention to

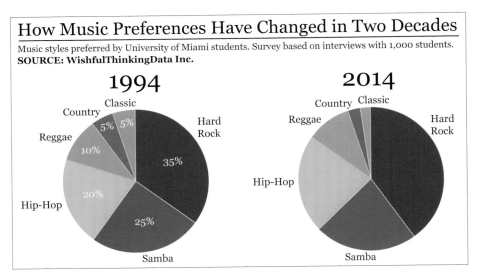

Figure 2.6 Notice the source of the graphic. Quite a bit of wishful thinking on my part was involved in making up the data, as I like hard rock.

---

15 Here's design theorist Edward Tufte: "The only worse design than a pie chart is several of them."

the numbers in the graphics rather than focusing on the size of their segments. And **if you need to read all of the numbers in a chart to understand it, why do you need the chart in the first place?**

The reason why pie charts are still so widespread despite their obvious shortcomings escapes me. I think that people keep using them because they are fun and aesthetically pleasing. Also, as kids we got used to representing part-to-whole relationships using this kind of graphic, even if it is inefficient when you have more than two or three segments.

Now read **Figure 2.7**, in which I display exactly the same data as a **slope chart.** Isn't answering the questions I posed before much easier now? You don't even need to read the labels on the vertical axis to identify what went up and what went down. The purpose (or function) of my graphic is to display change, so I show change in a way that our brains can grasp: what grows bigger goes up, and what becomes smaller goes down.

This is what functional visualization means: choose graphic forms according to the tasks you wish to enable. **The purpose of your graphics should somehow guide your decision of how to shape the information.**

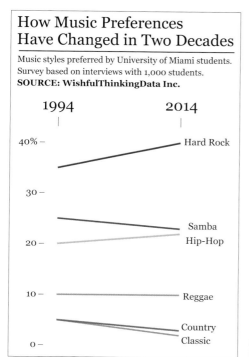

Figure 2.7 A slope chart is much better to represent change between two points in time.

HOW CHICAGO CHANGED THE COURSE OF ITS RIVERS

Between 1889 and 1900, the newly created Sanitary District of Chicago changed the direction of the flow of the city rivers to improve the quality of the water citizens had access to.

Before 1889

Chicago sewage was discharged in the rivers, which flowed into Lake Michigan. The lake was Chicago's main source of drinking water.

After 1900

The Chicago River was diverted by means of control structures and new canals. Water started flowing to the Des Plaines River.

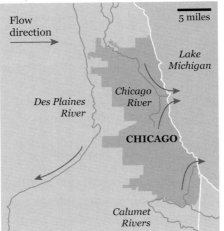

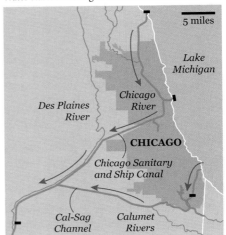

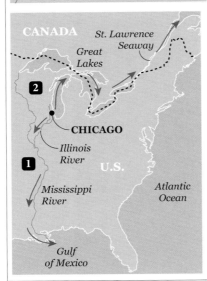

As a result

Water from rivers and lakes in the Chicago area flows in two opposite directions nowadays:

1 Lake Michigan flows into the Chicago River. The Chicago Area Waterway System connects the rivers of Chicago to the Mississippi through the Des Plaines and Illinois Rivers. The water ends in the Gulf of Mexico.

2 Lake Michigan also flows into Lake Huron, Lake Erie, Lake Ontario, and then into the Saint Lawrence Seaway, to end in the Atlantic Ocean.

(Maps have been greatly simplified for clarity.)

SOURCE: United States Environmental Protection Agency

Figure 2.8 An infographic of how the course of rivers in Chicago was changed.

Beautiful

If you ever visit Chicago, make some time for a walk in the Near North Side area, downtown. Find the Chicago River—not a hard feat—and head east toward Lake Michigan. On the north bank of the river, you'll see the Centennial Fountain. There's a picture of it on the following pages, but don't look at it just yet.

When passing by, most tourists are impressed by the huge water arc that the fountain shoots every hour, but they miss the story it tells. The first time I traveled to Chicago, I was lucky to be in the company of two knowledgeable friends, ProPublica's **Scott Klein** and NPR's **Brian Boyer**. They pointed out to me that the Centennial Fountain isn't just an intriguing piece of architectural art. It's also an explanatory visualization.

Before I show the fountain, I'd like you to read an infographic I designed (**Figure 2.8**). This is similar to many other slightly dull news graphics: a handful of simple maps, perhaps one chart or two, some copy to provide context, and that's it. It gets the job done, but it's not particularly exciting.

The Centennial Fountain was built to commemorate the 100th anniversary of the Sanitary District of Chicago. Between 1889 and 1900, that entity reversed the flow of several rivers in Chicago as part of an ambitious plan to solve the many sewage challenges the city had faced in the past. Before this great feat of civic engineering, sewage was discharged into Lake Michigan, which is the city's main source of water, too.

Now see the fountain (**Figure 2.9**) and the explanation of how it should be interpreted (**Figure 2.10**). The central and highest point of the fountain is the city of Chicago. The arms at either side represent the watersheds that originate in it: one goes from Lake Michigan to the Atlantic Ocean, and the other was designed by the Sanitary District of Chicago at the end of the nineteenth century, taking water from the local rivers to the Gulf of Mexico.

Which visual explanation do you prefer? My version (Figure 2.8), which is precise—to be fair, it's as precise as any infographic designed in 45 minutes can be—or the fountain?

Depending on the purpose of the visualization and its audience, I might choose the fountain. This highly schematic map of the watersheds isn't to scale, so it's not precise at all. But does it need to be? The fountain is a physical diagram

Figure 2.9 The Centennial Fountain, Chicago. (Panoramic by Scott Klein.)

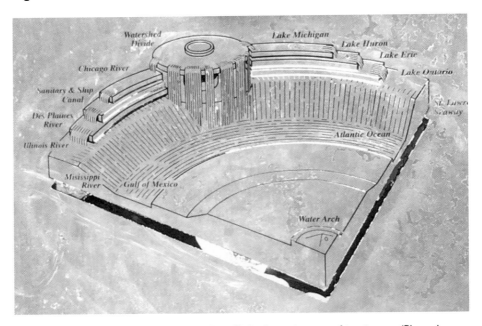

Figure 2.10 An explanation of how to "read" the fountain, part of its signage. (Photo by Scott Klein.)

depicting a system after all, so being true to the underlying geography may not be necessary, particularly if the tourists who visit it more often already know where those rivers and lakes are because they studied them in primary school.[16]

16 If we predict that many among the fountain's audience don't know much about U.S. geography, then it would be advisable to show the abstract diagram and something similar to my infographic side by side.

The Centennial Fountain is arresting, at least for the people I saw passing by during my visit. You cannot fail to notice it, to stop and contemplate its elegant symmetry, which can be appreciated without knowing anything about what it's intended to represent.

These are the essential components of the *feeling* **of beauty**: the way we perceive the appearance of an object and its deep connection to its purpose. Beauty always consists of a balanced mix of sensual and intellectual pleasure. In the words of philosopher **Roger Scruton**, "Art moves us because it is beautiful, and it is beautiful because it means something. It can be meaningful without being beautiful; but to be beautiful it must be meaningful."

Saying that beauty is subjective, as I'm anticipating that some of you will be quick to argue, is trivial. As any triviality, it contains a grain of truth, but think about it this way: *anything* that depends on human brains experiencing and interpreting our surroundings is subjective, as our experience is always mediated by complex interactions between sensation, perception, emotion, and feeling.[17] What matters is to what degree that interaction is particular or universal, parochial, or broad. In other words, **what matters isn't if the objects of our creation are beautiful or not per se, but if they are experienced as beautiful by as many people as possible**.

I am sure that an overwhelming majority of readers, regardless of age, gender, race, or educational background would agree that the second chart in **Figure 2.11**

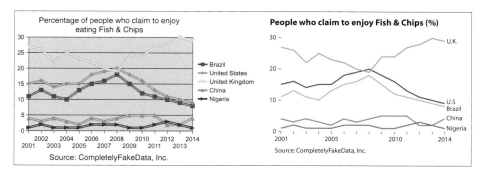

Figure 2.11 Which chart is more aesthetically pleasing?

---

17 The way I commonly use those terms, which aren't synonyms, has been influenced by Antonio Damasio's book *The Feeling of What Happens: Body and Emotion in the Making of Consciousness* (1999).

feels more aesthetically pleasing (and, therefore, closer to being beautiful) than the first one. Both of them present exactly the same content, but the second one does it in a much simpler, clearer, and more elegant way.

Beauty is, thus, not a thing, or a property of objects, but a measure of the emotional experience of awe, wonder, pleasure, or mere surprise that those objects may unleash. The very word "aesthetics" comes from the Greek *aísthēsis*, which means sensation or feeling. As **Donald A. Norman** wrote in his book *Emotional Design* (2003), beauty matters because attractive and pleasing things work better. They put us in a good mood, and so they invite us to invest some effort in understanding how to operate them.

Some things can be beautiful just by virtue of being efficient: they deliver a lot using a minimum amount of elements. Many visualization designers and theorists have stressed the importance of simplicity, and I tend to agree with them. As I've pointed out elsewhere,[18] data visualization isn't the same as data decoration.

Unfortunately, there are people out there who call themselves infographics or data visualization designers but who are in reality data decorators. They deliver charts like **Figure 2.12** with relentless and terrifying consistency. They ignore the advice of the likes of critic **Alice Rawsthorn**: "Design has been

Share of worldwide urban population growth 2010-2050

Figure 2.12 Never do this!

---

18 "Don't call yourself an infographics designer if what you do is data decoration." From http://www.thefunctionalart.com/2014/10/dont-call-yourself-infographics.html

(...) trivialized, misunderstood, and misused. It is routinely confused with styling (...) Few things infuriate designers more [than feeling relegated to the role of styling or decorating]."[19]

That said, personal aesthetic preferences can play a role in visualization, and not all design choices that are unrelated to the data can be deemed as useless, whimsical decoration, or chart junk. The work of the design studio **Accurat** is paradigmatic. It stands in the blurry boundary between data visualization and art. In **Figure 2.13**, Accurat sacrificed some clarity to come up with an artistically expressive display.

Compare Accurat's graphic to a quick redesign I've just made, in **Figure 2.14**, which is just a draft based on a small sample of authors. Mine, if it was finished

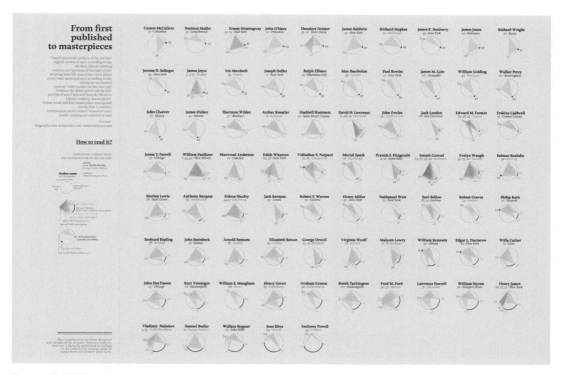

Figure 2.13 Visualization by Accurat.it.

---

19 This comes from Alice Rawsthorn's book *Hello World: Where Design Meets Life*. See references at the end of this chapter.

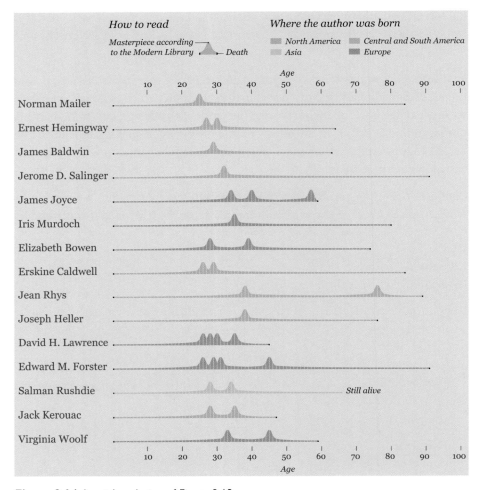

Figure 2.14 A quick redesign of Figure 2.13.

and the writers were sorted correctly, would be more efficient at letting readers extract patterns and make accurate comparisons. However, to me it also looks less intriguing, surprising, and elegant than the original.

Which one do you think I'd print if I were the owner of a publication, mine or Accurat's? Is it appropriate to make a graphic less readable—or more complicated—if that increases its novelty and visual appeal? Are there strategies to make function and beauty reinforce each other? How do we balance them out? I will withhold my answers to those questions for now. I'll just give you a heads-up, also coming from critic Alice Rawsthorn:

> Of all the many thousands of words devoted to untangling the tortuous relationship between art and design, my favourites are those of Charles Eames, who, when asked if design was "an expression of art," said: "I would rather say that it is an expression of purpose. It may (if it is good enough) later be judged as art."

Insightful

"The purpose of visualization is insight, not pictures," proclaims a classic book.[20] This means that good visualizations clear the path to making valuable discoveries that would be inaccessible if the information were presented in a different way. Visualizations that offer just obvious and trivial messages are worthless. Implicitly, their designers ask you to invest effort in reading them in exchange for very little return.

Designers of visualizations, and scholars who study them have struggled to give a coherent definition of *insight*. A group of researchers from the University of North Carolina–Charlotte proposed that there are several kinds of insight.[21] One of them, spontaneous insight, is equivalent to a "eureka" or "a-ha" moment. It's sudden, surprising, and unexpected. Another one, called knowledge-building insight, is based on a gradual and deliberate process of exploration of the information that doesn't necessarily lead to "wow" moments.

The two kinds of insight are related. Talking about science, the authors write, "The major paradigm shifts associated with spontaneous insight can create new structures and relationships in a user's understanding of a problem, which can then serve as the schematic structures needed for generating future knowledge-building insights." This newly acquired knowledge can then open the door to even more spontaneous insights, in a virtual cycle akin to the island of knowledge metaphor I discussed earlier.

---

20 *Readings in Information Visualization: Using Vision to Think*, co-edited by Stuart K. Card, Jock D. Mackinlay, Ben Shneiderman

21 "Defining Insight for Visual Analytics," by Remco Chang, Caroline Ziemkiewicz, Tera Marie Green, and William Ribarsky: http://www.cs.tufts.edu/~remco/publications/2009/cga-viewpoints-insight.pdf.

The hockey stick chart at the beginning of this chapter is an example of how spontaneous insight works. It's likely that many readers experienced a eureka moment the first time they saw it: "Whoa, take a look at *that* steep slope! What's going on there?" Suddenly, what hid behind a veil of complexity became evident; meaningful patterns and trends turned into something they couldn't ignore.

Knowledge-building insight is much more common in interactive visualizations. Consider the graphic in **Figure 2.15**, and go to the link in its caption. First, you'll see the global PhD gender gap. Now, click the little arrow to the left of "All PhDs" and you'll access "Non-science PhDs." Did you notice something? The gender gap is wide, but now there are more women than men in most countries. Women tend to choose graduate programs in the social sciences and the humanities more than men do.

Click the same arrow again, and you'll be as struck as I was by the huge gender imbalance in science and engineering. In places like Taiwan and South Korea, more than 75 percent of graduates are men. If you ever believed that the lack of gender diversity in the tech industry worldwide was a hoax, check the evidence. This interactive visualization will be of great help with that.

Enlightening

Ultimately, the goal of any candid visual communicator is to give people access to the information they need to increase their well-being. Great visualizations change people's minds for the better. They are enlightening.

An enlightening graphic is a consequence of paying attention to the previous four qualities. A graphic that is truthful, functional, beautiful, and insightful has the potential of being enlightening as well. But there's something else to consider at this point: the topic of the visualization. **Choosing topics ethically and wisely—casting light over relevant issues—matters a lot**.

Every semester I mentor several students who want to pursue careers in data visualization or news infographics. One of the projects I'm most proud of was made by a Spanish designer and programmer, **Esteve Boix**, who is very passionate about geeky movies and TV shows.

Esteve wanted to quantify the first season of *Buffy the Vampire Slayer*, the television series that brought fame to writer-director **Joss Whedon**. I agreed on the topic, although I knew close to nothing about Buffy. My experience tells me that students do much better when they can work on things they care about.

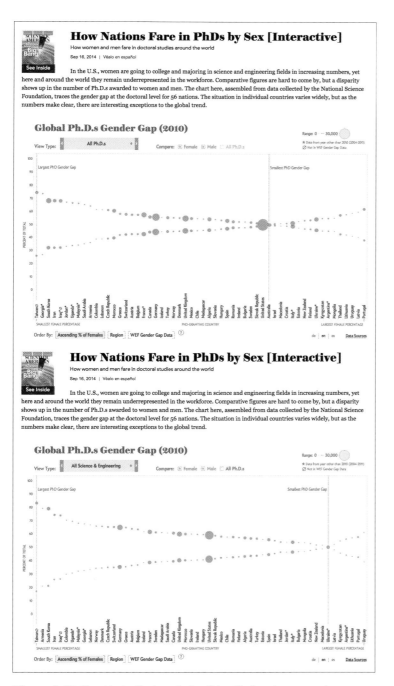

Figure 2.15 Graphic by Periscopic for *Scientific American* magazine: http://www.scientificamerican.com/article/how-nations-fare-in-phds-by-sex-interactive/.

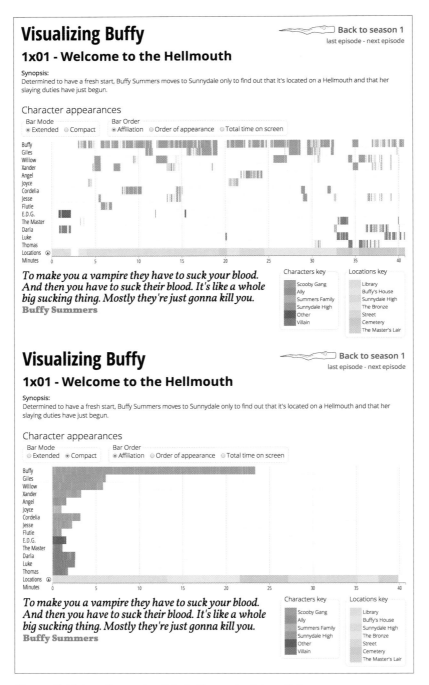

Figure 2.16 http://www.visualizingbuffy.com by Esteve Boix.

The results were impressive (**Figure 2.16**). Esteve turned in a project that explores every episode of the first season of Buffy. You can see which characters were onscreen in each scene and sort and filter the data in different ways. Esteve didn't work with an existing database, by the way. He watched *all* episodes repeatedly to time each character's appearances.

Now, read the following paragraph, which opens an article by Pulitzer Prize winner **David K. Shipler**, written after Hurricane Katrina devastated the coast of Louisiana:

> There is no more telling indictment of reporters and editors than the surprise felt by most Americans in seeing the raw poverty among New Orleans residents after Hurricane Katrina. In an open society, nobody who had been watching television or reading newspapers should have been surprised by what Katrina "revealed," to use the word so widely uttered in the aftermath. The fissures of race and class should be "revealed" every day by America's free press. Why aren't they?[22]

Nowadays, as any of us can potentially be part of that "free press," we can also ask ourselves: which of these topics matters more, Buffy or New Orleans? The easy response is to succumb to relativism: "It depends on who you are and on your audience. Besides, those topics aren't comparable!"

I honestly believe that that's not what you *really* want to answer. Those topics *are* comparable. We humans love to have fun instead of worrying about somber realities—to eat doughnuts instead of broccoli, so to speak—and we'll make any excuse we can to justify our behavior and rationalize it, no matter how well we know, deep inside, that we're fooling ourselves consciously and unashamedly. **Some topics do matter more than others indeed because they are more critical to the well-being of more people**.

I'm not saying that visualizing Buffy is wrong, mind you. It's great, in fact. Lifestyle and popular culture sections in newspapers and magazines exist for that reason. But life is short and time is limited, so given the choice of tweaking our priorities as visual communicators, we perhaps could work a bit more on the New Orleans of this world and a bit less on the vampire slayers. If Esteve wanted to do a second visualization project, I'd suggest being inspired by the work of the **Pulitzer Center**, such as its visualization about childhood mortality (**Figure 2.17**).

---

22 "Monkey See, Monkey Do": http://nhi.org/online/issues/145/monkeyseemonkeydo.html.

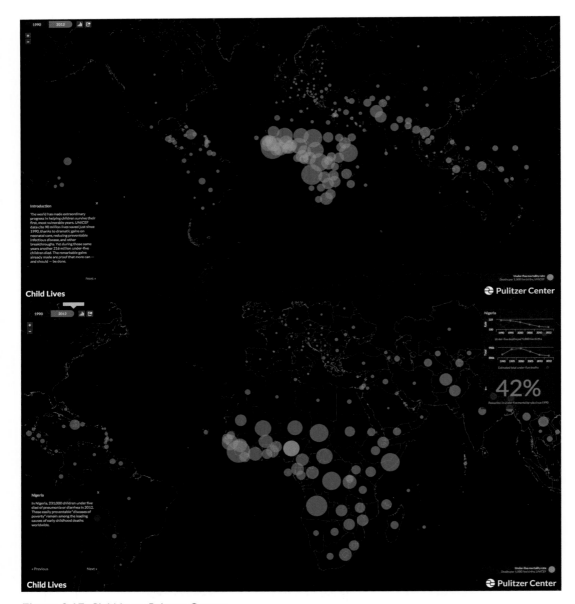

Figure 2.17: Child Lives. Pulitzer Center:
http://pulitzercenter.org/blog/child-lives-visualization-mortality-global-aid-public-health

Caring about social good doesn't mean that we need to become ideologues or activists, which is a quite tempting prospect. The motto of one of the visualization companies that I admire the most, **Periscopic**, is **"do good with data."** I wholeheartedly support that motto, but I also feel uncomfortable with it, as the road to hell is paved with good intentions. Most activists I've met are noble and honest people, but some, like anti-vaccine campaigners, are deeply misguided.

We should certainly do good with data, but only after we've thoroughly made sure that our data is good. Let's see how.

To Learn More

- Papanek, Victor. *Design for the Real World: Human Ecology and Social Change.* Chicago: Chicago Review Press, 2nd ed., 2005. A vigorous manifesto about ethical choices in design.

- Rawsthorn, Alice. *Hello World: Where Design Meets Life.* New York: The Overlook Press, 2013. An overview of what design—graphic and otherwise—really is.

- Scruton, Roger. *Beauty.* New York: Oxford University Press, 2009. A brief and intriguing essay about aesthetics.

- Tufte, Edward R. *The Visual Display of Quantitative Information.* Cheshire, CT: Graphics Press, 1983. Tufte has written four books about visualization design. His first one is still the best.

PART II

truthful

3

The Truth Continuum

To believe that truth is true is not due to daring, but due to humility: the honest man does not think he gets a veto over reality.

—John C. Wright. *Transhuman and Subhuman: Essays on Science Fiction and Awful Truth*

I'll begin with an axiom:

Any visualization is a model.

Think of a locator map. A map is always a simplified depiction of a particular area. It doesn't look exactly like the area itself. Mapmakers remove needless features and emphasize the ones that matter to them in a process of rational and systematic abstraction. Road maps, for instance, highlight roads, cities, towns, and boundaries. Their function is to help you find your way around, not to display every single mountain, valley, or river.

The idea of model can be extended to any act of thinking and communication. We humans use models for perception, cognition, and reasoning because our limited brains are incapable of grasping reality in all its glorious complexity. Our senses and brain mediate our relationship with the world. Our vision doesn't consist of a high-resolution animation of what we have in front of our eyes. That's just a convenient illusion that our brains concoct.[1]

A model is a sign—or a set of signs and their relations—that describes, explains, or predicts something about how nature works with a variable degree of accuracy. Good models abstract reality while keeping its essence at the same time.

Numerical thinking and communication are also based on models. Think of a statistic like the average. If I tell you that the average height of adult U.S. females is 63.8 inches, I am giving you a model that is intended to summarize *all* heights of *all* adult women in the United States. It's not a perfect model, just an approximation. It can be a fair one if a majority of female heights are close to this average.

If I showed you the entire data set of roughly 158 million women's height records, you wouldn't be able to understand anything. It would be too much information for a single human brain to compute. It is chimerical to think that we can make *perfect* models to observe, analyze, and represent reality. Designing incomplete but still informative ones is the most we can achieve.

Therefore, my axiom has an important coda:

The more adequately a model fits whatever it stands for without being needlessly complex, *and* the easier it is for its intended audience to interpret it correctly, the better it will be.

Some models, therefore, are better than others. "Better" means, in this context, more truthful, accurate, informative, and understandable.

---

1   For more details about how and why the brain does this, see my previous book, *The Functional Art*. The stance I am adopting in this chapter is based on a philosophy of science called "model-dependent realism," outlined in Stephen Hawking's and Leonard Mlodinow's book *The Grand Design*: "There is no picture- or theory-independent concept of reality. Instead we will adopt a view that we will call model-dependent realism: the idea that a physical theory or world picture is a model (…) and a set of rules that connect the elements of the model to observations. We make models in science, but we also make them in everyday life. Model-dependent realism applies not only to scientific models but also to the conscious and subconscious mental models we all create in order to interpret and understand the everyday world. There is no way to remove the observer—us—from our perception of the world, which is created through our sensory processing and through the way we think and reason. Our perception—and hence the observations upon which our theories are based—is not direct, but rather is shaped by a kind of lens, the interpretive structure of our human brains."

Dubious Models

For **Figure 3.1**, I used data from the National Cable & Telecommunications Association (NCTA) mentioned in Chapter 2. The subtitle the NCTA originally wrote, which I'm reproducing verbatim, makes its message explicit, in case you had any doubts: broadband cable connections in the United States have improved quite a lot in the past few years. But have they?

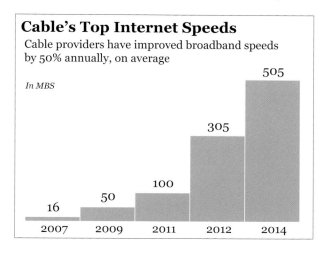

Figure 3.1 Misleading your audience may yield benefits in the short term. In the long term, however, it may destroy your credibility.

This isn't really a satisfactory model if we wish to understand the overall growth of Internet access speeds. This graphic is showing just top speeds! We are missing important information. How about minimum speeds, average speeds, and, more importantly, the number of people who have access to those top, average, and minimum speeds? That would make the model—the chart—more truthful. By the way, it'd also be necessary to show all years, rather than what seem to be carefully picked ones.

Some people devise bad visual models on purpose, to mislead their audience, but more often a faulty model is the result of a well-intentioned designer not paying proper attention to the data. **Figure 3.2** is a chart of traffic fatalities between 1975 and 2012. Consider it for a minute. I live in Florida, so I find it worrying that road deaths have increased so much, while most other states have improved noticeably. But is this what really happened?

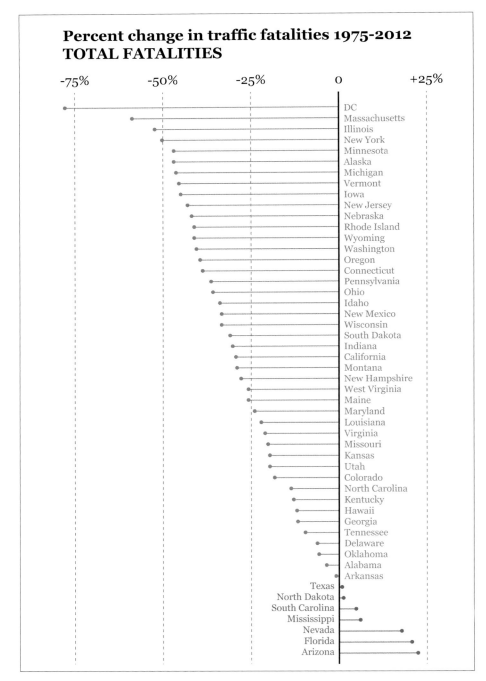

Figure 3.2 Source:
http://graphzoo.tumblr.com/post/85330752462/data-source-httpwwwnhtsagov-code.

An analogy may come in handy: let's say you design a graphic about motor vehicle accidents that compares Chicago, Ill. (population of 2.7 million), to Lincoln, Neb. (population of 269,000). Would that be fair? Not entirely. The absolute numbers—the actual case count—are relevant, but you'd also need to apply some control to them, generating a *relative* variable. In the case of Figure 3.2, it would be the ratio between accidents and population or number of vehicles.

$$(\text{Fatalities/Vehicles}) \times 100{,}000 = \text{Rate of fatalities per 100,000 vehicles}$$

We should apply that formula to both the 1975 and 2012 figures and then calculate the difference. It may well be that some states are experiencing a large drop in fatalities just because their populations have not changed that much and because roads and cars have become safer.

We can go even further. An exploration of this topic could take into account not just the number of vehicles but also how many miles those vehicles are driven, as commute distances in the United States vary a lot. You can see the results in **Figure 3.3**. I highlighted Florida in both charts. Also, notice North Dakota. I wonder if those figures are related to the oil boom in the late 2000s. According to the Pew Research Center, North Dakota added nearly 100,000 workers between 2009 and 2014 alone, and commutes are long.[2]

To make our visualization even better, we may want to apply more controls, like the effect of traffic regulations. For instance, seat belt laws in the United States began to be adopted in the mid-1980s. By the end of that decade, many states still didn't mandate seat belts for adults. New Hampshire still doesn't. Besides, in 16 states you won't get a ticket for not using your seat belt unless you're pulled over for another infraction. According to the Centers for Disease Control and Prevention, "Seat belts reduce serious crash-related injuries and deaths by about half."[3]

||||▮▮▮▮▮||||

---

2   "How North Dakota's 'man rush' compares with past population booms." http://www.pewresearch.org/fact-tank/2014/07/16/how-north-dakotas-man-rush-compares-with-past-population-booms/

3   I am taking this statistic at face value, but you may want to check it: "Seat Belts: Get the Facts." http://www.cdc.gov/motorvehiclesafety/seatbelts/facts.html

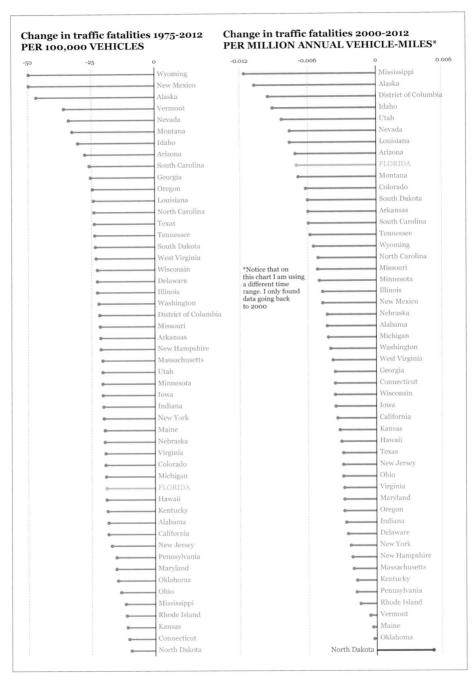

Figure 3.3 When we apply some controls, the results are quite different.

In 2010, *Wired* magazine proclaimed "The Web Is Dead. Long Live the Internet" on its front cover.[4] The point of the story was that Web browsers were in decline as a means of accessing data from the Internet. Other technologies, such as apps or video streaming, were on the rise.

Readers of that article were greeted by a stacked area chart similar to the first one in **Figure 3.4**. Web browsers were born in the early 1990s, saw their peak in 2000, when they accounted for more than 50 percent of Internet traffic, and declined later. In 2010, just 23 percent of the data downloaded from the Internet were accessed through a browser.

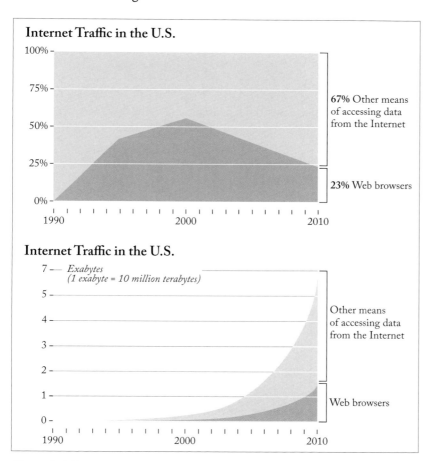

Figure 3.4 Two versions of the same story. (Sources: *Wired* magazine and BoingBoing.net.)

---

4   "The Web Is Dead. Long Live the Internet." http://www.wired.com/2010/08/ff_webrip/all/

Many of the problems with this chart—and with the story as a whole—were spotted by **Rob Beschizza**, managing editor of BoingBoing.net.[5] In the mid-90s, the number of Internet users was counted in *millions*. By 2010, it was counted in *billions*. Moreover, the kind of content people download has changed quite a lot. In the '90s, we mostly consumed text and low-resolution pictures. In 2010, video and file-sharing services were widespread. Many more people with much better connections were downloading much larger files. Those facts are reflected in the second chart in Figure 3.4, which is based on the one that Beschizza designed. The Web is hardly dying, after all.

The Mind, That Clumsy Modeler

A visualization is a model that serves as a conduit between a mental model in the designer's brain and a mental model inside the audience's brains.[6] Blunders, therefore, can originate on the designer's side but also on the reader's side. I've learned this the hard way, by being misled by wonderful and accurate visualizations numerous times.

Every year I travel to Kiev, Ukraine, to teach a one-week introduction to visualization workshop. As I write this, Ukraine is suffering the consequences of a chain of destabilizing events: a pro-Russian president was expelled by popular protests, a pro-Western government was democratically elected, Russia then annexed the region of Crimea, and, as of this writing, Russia's president, Vladimir Putin, continues supporting separatist militia groups in the eastern part of the country.[7]

None of this had happened in 2012, when I flew to Kiev for my regular gig. Before my trip I had been in touch with **Anatoly Bondarenko**, a programmer, journalist, and visualization designer who works for an online media organization called Texty (http://texty.org.ua).

I met Anatoly in person, and he showed me his work. I was enthralled by one map in particular (**Figure 3.5**), which displayed the results of the 2012 parliamentary elections. Orange circles correspond to districts won by pro-Western parties.

---

5   "Is the web really dead?" http://boingboing.net/2010/08/17/is-the-web-really-de.html

6   Designer and audience can be the same individual, of course. In some cases, you design a visualization to improve your mental models, to understand something better.

7   BBC News has a good recap of the crisis at http://www.bbc.com/news/world-europe-25182823.

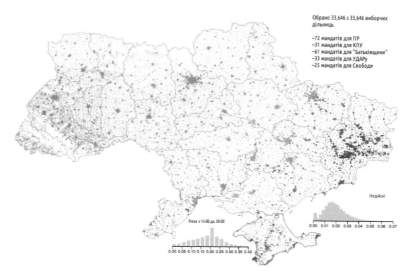

Figure 3.5 Results of the Ukrainian parliamentary elections, 2012. (Visualization by Texty: http://texty.org.ua/mod/datavis/apps/elections2012/.)

Blue circles identify districts where pro-Russian parties got a majority of the vote. In both cases, the intensity of the color is proportional to the percentage of the vote obtained by the winning parties. The size of each circle is proportional to the size of the voting population.

You don't need to understand a word of Ukrainian to immediately reach a striking insight: Ukraine, before the crisis began, was a fundamentally divided country. The west was (and still is) mostly pro-Western, and the east and south were mostly pro-Russian.

A year after my visit, Ukrainians in the western part of the country began protesting against President Viktor Yanukovych after he rejected an agreement with the European Union and proposed to strengthen ties with Russia. Yanukovych fled to Russia a few months later, when the protests turned into a full-blown uprising.

When the protests exploded, Western media began publishing maps like the ones in **Figure 3.6**. If you compare them to Figure 3.5, which had had such an impact on me one year earlier, you'll perceive an almost perfect overlap: pro-Western vote corresponds with protests and with fewer people who have Russian as their primary language. What a conspicuous pattern!

Presidential Election Results 2010
51% or more of the vote
■ Tymoshenko (pro-Western)
■ Yanukovych (pro-Russian)

Main native language
20% or more of the citizens
■ Ukrainian
■ Russian

Cities where the protests against president Yanukovych began

Kiev

Figure 3.6 Ukraine seems to be a completely divided country.

I immediately shot an e-mail to Anatoly asking, "Do you remember the map that you showed me when I was in Kiev? It explains *everything* that is going on right now in your country! It's so prescient! Ukraine is clearly two completely different countries!"

A few hours later, Anatoly replied. His suggestion, which I am not reproducing verbatim, became a motto that I share with my students every semester: **"It's more complicated than that."** I usually add: "And if it's really more complicated than that, then that complexity, which is crucial for understanding the story, needs to be shown in the visualization." **Good visualizations shouldn't over-simplify information. They need to clarify it. In many cases, clarifying a subject requires *increasing* the amount of information, not *reducing* it**.[8]

What could have been added to my mental model was the results of polls like the one that Anatoly attached to his e-mail (**Figure 3.7**). Voting patterns may reveal a sharp ideological divide in Ukraine, but when you ask people if they want to strengthen ties with the European Union or with Russia, the portrait you get is much more interesting. In the east, the most pro-Russian region of Ukraine, just 51 percent of people were in favor of a trade agreement with Russia. In the south, where Crimea is, people's preferences are split almost equally.

According to Anatoly, Western media were not presenting a nuanced account of the situation. Everyone in Ukraine knows that their country is contradictory and messy—is there any country that isn't?—and that the "Westernized people

---

8   The difference between simplifying and clarifying was suggested to me by famous explanation graphics designer Nigel Holmes (http://www.nigelholmes.com).

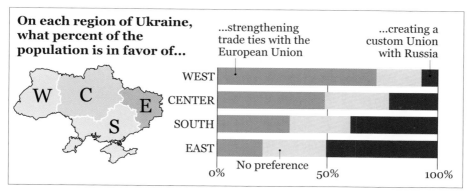

Figure 3.7 What Ukrainians want.

here, Russianized people there" narrative is a gross mischaracterization. The divide exists, but it's not as clear-cut as it seems. When Ukrainians see Texty's election results map, they know how to put it in context. They see beyond the visualization because they come to it with previously acquired knowledge.

That doesn't happen with readers in other parts of the world. When they see Texty's map, they may create faulty mental models, like I did. They jump to conclusions. **What you design is never exactly what your audience ends up interpreting, so reducing the chances for misinterpretation becomes crucial.** In a case like this, adding a textual explanation to the map can really help. The map would still show the divide. Text would warn people against making far-fetched inferences.

Why Are We So Often Mistaken?

In the past decade, books about how prone to error human reasoning is have proliferated wildly.[9] The portrait of the human mind that those books outline is humbling. Here's the scenario that they describe:

1. I detect interesting patterns, regardless of whether or not they are real. I'll call this **the patternicity bug**.

---

9   After writing this line, I looked at the shelves in my home office and saw Daniel Kahneman's *Thinking Fast and Slow*; Michael Shermer's *The Believing Brain*; Christopher Chabris' and Daniel Simons' *The Invisible Gorilla*; Carol Travis' and Elliot Aronson's *Mistakes Were Made (but not by me)*; Robert Kurzban's *Why Everyone (Else) Is a Hypocrite*; Dean Buonomano's *Brain Bugs*; Will Storr's *The Unpersuadables*; Mahzarin R. Banaji's and Anthony G. Greenwald's *Blindspot*; and David Eagleman's *Incognito*. And there are more in my office at the University of Miami.

2. I immediately come up with a coherent explanation for those patterns. This is **the storytelling bug**.

3. I start seeing all further information I receive, even the one that conflicts with my explanation, in a way that confirms it. I refuse to give my explanation up, no matter what. This is **the confirmation bug**.

A caution is pertinent at this point. These are indeed bugs or biases, but they play a key role in our survival. Many authors have pointed out that the human mind didn't evolve to discover the truth, but to help us survive in a world where we needed to make quick, intuitive, life-or-death decisions even when information was punily incomplete. The consequence is that we have all inherited what we could call the "Faint noise behind those bushes > Possible predator > Run or prepare to defend yourself" algorithm.

Snap judgments and intuitions are still a crucial component of reasoning. Risk expert **Gerd Gigerenzer** has written that, "Intuition is unconscious intelligence based on personal experience and smart rules of thumb."[10] To develop good models of reality—descriptive, explanatory, predictive, and so on—we use both intuition and deliberate thinking. Even the most hard-nosed scientific theories begin as gut feelings that are thoroughly tested later.

In the face of patchy evidence, which may make testing impossible, making guesses can be a good option if we have the domain-specific knowledge to do so with accuracy. For instance, after 20 years of designing visualizations, I have developed a gut feeling for when a graphic will work. However, if experiments— even unscientific ones, where I simply show a graphic to friends—show that any of my intuitive design choices is wrong, I need to be prepared to discard it.

Our challenge is that **we snap-judge whether we have the necessary knowledge for it or not**. This is why I created a simplistic mental model of Ukraine after casually comparing several maps of the country: I lacked the domain-specific information to make good inferences from the data, but *I made them anyway*. The very faculties that aided our survival in the past are the ones that can lead us to mistakes in the modern world. As visualization designers and data communicators, it is of utmost importance to be aware of this challenge.

---

10 Gigerenzer has written several books about risk and uncertainty. My favorite one, from which this quote is extracted, is *Risk Savvy: How to Make Good Decisions* (2014).

Mind Bug 1: Patternicity

The first mental bug in our list is our astonishing capacity for detecting patterns, visual and otherwise. This is the very faculty that makes visualization such a powerful tool: transform tons of numbers into a chart or a data map and, suddenly, you'll see those numbers under a completely different light.

However, many patterns that your eyes and brain detect in data are the result of pure coincidences and noise. Author **Michael Shermer** calls our tendency to perceive patterns, even when there's nothing meaningful in front of us, **patternicity**. Other scientists call it **apophenia**. Start tossing a dice, and if you get the same number three or four times in a row, you will automatically begin to suspect that there's something wrong with it. It may be amiss, but all may be normal, too. Randomness makes that result possible. Besides, randomness rarely looks truly random to us.

See **Figure 3.8**. It's not very elegant, I know, but don't worry about that. Those are unemployment rates in nine fictional countries between 2010 and 2015. If you just take a quick look at them, you may not notice anything, but stare at them for 30 seconds, and you'll likely begin seeing patterns. Do you notice that some data points repeat regularly over time, that some highs and lows tend to

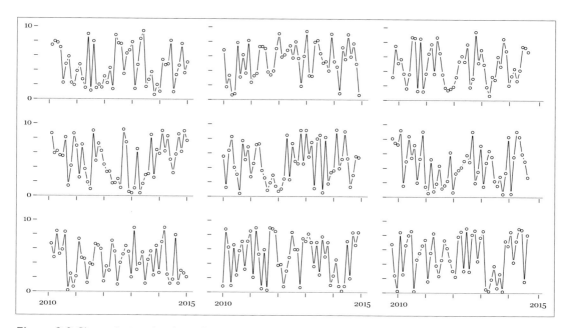

Figure 3.8 Charts designed with random numbers.

appear in the same years in some of these countries? The more you scrutinize this array of charts, the more you'll get to see.

Well, all those charts are completely random. I wrote a four-line script that generated 50 numbers between 1 and 10, ran it nine times, and designed the charts. Even if I *know* that they are based on meaningless data, my brain still *wants to see* something interesting in these charts. It whispers, "There are so many coincidences here.... It's impossible that they have appeared just as a result of nature playing dice, isn't it?"[11]

Randomness and uncertainty in data may render many news stories and visualizations (think of charts showing tiny changes in the unemployment rate or in the stock market) completely meaningless. Still, people keep making them because of our natural inclination for storytelling.

Mind Bug 2: Storytelling

Once we detect patterns, it is only natural that we'll try to find a cause-effect explanation for them. My reaction to comparing Texty's map of Ukraine to others in Western media was to jump to conclusions, to fill in the gaps, and to frame the results as a story—a made-up one. We humans feel patterns first, we build narratives based on them, and then we look for ways of justifying the rationality of our narrative.

Essayist **Will Storr** defines "story" this way in his book *The Unpersuadables* (2014):

> At its most basic level, a story is a description of something happening that contains some form of sensation, or drama. It is, in other words, an explanation of cause and effect that is soaked in emotion (...) We are natural-born storytellers who have a propension to believe our own tales.

We humans love exciting stories. We see a single event and we transform it into a general rule. We stereotype and generalize. We read about an Asian math genius, and we infer that all Asians are good at math. We see two events in sequential order, and we automatically infer a causal relationship between them. Many

---

11   Discussing the weird world of quantum mechanics, Albert Einstein claimed that God—a.k.a. "nature," as Einstein was an agnostic—doesn't play dice with reality. According to Stephen Hawking, "Einstein was very unhappy about this apparent randomness in nature (...) He seemed to have felt that the uncertainty was only provisional: but that there was an underlying reality in which particles would have well-defined positions and speeds, and would evolve according to deterministic laws, in the spirit of Laplace."
http://www.hawking.org.uk/does-god-play-dice.html.

among us still believe that cold weather causes colds, when the truth is that what makes cold transmission more likely is our habits: when it's cold outside, we tend to stay indoors more, closer to people who may be already sick.

It happens to me, to you, to all of us. Being aware of this mental bug is paramount for visualization designers, but we're generally oblivious to it, with dire consequences. In January 2014, infographics designer **Raj Kamal** wrote an article in which he explained his creative process:

> It's the "message" that decides the presentation. The numbers, visual, or text or a combination of these are to only support the way of putting the message across. This also changes the way one conceptualizes a graphic. The thought starts with the message and then gets into putting other related information together to support it instead of starting with the data and thinking of what to make of it (...) The advantage of taking this route is also that you are not just restricted by topics or numbers or just presenting "news." You can go a step further and air your "views," too, to make a point.[12]

Proceeding this way is a recipe for disaster, but it is one that is too common in the news industry. A managing editor comes up with a headline—"We're going to show how raising the minimum wage increases unemployment"—and then asks her reporters to *just* look for data to support it. It is the flaw, I believe, behind *Wired*'s story about the death of Web browsers, discussed before.

Storytelling can be a potent tool for communicating effectively, but it is dangerous if it blinds us toward evidence that should compel us to tweak or discard our models. This is why the modern rise of uncritical advocacy and activism, as well as opinionated "journalism," worries me so much.

After we've grown enamored of our beautiful models, it's difficult to get rid of them. We all have a very sensitive mental trigger that reacts when we're challenged by contradicting information. If it could speak, that trigger might say, "I am a reasonable, well-read brain that thinks carefully about everything, weighing all evidence available. How do you even dare to *suggest* that I'm wrong?" This tunnel-vision effect is the result of cognitive dissonance, and the best way we humans have developed to cope with it is the confirmation bug, also called **confirmation bias**.

---

12 "Everyday Visuals as News." http://visualoop.com/16740/everyday-visuals-as-news-views-and-graphics. Kamal is a very talented Indian designer. He has recently recognized that those words don't really describe how infographics should be made.

Mind Bug 3: Confirmation

Once a good story takes over our understanding of something, we'll attach to it like leeches to warm, plump flesh. An attack on our beliefs will be seen as personal. Even if we are presented with information that renders our beliefs worthless, we'll try to avoid looking at it, or we'll twist it in a way that confirms them. We humans try to reduce dissonance no matter what.[13] To do it, we can selectively search just for evidence that backs our thoughts, or we may interpret any evidence, old and new, in a way that also achieves that goal.

Psychologists have observed these effects so many times that it's appalling that the general public isn't more aware of them. In a classic 2003 study, Stanford University social psychologist **Geoffey Cohen** presented welfare policies to groups of liberals and conservatives.[14] Liberal people endorsed conservative policies if they were presented as coming from the Democratic Party. The opposite was also true: conservatives favored liberal policies if they were told that they had been proposed by the Republican Party.

When asked about why they were in favor or against the policies, both liberals and conservatives said that they had carefully analyzed the evidence. All of them were blind to their own tendency to self-deception, but were ready to attribute self-deception to others.

Similar studies have been done about opinions on gun control, Israeli-Palestinian negotiations, supernatural beliefs, and so on. A very worrying result from some of them is that, in religiously or politically contentious issues, such as climate change, more and better information may not lead to better understanding, but to more polarization. A study titled "The Tragedy of the Risk-Perception Commons: Culture Conflict, Rationality Conflict, and Climate Change" is worth quoting extensively:

> The principal reason people disagree about climate change science is not that it has been communicated to them in forms they cannot understand. Rather, it is that positions on climate change convey values—communal concern versus individual self-reliance; prudent self-abnegation versus the heroic pursuit of reward; humility versus ingenuity; harmony with

---

13 The literature on cognitive dissonance and confirmation bias is also abundant. *Mistakes Were Made (but not by me)*, by Carol Travis and Elliot Aronson, is a good primer. The examples mentioned in this section come from this book.

14 Geoffrey L. Cohen, "Party Over Policy: The Dominating Impact of Group Influence on Political Beliefs." https://ed.stanford.edu/sites/default/files/party_over_policy.pdf

nature versus mastery over it—that divide them along cultural lines. Merely amplifying or improving the clarity of information on climate change science won't generate public consensus if risk communicators fail to take heed of the cues that determine what climate change risk perceptions express about the cultural commitments of those who form them.

In fact, such inattention can deepen polarization. Citizens who hold hierarchical and individualistic values discount scientific information about climate change in part because they associate the issue with antagonism to commerce and industry. (...) Individuals are prone to interpret challenges to beliefs that predominate with their cultural community as assaults on the competence of those whom they trust and look to for guidance. That implication—which naturally provokes resistance—is likely to be strengthened when communicators with a recognizable cultural identity stridently accuse those who disagree with them of lacking intelligence or integrity.[15]

Think about this the next time you feel tempted to call someone you disagree with an idiot during a discussion in social media. **The way we present information matters as much as the soundness of the information itself.**

Do you want to get an even better example of dissonance reduction and confirmation bias? Think of your own media consumption. My political opinions are those of a centrist in economic issues and those of a secular liberal in socio-cultural ones. Can you make a guess of which newspapers and weekly magazines I've read on a regular basis for years? I bet that many of you immediately said *The New York Times* and the *New Yorker* magazine.

I don't read those publications just because they are high-quality journalistic products. I also enjoy them because I can read them with my unconscious ideological outrage alarm on standby mode. That's much harder to do when I read quality conservative publications, such as *The Weekly Standard* or *The American Spectator*. But I do read these, too, consciously silencing the annoying little imp who whines, "This is bonkers," before evaluating the arguments.[16] It is hard work, but it's work that needs to be done. My mind, as yours, as anyone's, needs to be disciplined. Left to its own will, when contradicted, it becomes a toddler prone to vociferous tantrums.

|||▌▌▌▉▌||||

---

15 Available online at https://www.law.upenn.edu/live/files/ 296-kahan-tragedy-of-the-riskperception1pdf

16 Notice the "quality" adjective. I avoided suggesting cable networks of any ideological stripe on purpose.

Exposing yourself to contradicting evidence isn't enough. You also need to use tools and methods to evaluate it, as not all opinions and interpretations of evidence and models of reality are equally valuable. The books mentioned in this chapter can help a lot with that, but I'd like to at least share with you two quotes and a graphic that I like to bring to my classes when discussing the many challenges we face when designing visualizations.

Here are the quotes:

> "The first principle is that you must not fool yourself—and you are the easiest person to fool." Richard Feynman.[17]

> "(...) The great tragedy of Science—the slaying of a beautiful hypothesis by an ugly fact." Thomas Henry Huxley.[18]

Both Feynman and Huxley were referring to science, but I believe that neither was talking *just* about science. They were talking about life in general. The first principle in life is that you must not fool yourself, and a great tragedy in life is that beautiful ideas must be slayed by ugly facts, whenever they appear.

And now, the graphic, which I call **the truth continuum**.

Truth Is Neither Absolute, Nor Relative

Let's go back to the beginning of the chapter, when I wrote that every visualization is a model and that the quality of any model is higher the better that model fits the reality it stands for, without being needlessly complicated. Remember that a model is an abstraction that describes, explains, or predicts something about the workings of nature.[19]

For the next mental exercise, forget that this book is about data and visualization. Imagine that I use the word "model" to refer to *any* kind of model, from mere opinions to scientific theories, or to the different ways to communicate them, from text to visualizations.

Unless you're a pathological liar or a very particular kind of journalist or strategic communicator, whenever you create a model, you want it to be as close to

---

17 Caltech commencement address, 1974. http://tinyurl.com/h9v3fyp

18 "Biogenesis and Abiogenesis," 1870. http://aleph0.clarku.edu/huxley/CE8/B-Ab.html

19 Some of my thoughts in this section have been greatly influenced by David Deutsch's book *The Beginning of Infinity*. See "To learn more" at the end of the chapter.

the truth as possible. Let's suppose that we create a continuum and that we put our model in the middle, like this:

Absolutely ◄---//--------------------•--------------------//--► Absolutely
untrue *My model* true

How can we make this model move further to the right? By applying rigorous thinking tools such as logic, statistics, experiments, and so on. More and better information begets better models.[20] A model solidly grounded on these methods is likely to be closer to being true than to being false. I say "likely" because in this little mental exercise I'm assuming that we don't know what "absolutely true" really means. We can't. We are humans, remember?

Nonetheless, almost 400 years after Sir Francis Bacon created empirical and experimental science, we have collected enough evidence to know that these methods work. They never give us a perfect understanding of reality but, based on their inherent self-correcting nature (good theories are inevitably killed by *better* theories), they do give us a series of better *approximations*.

Notice that the scale in the diagram is truncated. To understand why, I will refer you to the metaphor of the Island of Knowledge in the prologue. Here you have it again: our island expands and expands, eating away the Sea of Mystery, but the Shoreline of Wonder will never touch the coveted horizon that we long for. For the same reason, on this linear diagram, we'll never know for sure how far we still are from the left or right ends.

It's possible to visualize a comparison between two models that describe, explain, or predict the same reality: one based on applying rigorous methods and another one that is the product of pure guesswork. The diagram would look like this:

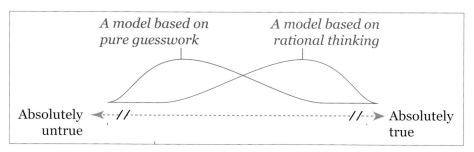

A model based on
pure guesswork

A model based on
rational thinking

Absolutely ◄---//--------------------------------//--► Absolutely
untrue true

---

20 If we are able to interpret it appropriately, needless to say.

Some clarification is necessary. First of all, the models aren't represented by dots anymore, but by lines with a smooth bump. Here's what this means: when you devise a model, it's never possible to know exactly where it lies in the continuum. All you know is that evidence-based reasoning may move you closer to the right-most end. That's what the bump represents: the higher the curve, the larger the likelihood of the model being in that point in the continuum. Still, there's a possibility that, no matter how rigorous you have been, your model is still inadequate. That's why the blue line extends all the way to the left end.

The bump of the red line is on the left because there are more ways of getting things wrong than right when your only thinking strategy is wacky guesswork. The red line extends all the way to the right end of the continuum because everyone can have a lucky day and hit truth by pure chance.

But it is not true, in science and in other realms of rational inquiry, that there may be competing explanations for the same reality, for the same event, phenomenon, and so on? Absolutely. How do you then decide which one is better?

A good evaluation of the tools and methods used to reach them (logic, statistics, experimentation, and so on) can help in choosing an explanation. However, just to continue with our idea of a truth continuum, it may happen that *multiple good models* exist at the same point on the scale. If they are all based on sound reasoning, *they will all be provisionally true* until more evidence is collected and analyzed. They are all true in the sense that they are equally rigorous, and equally effective, precise, and accurate at describing or explaining a reality, or at making predictions about it.

We can visualize this. See the diagram below, but instead of dots, imagine that you have brackets and curves, like in the previous one. I didn't use them here because the picture got very messy.

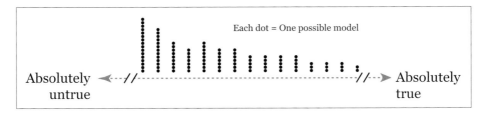

There are many more dots on one side than on the other because there are many more ways of screwing up than of being right about anything.

At this point you may be feeling tempted to send me an e-mail to ask why I bore you with this philosophical discussion. Here's the reason: **the way we think about theories and opinions being more or less true is identical to the way we can think of truer or untruer visualizations**. And the strategies that we apply to make our opinions truer are similar to the strategies that we can apply to make better visualizations.

On the morning of August 15, 2013, my breakfast was ruined by an alarming headline: "Study finds more than a quarter of journalism grads wish they'd chosen another career." It belonged to a story on the website of the Poynter Institute, one of the most distinguished United States journalism education institutions.

I immediately clicked the link and started reading.[21] I have three appointments in the University of Miami, and one of them is in the department of journalism. Was I going to lose one-third of my students in the near future?

The story began with this data point:

"About 28 percent of journalism grads wish they'd chosen another field, the annual survey of grads by the University of Georgia's Grady College says."

A percentage isn't bad per se, as I am sure that the people who conducted the survey and the person who wrote the story know their math. But is this percentage truthful enough? A single figure alone is rarely meaningful, so, at least for now, until we think more about the evidence we have, let's put this story to the left on the truth continuum.

Absolutely untrue ← //---●----------------------//--→ Absolutely true

Model 1
28% wished that they'd chosen a different field

---

21 Here's the story: http://www.poynter.org/news/mediawire/221280/ more-than-one-quarter-of-journalists-wish-theyd-chosen-another-career/. An important caveat: the headline mentions journalism grads, but the data represent journalism and mass communication grads. Mass communication comprises also marketing, advertisement, public relations, etc.

How can we create a more truthful model? An obvious strategy would be to explore the data set further. **When doing a visualization, or the analysis that precedes it, always ask yourself: compared to what, to whom, to when, to where…?**[22]

In our case, we can begin with the "when" factor, as it's present in the survey. The first graphic in **Figure 3.9** shows the variation of our percentage since 1999, which is minimal, despite dramatic changes in the job market. This is something worth analyzing.

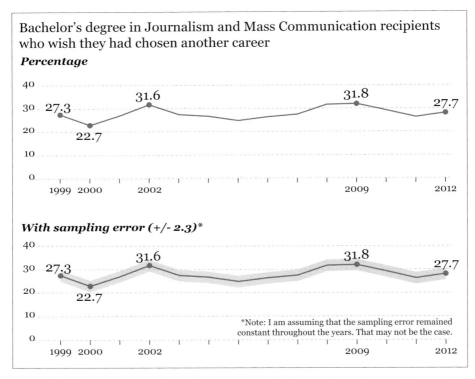

Figure 3.9 How many journalism and mass communication grads say they aren't happy with their choice of major? I am assuming that the error was the same in all years, which may not be the case.

---

22 Here's Edward Tufte in *Envisioning Information* (1990): "At the heart of quantitative reasoning is a single question: Compared to what?"

We could go even further and reveal the sampling error, something done in the second chart in that same figure. Any study based on sampling a population won't give you a precise number, but a range.[23] The sampling error here is 2.3 percentage points. That means that if the graphic shows a value of 30, what you're actually saying is that you are reasonably confident that the actual value in that moment in time was between 27.7 percent (30 minus 2.3) and 32.3 percent (30 plus 2.3). We have made our model/story/graphic a bit better. Let's move it closer to the right.

Now, if you were to give an even more accurate assessment of how badly journalism and mass communication grads feel about their career choice, what else would you need to look into?

I'd say that we'd need to compare them to other grads. I wonder, for instance, how many philosophy majors—to choose a major at random, ahem—now regret not double-majoring in computer science, or vice versa. The study I am using as a source itself recognizes that not comparing to other disciplines is a shortcoming.

Imagine that we can survey other grads, talk about it in the story, and display it in our visualization. The result would likely stand a bit further to the right.

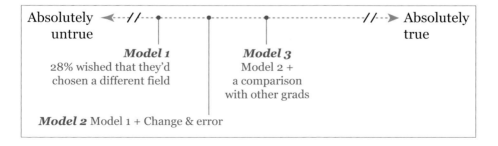

---

23 We'll talk about what "error" is in the next chapters.

What I've done so far is to increase **depth**, not just in my informal analysis of the data behind the story. All those multiple levels of depth should be revealed and explained to readers if we want them to generate a mental model that is similar to ours.

But is increasing depth enough? Not always. We also need to think of **breadth**. So far, I have toyed with just one variable, the percentage of grads who claim that they wish they had chosen another career. But aren't there other important factors that should become part of our model?

In **Figure 3.10**, I have summarized just a few, such as median annual wages. I've added the median for all occupations and a few other jobs in media (just a portion of journalism grads end up being reporters and editors). Many other variables could also be evaluated, including the number of news organizations, which has been in decline for years, versus the relative health of the marketing and public relations industry, which also employs journalists.

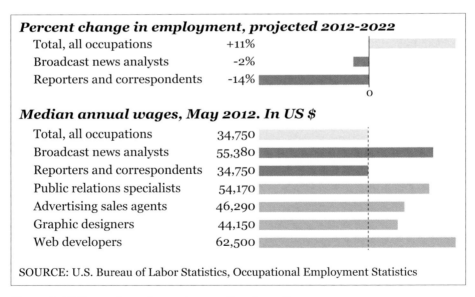

Figure 3.10 Comparison of several occupations in media.

If we reach this point, we're ready to update our truth continuum diagram again.

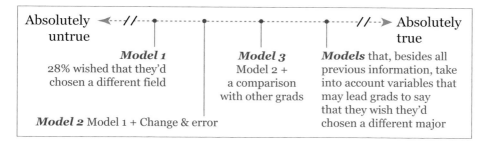

Absolutely ◀--//--•----------•----------•-----//--▶ Absolutely
untrue | | | true

Model 1
28% wished that they'd
chosen a different field

Model 3
Model 2 +
a comparison
with other grads

Models that, besides all
previous information, take
into account variables that
may lead grads to say
that they wish they'd
chosen a different major

Model 2 Model 1 + Change & error

Let's do a quick recap:

1. Job and wage prospects for journalism and mass communication grads who wish to be reporters and achieve that goal aren't great, to say the least. The situation may be a bit better for those few who land jobs as broadcast analysts or news graphic designers or Web developers, and even better for those who work in strategic communication.

2. The number of large- and medium-sized news organizations in the United States has been in decline in the past few years. This is due to shrinking circulations and audiences, as well as diminishing ad revenue. Salaries in other industries that hire journalism grads (marketing, for instance) are better, but not enormously different.

3. In spite of all that, the percentage of journalism grads who say that they wish they had chosen another career has changed very little since 1999. It's just 0.4 percentage points higher in 2012 than it was in 1999, and the sampling error of this survey is 2.3 percentage points.

My tentative conclusion is that, if we refer specifically to journalists, the headline and the angle of the story could adopt a positive tone. Instead of "More than a quarter of journalism grads wish they'd chosen another career," we could say, "Even if job prospects for journalists have worsened substantially and they may worsen even further in the future, the percentage of grads who wish they'd chosen another career hasn't changed at all in more than a decade." Is my model, the analysis, and the presentation of that analysis perfect? It isn't—far from it, as I haven't paid a lot of attention to those grads who didn't study journalism, but other areas of mass communication. That may change my headline quite a lot. More work to do!

I am a visual person who is unable to think without scribbling little diagrams, so let me show you what I drew when I was writing the previous few pages (**Figure 3.11**). I'm aware that it's a bit obscure. Remember that I designed it to clarify my own messy ideas, so it's a visual model to improve just my own mental model. It led me to the key takeaway of this chapter:

Don't rush to write a headline or an entire story or to design a visualization immediately after you find an interesting pattern, data point, or fact. Stop and think. Look for other sources and for people who can help you escape from tunnel vision and confirmation bias. Explore your information at multiple levels of depth and breadth, looking for extraneous factors that may help explain your findings. Only *then* can you make a decision about what to say, and how to say it, and about what amount of detail you need to show to be true to the data.

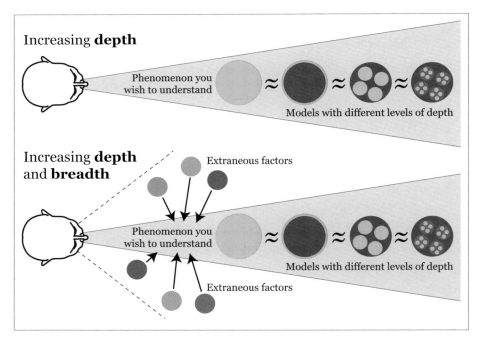

Figure 3.11 Levels of depth and breadth.

The last portion of that paragraph addresses some objections that I've found repeatedly when presenting these ideas to journalists and designers. The main objection goes like this: "I buy the idea of increasing depth and breadth when analyzing my information, but when it comes to presenting the results, **I need to *simplify***. People have short attention spans! Doesn't your suggestion force us to increase the complexity of visualizations endlessly?"

No, it doesn't.

I am very aware that some inescapable constraints may get in the way of creating a great visualization or story: the space available for it, the time that you have to produce it, and the time that you guess engaged readers will spend reading it.

I'm also aware that we can't present all the information we've collected—at least, not all at once. We need to show a summary first, but this summary needs to accurately reflect reality, and it cannot be *the only* thing we show. We should let people explore as many layers of depth and breadth as is appropriate and reasonable, given the time and space constraints mentioned.

When designing a visualization, we'll always need to make an informed choice about the amount of information that is needed for the audience to understand its messages well. Then, we can weigh that estimate against the time that we have to create our visualization and the room we have for it on the page or on screen.

This compromise reflects something mentioned at the beginning of this chapter: **it's unrealistic to pretend that we can create a *perfect* model. But we can certainly come up with a *good enough* one**.

Finally, unless there's a very good reason not to, we must disclose our sources, data, and the methods used to analyze them and to design our visualizations. Organizations like ProPublica are doing it already (**Figure 3.12**).

Figure 3.12 Visit the visualization: http://projects.propublica.org/graphics/ny-millions and note the "see our methodology" button at the bottom, which will take you to an in-depth discussion about how the data were gathered and analyzed.

The Laws of Simplicity, by John Maeda, is one of those books that everyone reads and many misinterpret. This is one of its most famous passages:

Simplicity is about subtracting the obvious and adding the meaningful.

Many people memorize the first half and conveniently forget the second. **Simplicity isn't just about *reduction*. It can** (and should) **also be about *augmentation*. It consists of removing what isn't relevant from our models but also of bringing in those elements that are essential to making those models truer.**

The Skills of the Educated Person

In his book *Mapping It Out*, cartographer Mark Monmonier, whom we'll find again in the chapter about maps, outlined the main skills that any educated person should cultivate. They are:

- **Literacy,** or fluency in written expression and understanding of texts.

- **Articulacy,** or fluency in oral communication.

- **Numeracy,** or fluency in analyzing, summarizing, and presenting data.

- **Graphicacy,** or fluency in interpreting and using visuals.

If you've reached this page, you probably understand why I completely agree with him, and you're ready for the next phase of our trip: understanding data.

To Learn More

- Deutsch, David. *The Beginning of Infinity: Explanations That Transform the World*. New York: Viking, 2011. This is the book that influenced me the most when writing this chapter.

- Godfrey-Smith, Peter. *Theory and Reality: An Introduction to the Philosophy of Science*. Chicago: University of Chicago Press, 2003. A concise and profound introduction to the subject.

- Shermer, Michael. *The Believing Brain: From Ghosts and Gods to Politics and Conspiracies—How We Construct Beliefs and Reinforce Them as Truths*. New York: Times Books, 2011. My favorite introduction to brain bugs—or features.

4

Of Conjectures and Uncertainty

We live in a world with a surfeit of information at our service. It is our choice whether we seek out data that reinforce our biases or choose to look at the world in a critical, rational manner, and allow reality to bend our preconceptions. In the long run, the truth will work better for us than our cherished fictions.

—Razib Khan, "The Abortion Stereotype,"
The New York Times (January 2, 2015)

To become a visualization designer, it is advisable to get acquainted with the language of research. Getting to know how the methods of science work will help us ascertain that we're not being fooled by our sources. We *will* still be fooled on a regular basis, but at least we'll be better equipped to avoid it if we're careful.

Up to this point I've done my best to prove that interpreting data and visualizations is to a great extent based on applying simple rules of thumb such as "compared to what/who/where/when," "always look for the pieces that are missing in the model," and "increase depth and breadth up to a reasonable point." I stressed those strategies first because in the past two decades I've seen that many designers and journalists are terrified by science and math for no good reason.[1]

It's time to get a bit more technical.

The Scientific Stance

Science isn't only what scientists do. Science is a stance, a way to look at the world, that everybody and anybody, regardless of cultural origins or background, can embrace—I'll refrain from writing "should," although I feel tempted. Here's one of my favorite definitions: "Science is a systematic enterprise that builds, organizes, and shares knowledge in the form of testable explanations and predictions."[2] **Science is, then, a set of methods, a body of knowledge, and the means to communicate it.**

Scientific discovery consists of an algorithm that, in a highly idealized form, looks like this:

1. You grow curious about a phenomenon, you explore it for a while, and then you formulate a plausible **conjecture** to describe it, explain it, or predict its behavior. This conjecture is just an informed hunch for now.

2. You transform your conjecture into a formal and testable proposition, called a **hypothesis**.

3. You thoroughly study and measure the phenomenon (under controlled conditions whenever it's possible). These measurements become **data** that you can use to **test** your hypothesis.

4. You draw **conclusions**, based on the evidence you have obtained. Your data and tests may force you to reject your hypothesis, in which case you'll need go to back to the beginning. Or your hypothesis may be tentatively corroborated.

---

1   Journalists and designers aren't to blame. The education we've all endured is. Many of my peers in journalism school, back in the mid-1990s, claimed that they weren't "good at math" and that they only wanted to write. I still hear this from some of my students at the University of Miami. I guess that something similar can be seen among designers ("I just want to design!"). My response is usually, "If you cannot evaluate and manipulate data and evidence at all, what are you going to write (design) about?"

2   From Mark Chang's *Principles of Scientific Methods* (2014). Another source to consult is "Science and Statistics," a 1976 article by George E. P. Box.
http://www-sop.inria.fr/members/Ian.Jermyn/philosophy/writings/Boxonmaths.pdf

5. Eventually, after repeated tests and after your work has been reviewed by your peers, members of your knowledge or scientific community, you may be able to put together a systematic set of interrelated hypotheses to describe, explain, or predict phenomena. We call this a **theory**. From this point on, always remember what the word "theory" really means. A theory isn't just a careless hunch.

These steps may open researchers' eyes to new paths to explore, so they don't constitute a process with a beginning and an end point but a loop. As you're probably guessing, we are returning to themes we've already visited in this book: good answers lead to more good questions. The scientific stance will never take us all the way to an absolute, immutable truth. What it may do—and it does it well—is to move us further to the right in the truth continuum.

From Curiosity to Conjectures

I use Twitter a lot, and on days when I spend more than one hour on it, I feel that I'm more distracted and not as productive as usual. I believe that this is something that many other writers experience. Am I right or am I wrong? Is this just something that I feel or something that is happening to everyone else? Can I transform my hunch into a general claim? For instance, can I say that an X percent increase of Twitter usage a day leads a majority of writers to a Y percent decrease in productivity? After all, I have read some books that make the bold claim that the Internet changes our brains in a negative way.[3]

What I've just done is to notice an interesting pattern, a possible cause-effect relationship (more Twitter = less productivity), and made a conjecture about it. It's a conjecture that:

1. It makes sense intuitively in the light of what we know about the world.

2. It is testable somehow.

3. It is made of ingredients that are naturally and logically connected to each other in a way that if you change any of them, the entire conjecture will crumble. This will become clearer in just a bit.

---

3 The most famous one is *The Shallows* (2010), by Nicholas Carr. I am quite skeptical of this kind of claim, as anything that we do, see, hear, and so on, "changes" the wiring inside our skulls.

These are the requirements of any rational conjecture. **Conjectures first need to make sense** (even if they eventually end up being wrong) based on existing knowledge of how nature works. The universe of stupid conjectures is infinite, after all. Not all conjectures are born equal. Some are more plausible *a priori* than others.

My favorite example of conjecture that doesn't make sense is the famous *Sports Illustrated* cover jinx. This superstitious urban legend says that appearing on the cover of *Sports Illustrated* magazine makes many athletes perform worse than they did before.

To illustrate this, I have created **Figure 4.1**, based on three different fictional athletes. Their performance curve (measured in goals, hits, scores, whatever) goes up, and then it drops after being featured on the cover of *Sports Illustrated*.

Saying that this is a curse is a bad conjecture because we can come up with a much more simple and natural explanation: athletes are usually featured on magazine covers when they are at the peak of their careers. Keeping yourself in the upper ranks of any sport is not just hard work, it also requires tons of good luck. Therefore, after making the cover of *Sports Illustrated*, it is more probable that the performance of most athletes will worsen, not improve even more. Over time, an athlete is more likely to move closer to his or her average performance rate than away from it. Moreover, aging plays an important role in most sports.

What I've just described is **regression toward the mean**, and it's pervasive.[4] Here's how I'd explain it to my kids: imagine that you're in bed today with a cold. To cure you, I go to your room wearing a tiara of dyed goose feathers and a robe made of oak leaves, dance Brazilian samba in front of you—feel free to picture this scene in your head, dear reader—and give you a potion made of water, sugar, and an infinitesimally tiny amount of viral particles. One or two days later, you

---

4   When playing with any sort of data set, if you randomly draw one value and obtain one that is extremely far from the mean (that is, the average value), the next one that you draw will probably be closer to the mean than even further away from it. Regression toward the mean was first described by Sir Francis Galton in the late nineteenth century, but under a slightly different name: regression toward mediocrity. Galton observed that parents who were very tall tended to have children who were shorter than they were and that parents who were very short had children who were taller than them. Galton said that extreme traits tended to "regress" toward "mediocrity." His paper is available online, and it's a delight: http://galton.org/essays/1880-1889/galton-1886-jaigi-regression-stature.pdf.

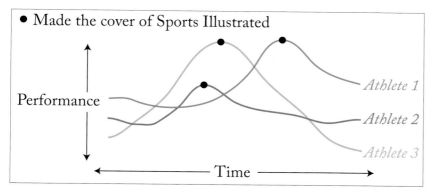

Figure 4.1 Athletes tend to underperform after they've appeared on the cover of *Sports Illustrated* magazine. Does the publication cast a curse on them?

feel better. Did I cure you? Of course not. It was your body regressing to its most probable state, one of good health.[5]

For a conjecture to be good, it also needs to be testable. In principle, you should be able to weigh your conjecture against evidence. Evidence comes in many forms: repeated observations, experimental tests, mathematical analysis, rigorous mental or logic experiments, or various combinations of any of these.[6]

Being testable also implies being *falsifiable*. A conjecture that can't possibly be refuted will never be a good conjecture, as rational thought progresses only if our current ideas can be substituted for better-grounded ones later, when new evidence comes in.

Sadly, we humans love to come up with non-testable conjectures, and we use them when arguing with others. Philosopher **Bertrand Russell** came up with a splendid illustration of how ludicrous non-testable conjectures can be:

> If I were to suggest that between the Earth and Mars there is a china tea-pot revolving about the sun in an elliptical orbit, nobody would be able to

---

5 Think about this next the time that anyone tries to sell you an overpriced "alternative medicine" product or treatment. The popularity of snake oil-like stuff is based on our propensity to see causality where there's only a sequence of unconnected events ("follow my unsubstantiated advice—feel better") and our lack of understanding of regression toward the mean.

6 If you read any of the books recommended in this chapter, be aware that many scientists and philosophers of science are more stringent than I am when evaluating if a particular procedure really qualifies as a test.

disprove my assertion provided I were careful to add that the teapot is too small to be revealed even by our most powerful telescopes. But if I were to go on to say that, since my assertion cannot be disproved, it is intolerable presumption on the part of human reason to doubt it, I should rightly be thought to be talking nonsense. (*Illustrated* magazine, 1952)

Making sense and being testable alone don't suffice, though. **A good conjecture is made of several components, and these need to be hard to change without making the whole conjecture useless**. In the words of physicist David Deutsch, a good conjecture is "hard to vary, because all its details play a functional role." The components of our conjectures need to be logically related to the nature of the phenomenon we're studying.

Imagine that a sparsely populated region in Africa is being ravaged by an infectious disease. You observe that people become ill mostly after attending religious services on Sunday. You are a local shaman and propose that the origin of the disease is some sort of negative energy that oozes out of the spiritual aura of priests and permeates the temples where they preach.

This is a bad conjecture not just because it doesn't make sense or isn't testable. It is testable, actually: when people gather in temples and in the presence of priests, a lot of them get the disease. There, I got my conjecture tested and corroborated!

Not really. This conjecture is bad because we could equally say that the disease is caused by invisible pixies who fly inside the temples, the souls of the departed who still linger around them, or by any other kind of supernatural agent. Changing our premises keeps the body of our conjecture unchanged. Therefore, a flexible conjecture is always a bad conjecture.

It would be different if you said that the disease may be transmitted in crowded places because the agent that provokes it, whether a virus or a bacterium, is airborne. The closer people are to each other, the more likely it is that someone will sneeze, spreading particles that carry the disease. These particles will be breathed by other people and, after reaching their lungs, the agent will spread.

This is a good conjecture because all its components are naturally connected to each other. Take away any of them and the whole edifice of your conjecture will fall, forcing you to rebuild it from scratch in a different way. After being compared to the evidence, this conjecture may end up being completely *wrong*, but it will forever be a *good* conjecture.

Hypothesizing

A conjecture that is formalized to be tested empirically is called a **hypothesis**.

To give you an example (and be warned that not all hypotheses are formulated like this): if I were to test my hunch that using Twitter for too long reduces writers' productivity, I'd need to explain what I mean by "too long" and by "productivity" and how I'm planning to measure them. I'd also need to make some sort of prediction that I can assess, like "each increase of Twitter usage reduces the average number of words that writers are able to write in a day."

I've just defined two variables. A **variable** is something whose values can change somehow (yes-no, female-male, unemployment rate of 5.6, 6.8, or 7.1 percent, and so on). The first variable in our hypothesis is "increase of Twitter usage." We can call it a **predictor** or **explanatory** variable, although you may see it called an **independent** variable in many studies.

The second element in our hypothesis is "reduction of average number of words that writers write in a day." This is the **outcome** or **response** variable, also known as the **dependent** variable.

Deciding on what and how to **measure** is quite tricky, and it greatly depends on how the exploration of the topic is designed. When getting information from any source, sharpen your skepticism and ask yourself: do the variables defined in the study, and the way they are measured and compared, reflect the reality that the authors are analyzing?

An Aside on Variables

Variables come in many flavors. It is important to remember them because not only are they crucial for working with data, but later in the book they will also help us pick methods of representation for our visualizations.

The first way to classify variables is to pay attention to the scales by which they're measured.

Nominal

In a nominal (or categorical) scale, values don't have any quantitative weight. They are distinguished just by their identity. Sex (male or female) and location (Miami, Jacksonville, Tampa, and so on) are examples of nominal variables. So are certain questions in opinion surveys. Imagine that I ask you what party you're planning to vote, and the options are Democratic, Republican, Other, None, and Don't Know.

In some cases, we may use numbers to describe our nominal variables. We may write "0" for male and "1" for female, for instance, but those numbers don't represent any amount or position in a ranking. They would be similar to the numbers that soccer players display on their back. They exist just to identify players, not to tell you which are better or worse.

Ordinal

In an ordinal scale, values are organized or ranked according to a magnitude, but without revealing their exact size in comparison to each other.

For example, you may be analyzing all countries in the world according to their Gross Domestic Product (GDP) per capita but, instead of showing me the specific GDP values, you just tell me which country is the first, the second, the third, and so on. This is an ordinal variable, as I've just learned about the countries' rankings according to their economic performance, but I don't know anything about how far apart they are in terms of GDP size.

In a survey, an example of ordinal scale would be a question about your happiness level: 1. Very happy; 2. Happy; 3. Not that happy; 4. Unhappy; 5. Very unhappy.

Interval

An interval scale of measurement is based on increments of the same size, but also on the lack of a true zero point, in the sense of that being the absolute lowest value. I know, it sounds confusing, so let me explain.

Imagine that you are measuring temperature in degrees Fahrenheit. The distance between 5 and 10 degrees is the same as the distance between 20 and 25 degrees: 5 units. So you can add and subtract temperatures, but you cannot say that 10 degrees is twice as hot as 5 degrees, even though 2 × 5 equals 10. The reason is related to the lack of a real zero. The zero point is just an arbitrary number, one like any other on the scale, not an absolute point of reference.

An example of interval scale coming from psychology is the intellectual quotient (IQ). If one person has an IQ of 140 and another person has an IQ of 70, you can say that the former is 70 units larger than the latter, but you cannot say that the former is *twice* as intelligent as the latter.

Ratio

Ratio scales have all the properties of the other previous scales, plus they also have a meaningful zero point. Weight, height, speed, and so on, are examples of ratio variables. If one car is traveling at 100 mph and another one is at 50, you can say that the first one is going 50 miles faster than the second, and you can also say that it's going twice as fast. If my daughter's height is 3 feet and mine is 6 feet (I wish), I am twice as tall as her.

Variables can be also classified into discrete and continuous. A **discrete** variable is one that can only adopt certain values. For instance, people can only have cousins in amounts that are whole numbers—four or five, that is, not 4.5 cousins. On the other hand, a **continuous** variable is one that can—at least in theory— adopt any value on the scale of measurement that you're using. Your weight in pounds can be 90, 90.1, 90.12, 90.125, or 90.1256. There's no limit to the number of decimal places that you can add to that. Continuous variables can be measured with a virtually endless degree of precision, if you have the right instruments.

In practical terms, the distinction between continuous and discrete variables isn't always clear. Sometimes you will treat a discrete variable as if it were continuous. Imagine that you're analyzing the number of children per couple in a certain country. You could say that the average is 1.8, which doesn't make a lot of sense for a truly discrete variable.

Similarly, you can treat a continuous variable as if it were discrete. Imagine that you're measuring the distance between galaxy centers. You could use nanometers with an infinite number of decimals (you'll end up with more digits than atoms in the universe!), but it would be better to use light-years and perhaps limit values to whole units. If the distance between two stars is 4.43457864... light-years, you could just round the figure to 4 light-years.

On Studies

Once a hypothesis is posed, it's time to test it against reality. I wish to measure if increased Twitter usage reduces book-writing output. I send an online poll to 30 friends who happen to be writers, asking them for the minutes spent on Twitter today and the words they have written. My (completely made up) results are on **Figure 4.2**. This is an **observational study**. To be more precise, it's a **cross-sectional study**, which means that it takes into account data collected just at a particular point in time.

If I carefully document my friends' Twitter usage and the pages they write for a long time (a year, a decade, or since Twitter was launched), I'll have a **longitudinal study**. On **Figure 4.3**, I plotted Twitter usage (X-axis) versus words written (Y-axis) every year by three of my 30 fictional author friends. The relationship becomes clear: on average, the more time they spend on Twitter, the less they write for their own books. That's very unwise!

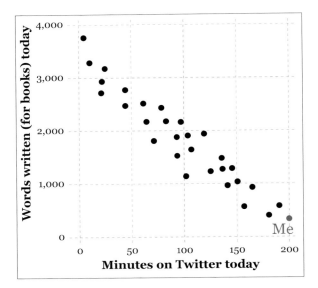

Figure 4.2 Writer friends don't let their writer friends use Twitter when they are on a deadline.

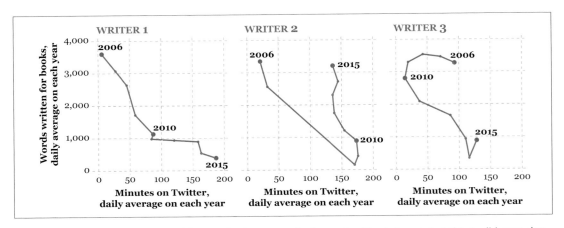

Figure 4.3 The more writers use Twitter, the fewer words they write. Don't forget that this is all bogus data.

The choice of what kind of study to conduct depends on many factors. Doing longitudinal studies is usually much more difficult and expensive, as you'll need to follow the same people for a long time. Cross-sectional studies are faster to build but, in general, their results aren't very conclusive.[7]

Going back to my inquiry, I face a problem: I am trying to draw an inference ("writers can benefit from using Twitter less") from a particular group of writers. That is, I am trying to study something about a **population**, *all* writers, based on a **sample** of those writers, my friends. **But are my friends representative of all writers? Are inferences drawn from my sample applicable to the entire population?**

Always be suspicious of studies whose samples have not been randomly chosen.[8] Not all scientific research is based on random sampling, but analyzing a random sample of writers chosen from the population of all writers will yield more accurate results than a cherry-picked or self-selected sample.

This is why we should be wary of the validity of things like news media online polls. If you ask your audience to opine on a subject, you cannot claim that you've learned something meaningful about what the public in general thinks. You cannot even say that you know the opinion of your own audience! You've just heard from those readers who feel strongly about the topic you asked about, as they are the ones who are more likely to participate in your poll.

Randomization is useful to deal with **extraneous variables**, mentioned in Chapter 3 where I advised you to always try to increase depth and breadth. It may be that the results of my current exploration are biased because a good portion of my friends are quite geeky, and so they use Twitter a lot. In this case,

---

7   Different kinds of studies beget different kinds of conclusions. For instance, in a cross-sectional study you might be able to conclude, "In the population we studied, the kind of people who tweet little are also the kind of people who write a lot," but you cannot add anything about time change or causality. If you do a longitudinal study, you might conclude, "In the population studied, the kind of people who choose to start tweeting less are also the kind who start writing more," but you cannot say anything about causality. If you then decide to conduct a controlled experiment, you might be able to say, "In the population studied, whichever kind of person you are, if you start tweeting less, then you'll start writing more." But even in this case you cannot say anything about how many of those people are naturally inclined to tweet or to write. Science is hard!

8   Many introduction to statistics textbooks include a section about how random sampling is conducted. I recommend that you take a look at a couple of them. Before you do so, though, you may want to read this nice introduction by Statistics Canada: http://tinyurl.com/or47fyr.

the geekiness level, if it could be measured, would distort my model, as it would affect the relationship between predictor and outcome variable.

Some researchers distinguish between two kinds of extraneous variables. Sometimes we can identify an extraneous variable and incorporate it into our model, in which case we'd be dealing with a **confounding variable**. I know that it may affect my results, so I consider it for my inquiry to minimize its impact. In an example seen in previous chapters, we controlled for population change and for variation in number of motor vehicles when analyzing deaths in traffic accidents.

There's a second, more insidious kind of extraneous variable. Imagine that I don't know that my friends are indeed geeky. If I were unaware of this, I'd be dealing with a **lurking** variable. A **lurking variable** is an extraneous variable that we don't include in our analysis for the simple reason that its existence is unknown to us, or because we can't explain its connection to the phenomenon we're studying.

When reading studies, surveys, polls, and so on, always ask yourself: did the authors rigorously search for lurking variables and transform them into confounding variables that they can ponder? Or are there other possible factors that they ignored and that may have distorted their results?[9]

Doing Experiments

Whenever it is realistic and feasible to do so, researchers go beyond observational studies and design **controlled experiments**, as these can help minimize the influence of confounding variables. There are many kinds of experiments, but many of them share some characteristics:

1. They observe a large number of subjects that are representative of the population they want to learn about. Subjects aren't necessarily people. A subject can be any entity (a person, an animal, an object, etc.) that can be studied in controlled conditions, in isolation from external influences.

---

9   One of the best quotes about the imperfection of all our rational inquiry methods, including science, comes from former Secretary of Defense Donald Rumsfeld. In a 2002 press conference about using the possible existence of weapons of mass destruction in Iraq as a reason to go to war with that country, he said, "Reports that say that something hasn't happened are always interesting to me, because as we know, there are known knowns; there are things we know we know. We also know there are known unknowns; that is to say we know there are some things we do not know. But there are also unknown unknowns—the ones we don't know we don't know. And if one looks throughout the history of our country and other free countries, it is the latter category that tends to be the difficult one." It's acceptable to argue that Rumsfeld was being disingenuous, as some of those "unknown unknowns" were actually "known unknowns" or even "known knowns."

2. Subjects are divided into at least two groups, an **experimental** group and a **control** group. This division will in most cases be made blindly: the researchers and/or the subjects don't know which group each subject is assigned to.

3. Subjects in the experimental group are exposed to some sort of condition, while the control group subjects are exposed to a different condition or to no condition at all. This condition can be, for instance, adding different chemical compounds to fluids and comparing the changes they suffer, or exposing groups of people to different kinds of movies to test how they influence their behavior.

4. Researchers measure what happens to subjects in the experimental group and what happens to subjects in the control group, and they compare the results.

   If the differences between experimental and control groups are noticeable enough, researchers may conclude that the condition under study may have played some role.[10]

We'll learn more about this process in Chapter 11.

When doing visualizations based on the results of experiments, it's important to not just read the abstract of the paper or article and its conclusions. Check if the journal in which it appeared is peer reviewed and how it's regarded in its knowledge community.[11] Then, take a close look at the paper's methodology. Learn about how the experiments were designed and, in case you don't understand it, contact other researchers in the same area and ask. This is also valid for observational studies. A small dose of constructive skepticism can be very healthy.

In October 2013, many news publications echoed the results of a study by psychologists David Comer Kidd and Emanuele Castano which showed that reading literary fiction temporarily enhances our capacity to understand other people's

---

10 To be more precise, scientists compare these differences to a hypothetical range of studies with the same sample size and design but where the condition is known to have no effect. This check (statistical hypothesis testing) helps to prevent spurious conclusions due to small samples or high variability. This check isn't about whether the effect is large in an absolute/pragmatic sense, as we'll see soon.

11 You can search for the impact factor (IF) of the publication. This is a measure of how much it is cited by other publications. It's not a perfect quality measure, but it helps.

mental states. The media immediately started writing headlines like "Reading fiction improves empathy!"[12]

The finding was consistent with previous observations and experiments, but reporting on a study after reading just its abstract is dangerous. What were the researchers really comparing?

In one of the experiments, they made two groups of people read either three works of literary fiction or three works of nonfiction. After the readings, the people in the literary fiction group were better at identifying facially expressed emotions than those in the nonfiction group.

The study looked sound to me when I read it, but it left crucial questions in the air: what *kinds* of literary fiction and nonfiction did the subjects read? It seems predictable that you'll feel more empathetic toward your neighbor after reading *To Kill a Mockingbird* than after, say, Thomas Piketty's *Capital in the Twenty-First Century*, a brick-sized treaty on modern economics that many bought—myself included—but just a few read.

But what if researchers had compared *To Kill a Mockingbird* to Katherine Boo's *Behind the Beautiful Forevers*, a haunting and emotional piece of journalistic reporting? And, even if they had compared literary fiction with literary non-fiction, is it even possible to measure how "literary" either book is? Those are the kinds of questions that you need to ask either to the researchers that conducted the study or, in case they cannot be reached for comment, to other experts in the same knowledge domain.

About Uncertainty

Here's a dirty little secret about data: it's always noisy and uncertain.[13]

To understand this critical idea, let's begin with a very simple study. I want to know my weight. I've been exercising lately, and I want to check the results. I step on the scale one morning and I read 192 lbs.

---

12 "Reading Literary Fiction Improves Theory of Mind." http://scottbarrykaufman.com/wp-content/uploads/2013/10/Science-2013-Kidd-science.1239918.pdf

13 Moreover, data sets are sometimes incomplete and contain errors, redundancies, typos, and more. For an overview, see Paul D. Allison's *Missing Data* (2002). To deal with this problem, tools like OpenRefine (http://openrefine.org/) may come in handy.

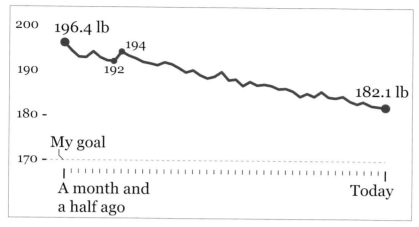

Figure 4.4 Randomness at work—weight change in a month and a half.

Out of curiosity, I decide to weigh myself again the day after. The scale shows 194 lbs. Damn it! How is that even possible? I've been eating better and running regularly, and my weight had already dropped from 196.4 lb. There's surely some sort of discrepancy between the measurements I'm getting and my true weight. I decide to continue weighing myself for more than a month.

The results are in **Figure 4.4**. There's a clear downward trend, but it only becomes visible when I display more than five or six days in a row. If I zoom in too much to the chart and just pay attention to two or three days, I'd be fooled into thinking that the noise in the data means something.

There may be different reasons for this wacky fluctuation to happen. My first thought is that my scale may not be working well, but then I realize that if there were some sort of technical glitch, it would bias *all* my measurements systematically. So the scale is not the source of the fluctuation.

It might be that I don't always balance my weight equally between my feet or that I'm weighing myself at slightly different times on each day. We tend to be a bit heavier in the afternoon than right after we wake up because we lose water while we sleep, and our body has already processed the food we ate the night before. But I was extremely careful with all those factors. I did weigh myself exactly at 6:45 a.m. every single day. And still, the variation is there. Therefore, I can only conclude that it's the result of factors that I can't possibly be aware of. I'm witnessing **randomness**.

Data always vary randomly because the object of our inquiries, nature itself, is also random. We can analyze and predict events in nature with an increasing amount of precision and accuracy, thanks to improvements in our techniques and instruments, but a certain amount of random variation, which gives rise to **uncertainty**, is inevitable. This is as true for weight measurements at home as it is true for anything else that you want to study: stock prices, annual movie box office takings, ocean acidity, variation of the number of animals in a region, rainfall or droughts—anything.

If we pick a random sample of 1,000 people to analyze political opinions in the United States, we cannot be 100 percent certain that they are perfectly representative of the entire country, no matter how thorough we are. If our results are that 48.2 percent of our sample are liberals and 51.8 percent are conservatives, we cannot conclude that the entire U.S. population is exactly 48.2 percent liberal and 51.8 percent conservative.

Here's why: if we pick a completely different random sample of people, the results may be 48.4 percent liberal and 51.6 percent conservative. If we then draw a third sample, the results may be 48.7 percent liberal and 51.3 percent conservative (and so forth).

Even if our methods for drawing random samples of 1,000 people are rigorous, there will always be some amount of uncertainty. We may end up with a slightly higher or lower percentage of liberals or conservatives out of pure chance. This is called **sample variation**.

Uncertainty is the reason why researchers will never just tell you that 51.8 percent of the U.S. population is conservative, after observing their sample of 1,000 people. What they will tell you, with a high degree of confidence (usually 95 percent, but it may be more or less than that), is that the percentage of conservatives seems to be indeed 51.8 percent, but that there's an error of plus or minus 3 percentage points (or any other figure) in that number.

Uncertainty can be represented in our visualizations. See the two charts in **Figure 4.5**, designed by professor **Adrian E. Raftery**, from the University of Washington. As they display projections, the amount of uncertainty increases with time: the farther away we depart from the present, the more uncertain our projections will become, meaning that the value that the variable "population" could adopt falls inside an increasingly wider range.

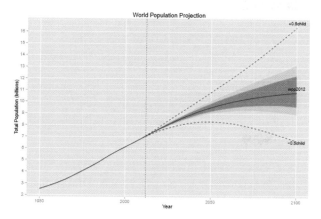

Figure 4.5 Charts by Adrian E. Raftery (University of Washington) who explains, "The top chart shows world population projected to 2100. Dotted lines are the range of error using the older scenarios in which women would have 0.5 children more or less than what's predicted. Shaded regions are the uncertainties. The darker shading is the 80 percent confidence bars, and the lighter shading shows the 95 percent confidence bars. The bottom chart represents population projections for each continent." http://www.sciencedaily.com/ releases/2014/09/140918141446.htm

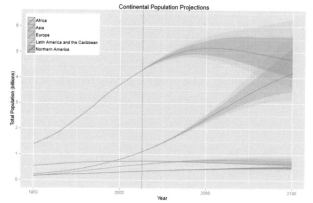

The hockey stick chart of world temperatures, in Chapter 2, is another example of uncertainty visualized. In that chart, there's a light gray strip behind the dark line representing the estimated temperature variation. This gray strip is the uncertainty. It grows narrower the closer we get to the twentieth century because instruments to measure temperature, and our historical records, have become much more reliable.

||||■ ■ ■ ■||||

We'll return to testing, uncertainty, and confidence in Chapter 11. Right now, after clarifying the meaning of important terms, it's time to begin exploring and visualizing data.

To Learn More

- Skeptical Raptor's "How to evaluate the quality of scientific research." http://www.skepticalraptor.com/skepticalraptorblog.php/how-evaluate-quality-scientific-research/

- *Nature* magazine's "Twenty Tips For Interpreting Scientific Claims." http://www.nature.com/news/policy-twenty-tips-for-interpreting-scientific-claims-1.14183

- Box, George E. P. "Science and Statistics." Journal of the American Statistical Association, Vol. 71, No. 356. (Dec., 1976), pp. 791-799. Available online: http://www-sop.inria.fr/members/Ian.Jermyn/philosophy/writings/Boxonmaths.pdf

- Prothero, Donald R. *Evolution: What the Fossils Say and Why It Matters.* New York: Columbia University Press, 2007. Yes, it's a book about paleontology, but, leaving aside the fact that prehistoric beasts are fascinating, the author offers one of the clearest and most concise introductions to science I've read.

PART III
functional

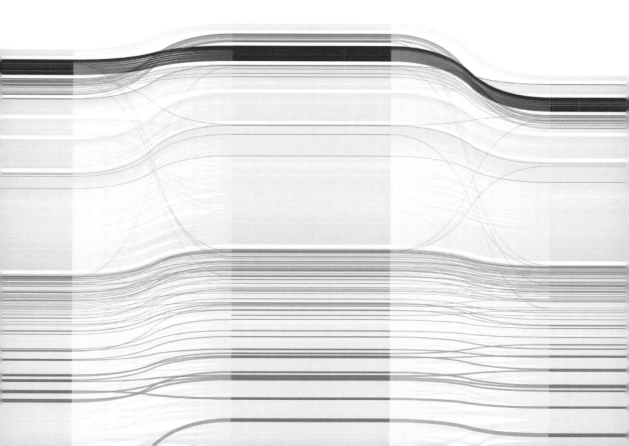

5

Basic Principles of Visualization

In the course of executing that design, it occurred to me that tables are by no means a good form for conveying such information…. Making an appeal to the eye when proportion and magnitude are concerned is the best and readiest method of conveying a distinct idea.

—William Playfair, *The Statistical Breviary*

There is a time in every class and workshop when someone raises her hand and asks: **How do you know that you have chosen the right graphic form to represent your data?** When is it appropriate to use a bar chart, a line chart, a data map, or a flow diagram? Geez, if I had the answer to that, I'd be rich by now. I invariably reply, "I have no idea, but I can give you some clues to make your own choices based on what we know about why and how visualization works."

In his book *Misbehaving: The Making of Behavioral Economics* (2015), University of Chicago's **Richard H. Thaler** recounts an anecdote that may be useful for any teacher. At the beginning of his career as a professor, Thaler made many of his students mad by designing a midterm exam that was deemed too hard. The average score, on a scale from 0 to 100, was 72. He got a lot of complaints about it.

Thaler decided to run an experiment. In the next exam, he set the maximum score to 137 points. The average ended up being 96 points. His students were thrilled.

Thaler kept the 137 mark in subsequent exams and also added this line to his syllabus: "Exams will have a total of 137 points rather than the usual 100. This scoring system has no effect on the grade you get in the course, but it seems to make you happier." It certainly did. After he made this change, Thaler never got any pushback from students again—even if he told them beforehand that they were going to be tricked!

Try to mentally visualize these numbers: 72 versus 100, and 96 versus 137. The first pair is easy. The human brain performs nicely at simple arithmetic with rounded figures. But it is abysmal when forced to manipulate any other kind of number without aid. It's hard to picture 96 in comparison to 137 in your head. It's much more effective to do it on a piece of paper or on a screen (**Figure 5.1**; the figures are shown twice, as a linear plot and as a pair of pie charts).[1]

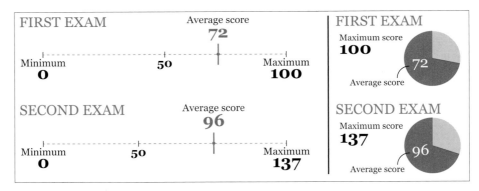

Figure 5.1 Seventy-two over 100 is a better score than 96 over 137. Funny, right?

---

1 This is a 2013 tweet by visualization author Edward R. Tufte, who got things wrong by trying to be too strict: "Pie chart users deserve same suspicion+skepticism as those who mix up its/it's, there/their. To compare, use little table, sentence, not pies." I am no fan of pie charts, but in this case, even if they are inferior to the linear plots, the two pie charts work better than a sentence or a table. This is why I usually say that there are no graphic forms that are intrinsically good or bad but graphic forms that are more or less effective.

It turns out that Thaler's second exam was *harder* than the first one. A score of 96 out of a maximum of 137 is a 70 percent score, in comparison to the 72 percent average of the first exam. But even if you're aware of that—because you know how to transform a raw score into a percentage— **96 over 137 still *feels* higher than 72 over 100**. That's a bug of the wetware sloshing inside your skull. **Most people grasp the truth of an assessment only when they unequivocally *envision* the evidence for it**, something that our kludgy brains alone often can't do well. **That's why visualization works**.

Visually Encoding Data

Vision is the most developed sense in the human species. A huge chunk of our brains is devoted to gathering, filtering, processing, organizing, and interpreting data collected from the retinas at the back of our eyes. We've evolved to be really fast at detecting visual patterns and exceptions to those patterns. It is only natural, then, that a set of methods consisting of **mapping data into visual properties**—spatial and otherwise—would prove to be so powerful.

"Mapping data into visual properties." That's quite a mouthful, so let me explain. Suppose that you want to compare the unemployment figures of five countries currently in economic recession. Let's call them A, B, C, D, and E because we need to organize them alphabetically for some reason.

These figures, which I am withholding for now, are our data. The mapping part consists of choosing properties that will let readers accomplish a particular goal ("comparing accurately") without being forced to read all numbers. I have encoded them in several ways in **Figure 5.2**. Which one of these graphics would you choose?

I'd go with length, height, or position, and here's why: if you don't know what the numbers are before you see the rest of the charts—the ones based on area, angle, weight, and color—can you quickly identify the highest or lowest unemployment rates and accurately compare them to the others? It's hard, isn't it?

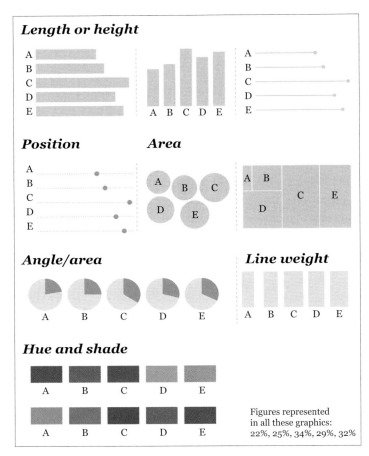

Figure 5.2 Different methods of encoding the same small data set. Remember that, perhaps because our client requested it, countries are organized alphabetically. Otherwise, it'd make more sense to arrange the figures from largest to smallest.

Thus, here are some preliminary suggestions to find the right graphic forms for your visualizations:

1. **Think about the task or tasks you want to enable**, or the messages that you wish to convey. Do you want to compare, to see change or flow, to reveal relationships or connections, to envision temporal or spatial

patterns and trends? We could summarize this point with a sentence that sounds tautological, but isn't: **plot what you need to plot.** And if you don't know what it is that you need to plot yet, plot many features of your data until the stories they may hide rise up.

2. **Try different graphic forms.** If you have more than one task on your wish list, you may need to represent your data in several ways.

3. **Arrange the components of the graphic** so as to make it as easy as possible to extract meaning from it. Whenever it's appropriate, add interactivity to your visualization so people can organize the data at will.

4. **Test the outcomes** yourself and with people who are representative of your audience—even if it is in a non-scientific, non-systematic manner.

Choosing Graphic Forms

Numerous authors have developed methods to choose appropriate ways of encoding data depending on what you want to reveal: Jacques Bertin, Katy Börner, William Cleveland, Stephen Few, Noah Iliinsky, Stephen Kosslyn, Isabel Meirelles, Tamara Munzner, Naomi Robbins, Nathan Yau... just to name a few off the top of my head.

In these pages I am showcasing **Severino Ribecca's** Data Visualisation Catalogue (**Figure 5.3**) and **Ann K. Emery's** Essentials website (**Figure 5.4**). They are both valuable starting points, but not perfect ones, as they include graphic forms that are rarely useful, such as the donut chart or the radar chart. Stephen Few's book *Show Me the Numbers* (2nd ed., 2012) is another worthy resource.

My favorite tool to make choices on how to present data, though, is a **hierarchy of elementary perceptual tasks,** or methods of encoding, that was put together in the 80s by two statisticians, **William S. Cleveland** and **Robert McGill**, and that was later redesigned by Cleveland himself to be included in his magnum opus *The Elements of Graphing Data.* You can see my own version of that scale on **Figure 5.5**, where I added a few examples of the graphics mainly associated with each step.

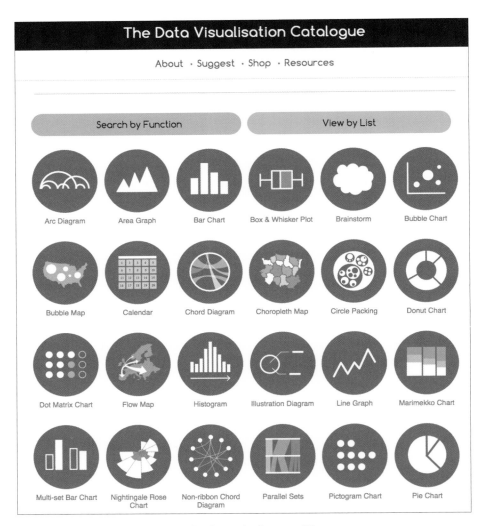

Figure 5.3 The Data Visualisation Catalogue, by Severino Ribecca:
http://www.datavizcatalogue.com.

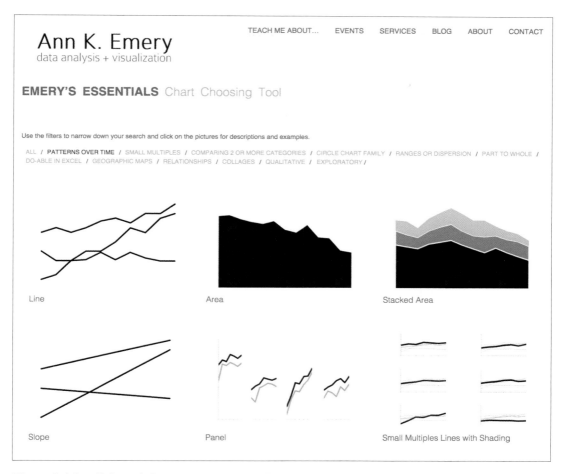

Figure 5.4 Ann K. Emery's Essentials website: http://annkemery.com/essentials/.

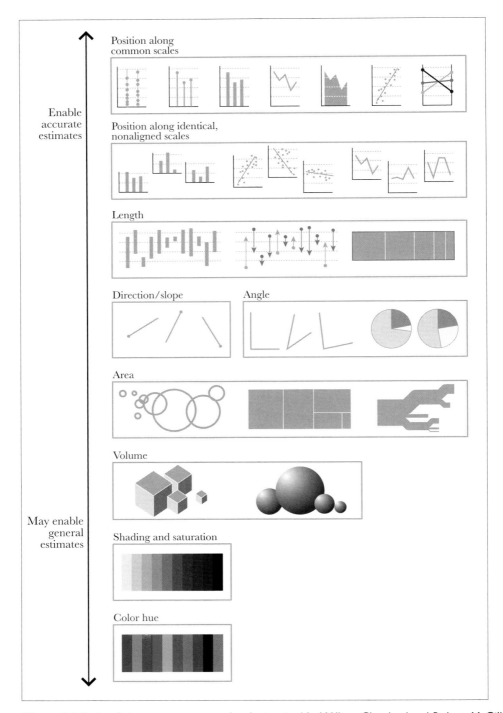

Figure 5.5 Scale of elementary perceptual tasks, inspired by William Cleveland and Robert McGill.

This is how Cleveland and McGill described their hierarchy: "We have chosen the term *elementary perceptual task* because a viewer performs one or more of these mental-visual tasks to extract the values of real variables represented on most graphs."[2]

In other words, to decode a pie chart, we try to use the angle or the area of the slices as cues. When seeing a bar chart, we may pay attention to the position of the upper edge of each bar or to its length or height. When trying to decode a bubble chart, we could try to compare areas (the right choice) or diameters (which would mislead us).

Cleveland and McGill tested the effectiveness of their perceptual tasks in several experiments. The conclusion was that **if you wish to create a successful chart, you need to construct it based on elementary tasks "as high in the hierarchy as possible."** The closer you move to the top of the scale, the faster and more accurate the estimates readers can make with your graphic. You can test that yourself going back to Figure 5.2. Area, color, and angle are much less effective than those graphic forms based on positioning objects on common scales.

A Grain of Salt

Two important caveats are in order at this point. First, **Cleveland and McGill were writing just about statistical charts**. What about data maps? After all, maps use many methods of encoding that belong to the bottom half of the hierarchy, such as area, hue, shading, and so on. Is this wrong? Hardly. **Methods of encoding on the bottom half of the scale may be appropriate when the goal isn't to enable accurate judgments but to reveal general patterns.**

Figure 5.6 is a **choropleth map** of unemployment rates by U.S. county. Its goal isn't to let you identify the counties with the highest or lowest rates or to rank counties in a precise manner. The map's purpose is to reveal geographic clusters, such as the very low rates in the North-South strip from North Dakota to Texas, or the very high rates in many counties in Southern states.

---

2 Cleveland and McGill's original 1984 paper can be read here:
https://www.cs.ubc.ca/~tmm/courses/cpsc533c-04-spr/readings/cleveland.pdf.

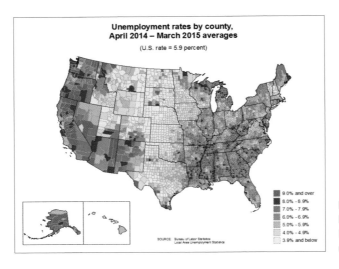

Figure 5.6 From the U.S. Bureau of Labor Statistics, http://www.bls.gov/lau/maps/twmcort.gif.

If the goal of this same graphic were to let readers compare counties, then the map wouldn't be the right choice. We'd need to pick a graphic form from the top of Cleveland's and McGill's scale, perhaps a bar chart or a lollipop chart, and then rank and group the counties in a meaningful way—from highest to lowest, alphabetically, per state, and so on.

And **what if our purpose is to show readers *both* the big picture and the details?** Then we'd need *both* the map *and* the chart on the same page or, if this were an interactive visualization, a menu that'd let people switch between them. **Multiple graphic forms may enable multiple tasks.**

The second caveat is that you cannot apply anyone's method of choosing graphic forms uncritically. A bit of critical judgment is paramount.

For instance, think of how hard it would be to use a method of encoding from the very top of Cleveland's and McGill's hierarchy to show the same data that **Figure 5.7** displays. Here, readers need to decode length and area, but that's not a huge problem, considering the purpose of the chart.

In **Figure 5.8**, I'm comparing several versions of a chart inspired by **Thomas Piketty's** 2014 bestseller *Capital in the Twenty-First Century*. The first one, on top, is similar to one that appears in Piketty's book. The second is my own version, spacing the years on the X-axis correctly. Notice how different the patterns look after doing this.

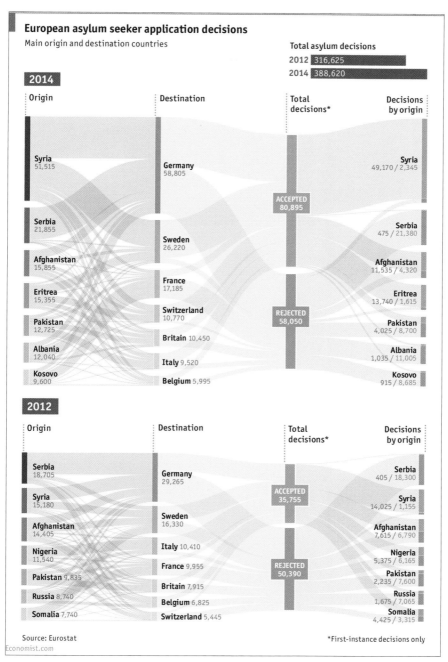

Figure 5.7 A Sankey diagram by *The Economist*,
http://www.economist.com/blogs/graphicdetail/2015/05/daily-chart-1

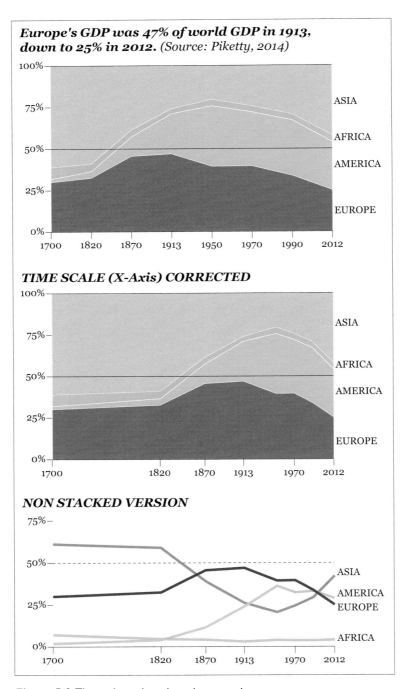

Figure 5.8 Three charts based on the same data.

Reading Piketty's **stacked area chart** forces you to perform perceptual tasks that belong to the middle of Cleveland's and McGill's scale. You need to either compare areas or distances between the top and bottom edges of each segment. The only changes that can be visualized accurately are Asia's and Europe's, as those two portions are sitting on a horizontal edge, either the o-baseline or the 100-line on top.

Africa's and America's baselines shift depending on how tall Asia's and Europe's segments are, and that makes detecting changes in those continents difficult. It may well happen that to your eyes it seems that Africa's output grew in the 1950s just because Africa's segment is being pushed up by the increasing size of American economies. But Africa's GDP barely changed in that decade.

This is all fine, though, because the purpose of this chart is explicit in its title: comparing Europe to the rest of the continents, besides making clear that figures add up to 100 percent. That's why in the original chart Europe's segment is emphasized and placed at the bottom, sitting on the o-baseline. The other continents are shown to provide context.

But what if the goal of the chart was to put all continents on the same footing and compare them in an accurate manner? In that case, the stacked area chart doesn't work well. Can you see, for instance, if America's contribution to world GDP was larger or smaller than that of Europe in 2012? You can't, unless you use your fingers to measure that last part of the chart. But see how easy this task is if we design a simple, non-stacked **time-series chart**, like the third one at the bottom?

Finally, what if you want to show *both* parts of a whole and all lines as individual entities, sitting on a common o-baseline? Then, you'd need to design both charts, as **National Public Radio (NPR)** did with its interactive visualization about college majors (**Figure 5.9**).[3] The designer, **Quoctrung Bui**, decided to first show readers the big picture—all majors together—stacked on top of each other. Then, if a reader decides that she needs more detail about a particular major, she can click it and see its change on a regular time-series chart.

---

3 The organization of majors in this chart is a bit confusing. As the segments are color-coded, I assumed that they were grouped somehow. It turns out that they are organized alphabetically and that colors are assigned somewhat arbitrarily.

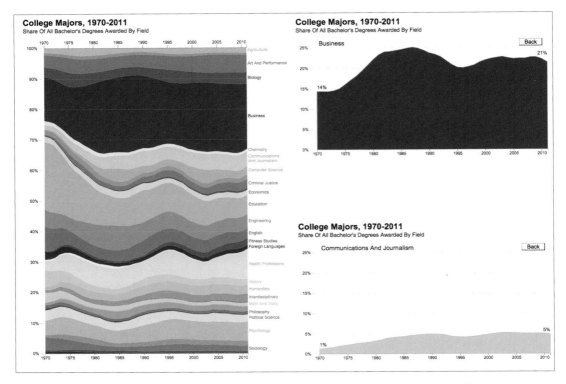

Figure 5.9 Visualization by NPR, http://www.npr.org/sections/money/2014/05/09/310114739/
whats-your-major-four-decades-of-college-degrees-in-1-graph.

The examples we've seen in this section will help you understand another important rule of thumb: if you need to show parts of a whole, show them, by all means. But if the purpose of your chart is to show *each* one of those parts individually, do that. Let's rephrase that as a more general rule: **always plot your data directly**.

In the first chart in **Figure 5.10**, I have chosen the right graphic form from Cleveland's and McGill's scale. All data are plotted on a common axis, so making accurate estimates is quite easy and fast. However, does it really matter to me to plot income and expenses as separate variables? Or does it matter more to see the *difference* between them? Depending on the answer, you'd need to choose either the first or the second chart. **If the difference matters more, plot the difference**, not income and expenses separately.

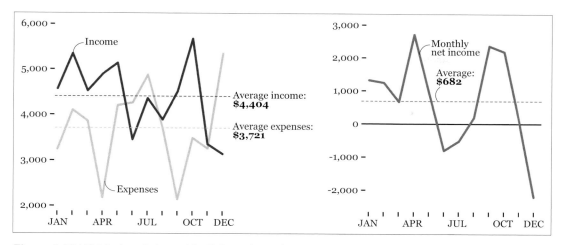

Figure 5.10 Which chart is better? It all depends on if you want to emphasize income versus expenses or if you wish to display the monthly net income.

Practical Tips About those Tricky Scales

Another factor to consider when deciding how to design a chart is its baseline and the scale on the X-axis (horizontal) and the Y-axis (vertical).

Look at the first two charts in **Figure 5.11** without reading the numbers on the Y-axis. Did you notice how large the differences are? Well, they really aren't! I truncated their Y-axis, so the baseline in both cases is set to 40 percent, rather than to 0 percent. It isn't acceptable to do so when the main visual cue to interpret the data is length or height measured from a common baseline. Bar charts,

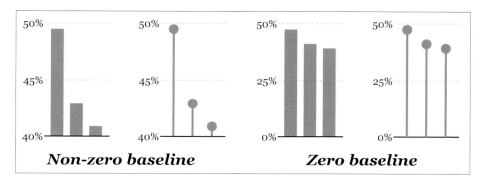

Figure 5.11 Don't truncate the Y-axis in bar charts and lollipop charts.

lollipop charts, histograms, and their variants should have a 0-baseline—unless you want to increase the chances of misunderstanding (which some people do, unfortunately!).

I should point out an exception: some data sets don't have a natural zero baseline. For instance, in economic analysis and finance, it's common to use indexed numbers, rather than just raw figures. Indexes often—not always, as we'll see in Chapter 8—have a base value of 100, as in **Figure 5.12**, which compares the cost of a product or service in different countries using the cost in the United States as the 100-baseline.

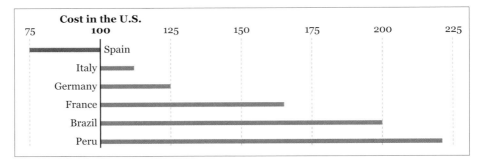

Figure 5.12 The cost of a product in different countries as a ratio of the cost of the same product in the United States.

You can think of the figures in the chart as percentage differences: 125 means 25 percent larger, and 200 means an increase of 100 percent (double). This plot would be a good choice for discussing the difference between costs in several countries in comparison to the United States. The difference between the U.S. and Brazil, for instance, is four times the difference between the United States and Germany.

We can derive a simple and flexible rule from this discussion: rather than trying to invariably include a 0-baseline in all your charts, **use logical and *meaningful* baselines** instead. This rule should help us decide what to do when designing charts in which length isn't the method of encoding. I am thinking of dot plots, scatter plots, line charts, and so on, which rather rely on position over common axes. For example, if you're talking about the historical unemployment rate in a country and this variable has never dropped below 5 percent, then 5 percent could be the baseline for your line chart.

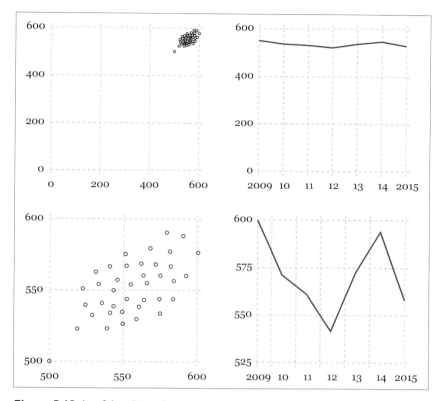

Figure 5.13 Are 0-baselines always necessary?

Compare the two sets of charts in **Figure 5.13**. It's a bit absurd to waste so much space just to show where the 0 point is, as I did on the two on top.

Another challenging situation appears when comparing widely different variables. See the first row of charts in **Figure 5.14**. The fact that a few data points are so large makes the smaller ones almost impossible to tell apart.

What to do? First, think of the purpose of these charts: is it just to highlight the largest values over the bulk of little ones? If that's what you need, leave the charts as they are. But what if you want readers to be able to clearly see both the large *and* the small values? You'll need at least two charts, each with its own scale, as shown in the second row of the same figure. **If your data vary so much that presenting them all on a single chart renders it useless, plot your data in several charts with dissimilar scales**.

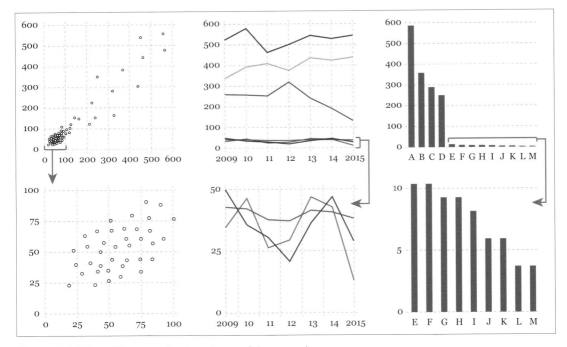

Figure 5.14 Two different scales for subsets of the same data.

Organizing the Display

Choosing the right graphic form isn't enough to design a great visualization. You also need to think of how your variables and categories are going to be organized: from highest to lowest, alphabetically, or by any other criteria. This decision also depends on the critical questions we have already asked ourselves: **what tasks should the graphic enable? What should I reveal with it?**

Imagine that you're doing some advertisement market analysis and you wish to know which kind of media influences teenagers and adults the most. You may conduct a survey and display the results as in **Figure 5.15**. This chart lets you compare the different methods of delivering ads *within each age group*.

But what if what you really wish to do is not compare media within age group but *across age groups*? In other words, what if you want to see which media becomes more or less trustworthy as people age?

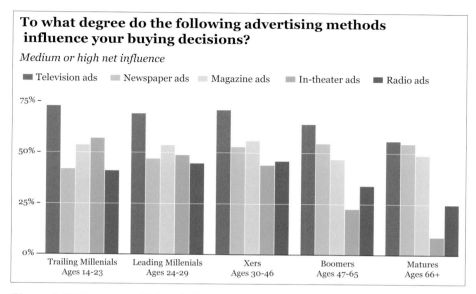

Figure 5.15 Data source: Deloitte's Digital Democracy Survey.

In that case, the current chart isn't that adequate. You can clearly spot TV's downward pattern, but that's just because the bar corresponding to TV ads is the first one of each cluster, and its color stands out over the others. If you want to see if magazine ads become more or less trusted later in life, your brain will be forced to isolate the blue bars in the middle of each group and then compare them to each other. That's way too much work. If seeing trends across age groups is the task we want to enable, let's group the bars not by age but by media (**Figure 5.16**).

We could further improve this chart. I love bar charts, but they tend to look a bit clunky when you have more than 10 bars or so. An intriguing alternative would be an unorthodox line chart (**Figure 5.17**), which doesn't put time on the X-axis, but a categorical variable, age groups. The beauty of this chart is that it gives us the best of both worlds: it doesn't just let us see trends across age groups, but it also lets us compare each medium within each group, as the dots are stacked on top of each other.

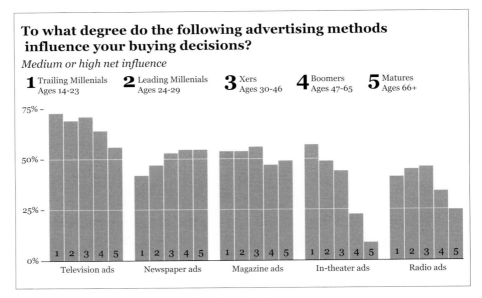

Figure 5.16 Reorganizing the data from Figure 5.15.

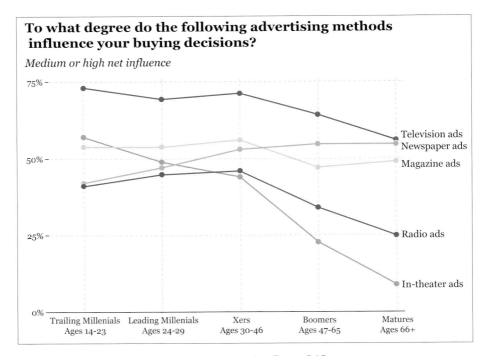

Figure 5.17 Line chart with the same data used in Figure 5.15.

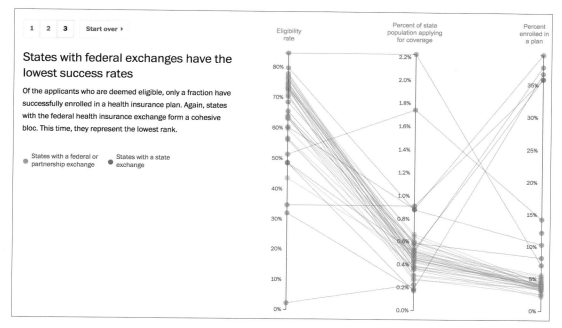

Figure 5.18 Visualization by *The Washington Post,*
http://www.washingtonpost.com/wp-srv/special/politics/state-vs-federal-exchanges/.

"Wait," you're probably thinking, "aren't line charts intended to display just trends over time intervals?" Many of us learned that rule in school. But that's just a convention, and conventions can and should change. Line charts can certainly be used to display time-series data, but time-series charts aren't the only kind of line charts that exist in the visualization designer's repertoire. Parallel coordinate charts, like the one in **Figure 5.18**, are pretty useful to visualize multi-dimensional data, as we'll see in Chapter 9.[4]

Put Your Work to the Test

There are certain graphic forms that I commonly avoid. One is the **radar chart**, as I consider it a feeble way of presenting information. Designers sometimes defend radar charts because they look pretty. I am not always against sacrificing a bit of clarity if the payoff in the form of allure is great, but I think that in the case presented in **Figure 5.19** we're sacrificing too much.

---

4 Visualization expert Robert Kosara has a good article about parallel coordinate charts: https://eagereyes.org/techniques/parallel-coordinates.

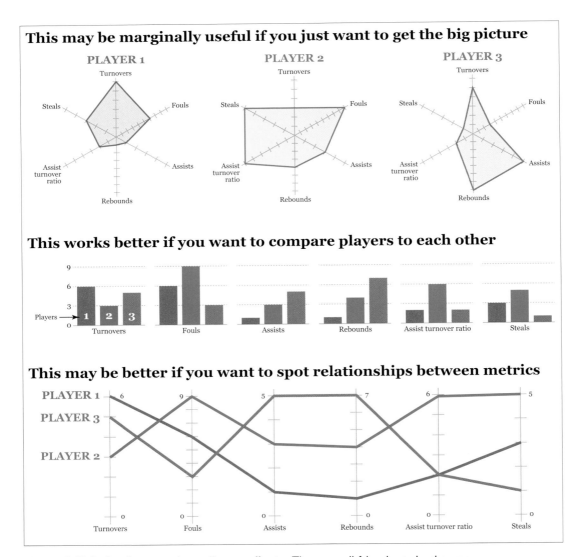

Figure 5.19 Radar charts aren't usually very effective. These are all fake charts, by the way.

On the three radar charts on top, I am presenting metrics of three basketball players. These charts are OK if all we need is a general and quick picture of the strengths and weaknesses of the players but little else.

Now see the same fake data on a bar chart, which makes it much easier to compare players to each other. Then I take a look at the parallel coordinates chart, which may be helpful to spot relationships between variables. For instance, it lets us see that there is a correlation between assists and rebounds. All these tasks can be completed with the radar charts, too, but it takes more effort: if you want to compare the performance of the three athletes in one metric, your eyes need to hop from radar chart to radar chart.

That said, I have used radar charts a couple of times in my career as an infographics and data visualization designer. Why did I break my own rule? Because sometimes a graphic form that is an inept choice in most circumstances may be fruitful in a very specific one.

Figure 5.20 is a poster-size infographic made by my team at the Brazilian weekly news magazine *Época*, where I was graphics director between 2010 and 2012. It shows the results of the 2010 presidential election with a combination of bar charts, **slope charts**—the ones at the bottom, comparing the 2010 results with the results of the previous election, state by state—and a choropleth map.

There's also a large radar chart on the upper-right corner. In this one, each radius corresponds to one of the 27 states Brazil is divided into. There are three color lines, one for each of the candidates. Red is for Dilma Rousseff (who ended up becoming president); blue is for José Serra; and green is for Marina Silva. The center of the radar is the 0 percent point, and the outmost ring corresponds to 100 percent of the vote. The farther away a joint of one of the lines is from the center, the larger the share of the vote that particular candidate got in that state.

Let me admit at the outset that these state-by-state results could also have been displayed using a set or traditional bar charts, but we decided on the radar chart because we wanted to highlight the fact that Dilma Rousseff, the left candidate, won by a very high margin in northeastern states. Notice that the radii on the radar chart are organized according to their geographic position: northeast on the upper-right corner, southeast on the bottom-right, and so forth. Someone familiar with Brazil's geography will be able to relate the choropleth map to the radar chart when they are placed side by side, like in this case.

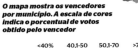

Os sinais da bússola eleitoral

A disputa de 2010 foi parecida com a de 2006

Alberto Cairo, Alexandre Mansur, Carlos Eduardo Cruz Garcia, Eliseu Barreira Junior, Marco Vergotti e Ricardo Mendonça

O PRIMEIRO turno da eleição presidencial de 2010 foi muito parecido com o da disputa de 2006. A petista Dilma Rousseff teve apenas 1,7 ponto porcentual a menos que o índice obtido pelo presidente Lula quatro anos atrás. A concentração maior de seus votos também foi no Nordeste. Desta vez, porém, a disputa foi um pouco menos polarizada. Os votos que provocaram segundo turno foram divididos entre o tucano José Serra e a verde Marina Silva.

Eleitores: 135.804.433, **abstenção:** *24.610.296 (18,12%),* **votos válidos:** *101.590.153 (91,36%),* **votos brancos:** *3.479.340 (3,13%) e* **votos nulos:** *6.124.254 (5,51%)*

Candidatos	50%	Votos
Dilma Rousseff **(PT)**	**46,9%**	47.651.434
José Serra **(PSDB)**	**32,6%**	33.132.283
Marina Silva **(PV)**	**19,3%**	19.636.359

Outros candidatos	%	Votos
Plinio **(PSOL)**	0,87%	886.816
José Maria Eymael **(PSDC)**	0,09%	89.350
Zé Maria **(PSTU)**	0,08%	84.609
Levy Fidelix **(PRTB)**	0,06%	57.960
Ivan Pinheiro **(PCB)**	0,04%	39.136
Rui Costa Pimenta **(PCO)**	0,01%	12.206

Fonte: Tribunal Superior Eleitoral (TSE)

O mapa mostra os vencedores por município. A escala de cores indica o porcentual de votos obtido pelo vencedor

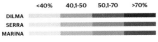

| | <40% | 40,1-50 | 50,1-70 | >70% |

DILMA
SERRA
MARINA

INFLUÊNCIAS REGIONAIS

Os cientistas políticos explicam algumas particularidades regionais na escolha entre Dilma, Marina e Serra

1 RORAIMA A preferência por Serra pode ser efeito da regularização das terras indígenas de Raposa-Terra do Sol, que teria afetado a economia local

2 ACRE No Estado de Marina, Serra venceu. Ela teve 35% em Rio Branco e drenou parte dos eleitores do governador Tião Viana (PT). Com as bases divididas, Dilma perdeu

3 MUNICÍPIOS DO NORDESTE No reduto mais forte do governo Lula, Serra venceu em poucas localidades. O motivo é a política municipal. Em Uruçuí, no Piauí, os eleitores puniram o prefeito Valdir Soares (PT), em uma fase impopular

4 PARÁ A política fundiária e ambiental do governo federal pode ter afetado interesses do setor pecuário e ter ajudado o PSDB local. O ex-governador e agora candidato novamente Simão Jatene (PSDB) puxou votos para Serra

DANÇA ESTADUAL Na comparação com a eleição presidencial de 2006, PT e PSDB tiveram votação menor na

COMO LER

% no 1º turno 2006	% no 1º turno 2010
Lula	Dilma
Alckmin	Serra
	Marina
Outros	Outros

AC
51,8% → 52,2%
42,6% → 23,8%
      → 23,5%
5,6% → 0,5%

AL
46,6% → 50,9%
37,8% → 36,5%
15,6% → 11,5%
      → 1,1%

AM
78,1% → 65,0%
      → 25,7%
12,5% → 8,5%
9,4% → 0,8%

AP
54,4% → 47,4%
32,2% → 29,7%
      → 21,4%
13,4% → 1,5%

BA
66,7% → 62,6
26,0% → 21,0
      → 15,7
7,3% → 0,7

DF
44,1% → 42,0%
37,1% → 31,7%
18,8% → 24,3%
      → 2,0%

ES
53,0% → 37,3%
37,2% → 35,4%
      → 26,3%
9,8% → 1,0%

GO
51,5% → 42,2%
40,2% → 39,5%
      → 17,2%
8,3% → 1,1%

MA
75,5% → 70,7%
18,8% → 15,1%
      → 13,6%
5,7% → 0,6%

MG
50,8% → 47,0%
40,6% → 30,8%
      → 21,3%
8,6% → 0,9%

MS
56,3% → 42,4
36,0% → 40,0
      → 16,9
7,7% → 0,7

Figure 5.20 Infographic published by *Época* magazine (Brazil).

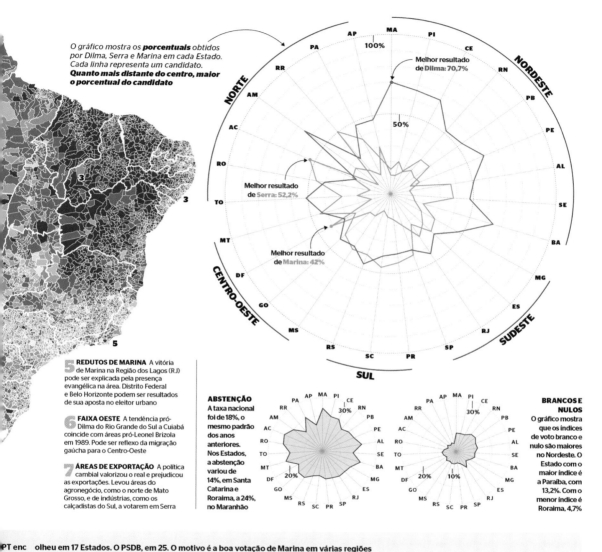

*O gráfico mostra os **porcentuais** obtidos por Dilma, Serra e Marina em cada Estado. Cada linha representa um candidato.* **Quanto mais distante do centro, maior o porcentual do candidato**

Melhor resultado de Dilma: 70,7%

Melhor resultado de Serra: 52,2%

Melhor resultado de Marina: 42%

5 **REDUTOS DE MARINA** A vitória de Marina na Região dos Lagos (RJ) pode ser explicada pela presença evangélica na área. Distrito Federal e Belo Horizonte podem ser resultados de sua aposta no eleitor urbano

6 **FAIXA OESTE** A tendência pró-Dilma do Rio Grande do Sul a Cuiabá coincide com áreas pró-Leonel Brizola em 1989. Pode ser reflexo da migração gaúcha para o Centro-Oeste

7 **ÁREAS DE EXPORTAÇÃO** A política cambial valorizou o real e prejudicou as exportações. Levou áreas do agronegócio, como o norte de Mato Grosso, e de indústrias, como os calçadistas do Sul, a votarem em Serra

ABSTENÇÃO
A taxa nacional foi de 18%, o mesmo padrão dos anos anteriores. Nos Estados, a abstenção variou de 14%, em Santa Catarina e Roraima, a 24%, no Maranhão

BRANCOS E NULOS
O gráfico mostra que os índices de voto branco e nulo são maiores no Nordeste. O Estado com o maior índice é a Paraíba, com 13,2%. Com o menor índice é Roraima, 4,7%

PT enc **olheu em 17 Estados. O PSDB, em 25. O motivo é a boa votação de Marina em várias regiões**

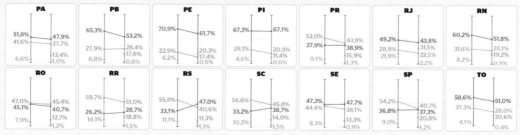

PA 51,8% / 47,9% / 41,6% / 37,7% / 6,6% / 13,4% / 1,0%	**PB** 65,3% / 53,2% / 27,9% / 28,4% / 17,6% / 6,8% / 0,8%	**PE** 70,9% / 61,7% / 22,9% / 20,3% / 17,4% / 6,2% / 0,6%

(PA) 51,8% — 47,9%, 41,6% — 37,7%, 6,6% — 13,4%, 1,0%
(PB) 65,3% — 53,2%, 27,9% — 28,4% — 17,6%, 6,8% — 0,8%
(PE) 70,9% — 61,7%, 22,9% — 20,3% — 17,4%, 6,2% — 0,6%
(PI) 67,3% — 67,1%, 28,1% — 20,9% — 11,4%, 4,6% — 0,6%
(PR) 53,0% — 43,9%, 37,9% — 38,9% — 15,9%, 9,1% — 1,3%
(RJ) 49,2% — 43,8%, 28,9% — 31,5% — 22,5%, 21,9% — 2,2%
(RN) 60,2% — 51,8%, 31,6% — 28,1% — 19,2%, 8,2% — 0,9%

(RO) 47,0% — 45,4%, 45,1% — 40,7% — 12,7%, 7,9% — 1,2%
(RR) 59,7% — 51,0%, 26,2% — 28,7% — 18,8%, 14,1% — 1,5%
(RS) 55,8% — 47,0%, 33,1% — 40,6% — 11,3%, 11,1% — 1,1%
(SC) 56,6% — 45,8%, 33,2% — 38,7% — 14,0%, 10,2% — 1,5%
(SE) 47,3% — 47,7%, 44,4% — 38,1% — 13,3%, 8,3% — 0,9%
(SP) 54,2% — 40,7%, 36,8% — 37,3% — 20,8%, 9,0% — 1,2%
(TO) 58,6% — 51,0%, 37,3% — 28,0% — 20,6%, 4,1% — 0,4%

It's hard to know if a graphic form will work well until you try it and you compare it to alternatives, so when designing this infographic, I also designed bar charts and a line chart (**Figure 5.21**). We discarded it at the end in favor of the radar chart because we tested the latter with some journalists and designers in the newsroom. I also showed it to friends and relatives. All of them got the message the radar chart was intended to convey in a few seconds: Dilma Rousseff's line looks like a rubber band that has been stretched out toward the northeast.

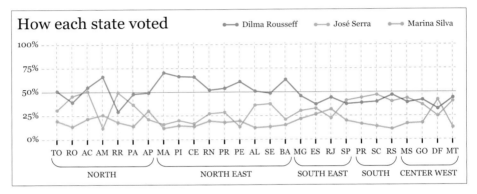

Figure 5.21 An alternative to the radar chart in Figure 5.20.

When the graphic was almost finished, *Época's* managing editor at the time, **Helio Gurovitz,** joked that the radar chart should actually be called a "compass chart" and suggested a title: The Signs of the Electoral Compass ("Os sinais da bússola eleitoral.") That made a lot of sense to me.

What I get from stories like this is that **rules of visualization matter as much as the results of the tests you may conduct with readers,** even those tests that are as informal as the one I've just described.

Tools like Cleveland's and McGill's hierarchy of methods of encoding are essential for our work, as they are grounded on empirical evidence obtained through experiments. They save time and energy that we can devote to better purposes, like plotting our data several times, giving this or that graphic form a try, putting the results side by side, showing them to as many people as possible, and then asking them about insights they get after exploring the graphic for a bit.

Some testing is critical, as **very often readers don't interpret our visualizations as we want them to**. In *Misbehaving: The Making of Behavioral Economics,* the book I mentioned at the beginning of this chapter, economist Richard H. Thaler describes an experiment he conducted in 1995. He asked employees at the University of Southern California to choose between two imaginary 401(k) retirement plans, a riskier one with higher expected returns (Fund A) and a safer one with lower ones (Fund B).

Thaler showed one group of employees the first two charts in **Figure 5.22**. These show the distribution of one-year returns. Each bar represents one of 35 possible changes (increase or decrease) from one year to the next.

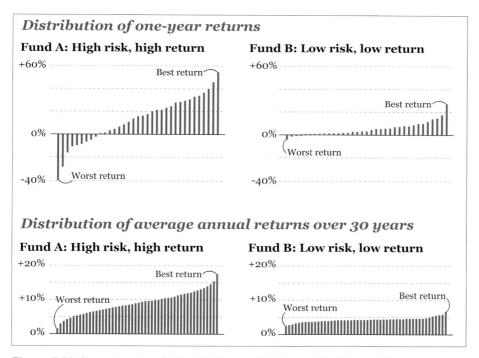

Figure 5.22 Charts based on Richard H. Thaler's *Misbehaving: The Making of Behavioral Economics* (2015).

The worst possible annual return of Fund A, the riskier one, is a -40 percent, and the best one is an increase of nearly 55 percent over the previous year. (Remember that these bars aren't organized chronologically, but from lowest to highest return.) Fund B shows less variation: the worst annual return is loss of -4 percent, while the best return is an increase of around 28 percent in one year.

Another group of subjects were shown the second set of two charts. These are all possible *total* returns over a period of more than 30 years. If you invest today and only take a look at your returns three decades from now, you may get anything from the lowest to the highest of the returns shown on the charts. There aren't negative returns in this case, as you can see.

The results of the experiments were impressive. People who saw the first two charts said that they weren't willing to take many risks, so they chose to put just 40 percent of their portfolio in Fund A (high risk, high return) and 60 percent in Fund B.

Those who were shown the second two charts said that they would prefer to invest *90 percent of their money in Fund A*, the risky one. The funniest thing of this experiment is that **both sets of charts are based on exactly the same underlying data**, coming from real portfolios made of a mixture of bonds and stocks.

Take notice: **The way data is visually presented has very real consequences on the lives of people who read your visualizations.**

To Learn More

- Bertin, Jacques. *Semiology of Graphics*. Redlands, CA: Esri Press, 2010. Bertin, a cartographer, was the founding father of modern visualization. This book, originally published in French in 1967, is his most famous one.

- Börner, Katy. *Atlas of Knowledge: Anyone Can Map*. Boston, MA: MIT Press, 2015. Börner, a professor of information science at Indiana University in Bloomington, is the author of two other books about visualization, but this is my favorite one by far. It's full of great examples, and it offers a thorough discussion of methods of encoding data.

- Cleveland, William S. *The Elements of Graphing Data*. Monterey, CA: Wadsworth Advanced and Software, 1985. An absolute classic of visualization.

- Few, Stephen. *Show Me the Numbers: Designing Tables and Graphs to Enlighten*. Oakland, CA: Analytics, 2004. My favorite book about statistical charts for business analytics.

- Meirelles, Isabel. *Design for Information: An Introduction to the Histories, Theories, and Best Practices behind Effective Information Visualizations.* Beverly, MA: Rockport, 2013. This beautiful book doesn't cover just quantitative or data visualization, but it also describes how to represent any kind of information by means of "structures:" hierarchical, relational, temporal, spatial, spatio-temporal, and textual.

- Steele, Julie, and Noah Iliinsky. *Designing Data Visualizations.* Sebastopol, CA: O'Reilly, 2011. A concise and dense introduction to good visualization practices.

6

Exploring Data with Simple Charts

The greatest value of a picture is when it forces us to notice what we never expected to see.

—John W. Tukey, *Exploratory Data Analysis*

The famous statistician **John W. Tukey** once wrote that exploring data is "graphical detective work."[1]

Tukey created an entire branch of data analysis almost singlehandedly. He called it **exploratory data analysis**. He explained that, before you can even begin testing your ideas against the evidence, it's essential to get a good feel for what your data look like. And the best way of doing so involves graphical displays, not just numerical summaries.

It would be presumptuous on my part to assume that I can explain everything about how to explore data. For that, you'll need to refer to the bibliography at the end of each chapter. However, I'd like to at least give you a glimpse of how it

---

1 These are the first lines in Tukey's 1977 classic *Exploratory Data Analysis*.

works and how exciting it can be. If you've ever thought that statistics is boring,[2] get ready for a pretty pleasant surprise.

Before we start, some advice: there's no better way of learning than doing. Think of a subject you care about and find data related to it. I'm interested in poverty, inequality, and educational attainment, so I'll be exploring related data sets in the following pages. In your case, it can be sports, science, the environment, politics, or whatever. It won't be hard to find tons of good data in the websites of governmental institutions, international organizations (the UN, the World Bank, the IMF, and so on), and even private companies.

Most of the data I'll be using can be found on my website, **www.thefunctionalart .com**. The simple calculations I'll discuss can be done in a few minutes with any decent software tool like LibreOffice or R (which are both open source and free), Tableau, Microsoft Excel, Apple's Numbers, JMP, and others. I've used R, Tableau, and Adobe Illustrator myself. On my website you'll also find video tutorials in which I explain how to design some of the charts in this book.

The Norm and the Exceptions

The process of visually exploring data can be summarized in a single sentence: **find patterns and trends lurking in the data and then observe the deviations from those patterns**. Interesting stories may arise from both the **norm**—also called the **smooth**—and the exceptions.

Let's begin with a simple data set. Every two years, the Brazilian Ministry of Education releases the **Ideb**, an index that measures quality in basic education in the country. The Ideb, a score between 0 and 10 assigned to each school, is based on formulas that take into account factors like infrastructure, teacher training, student tests, and so on.[3]

On a slow, boring Sunday a few weeks ago, I downloaded the 2009 Ideb scores. Why 2009? That was the year I moved to Brazil, where I lived until 2012, so the answer is just sheer curiosity. The spreadsheet, which you can partially see in

---

2 I hated statistics when I was in college. I later came to believe that this happened because some teachers tend to focus just on the more formal side of its methods rather than explaining the underlying logic of those methods, which is a much more interesting approach.

3 Read more about the Ideb here: http://portal.inep.gov.br/web/portal-ideb (use Google Translate if you don't understand Portuguese).

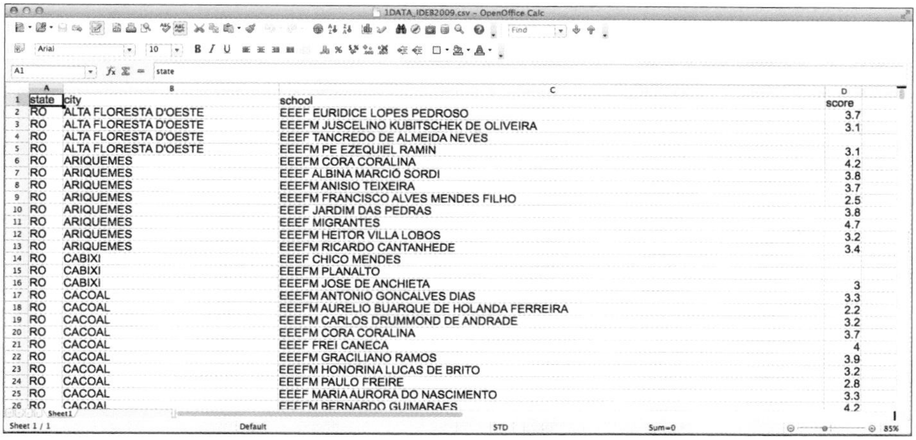

	state	city	school	score
2	RO	ALTA FLORESTA D'OESTE	EEEF EURIDICE LOPES PEDROSO	3.7
3	RO	ALTA FLORESTA D'OESTE	EEEFM JUSCELINO KUBITSCHEK DE OLIVEIRA	3.1
4	RO	ALTA FLORESTA D'OESTE	EEEF TANCREDO DE ALMEIDA NEVES	
5	RO	ALTA FLORESTA D'OESTE	EEEFM PE EZEQUIEL RAMIN	3.1
6	RO	ARIQUEMES	EEEFM CORA CORALINA	4.2
7	RO	ARIQUEMES	EEEF ALBINA MARCIÓ SORDI	3.8
8	RO	ARIQUEMES	EEEFM ANISIO TEIXEIRA	3.7
9	RO	ARIQUEMES	EEEFM FRANCISCO ALVES MENDES FILHO	2.5
10	RO	ARIQUEMES	EEEF JARDIM DAS PEDRAS	3.8
11	RO	ARIQUEMES	EEEF MIGRANTES	4.7
12	RO	ARIQUEMES	EEEFM HEITOR VILLA LOBOS	3.2
13	RO	ARIQUEMES	EEEFM RICARDO CANTANHEDE	3.4
14	RO	CABIXI	EEEF CHICO MENDES	
15	RO	CABIXI	EEEFM PLANALTO	
16	RO	CABIXI	EEEFM JOSE DE ANCHIETA	3
17	RO	CACOAL	EEEFM ANTONIO GONCALVES DIAS	3.3
18	RO	CACOAL	EEEFM AURELIO BUARQUE DE HOLANDA FERREIRA	2.2
19	RO	CACOAL	EEEFM CARLOS DRUMMOND DE ANDRADE	3.2
20	RO	CACOAL	EEEFM CORA CORALINA	3.7
21	RO	CACOAL	EEEF FREI CANECA	4
22	RO	CACOAL	EEEFM GRACILIANO RAMOS	3.9
23	RO	CACOAL	EEEFM HONORINA LUCAS DE BRITO	3.2
24	RO	CACOAL	EEEFM PAULO FREIRE	2.8
25	RO	CACOAL	EEEF MARIA AURORA DO NASCIMENTO	3.3
26	RO	CACOAL	EEEFM BERNARDO GUIMARAES	4.2

Figure 6.1 My data set, eagerly waiting to yield exciting stories.

Figure 6.1, has 19,387 rows, so it's hardly something you can extract meaning from by eyeballing it, unless you're some sort of replicant from *Blade Runner*.

The last column of the spreadsheet is the Ideb score. To refer to all values together I'll use the term **distribution**.

OK, we've got the data. Now, where to begin?

The Mode, the Median, and the Mean

Insights can arise simply by calculating **measures of central tendency**. In exploratory data analysis, these are sometimes called **the level** of the distribution, as they give you an idea of the average size of your numbers and of what their center point is.[4]

The simplest measure of central tendency is the **mode**. The mode is the value that appears most often in your distribution. Imagine that these are our Ideb scores:

1.2, 1.4, 1.8, 2.1, 2.1, 2.4, 2.7, 3.6, 3.8, 3.8, 4.0, 4.0, 4.0, 4.1, 4.5, 4.8, 4.9, 5.2, 5.6

The mode, highlighted above, is 4.0. That's the score that appears the most often. It appears three times. As it turns out, 4.0 also happens to be the mode of the Ideb variable in the actual data set.

4 I'm following B. H. Erikson's and T. A. Nosanchuk's *Understanding Data* (1992) in this section.

Distributions that have just one mode are called **unimodal**. It may happen that two or more scores are equally—or nearly equally—common, in which case we'd talk about a bimodal, trimodal, or even multimodal distribution.

The second statistic[5] we can calculate is the **median**. This is the value that divides our values in two halves. Going back to the scores before:

1.2, 1.4, 1.8, 2.1, 2.1, 2.4, 2.7, 3.6, 3.8, **3.8**, 4.0, 4.0, 4.0, 4.1, 4.5, 4.8, 4.9, 5.2, 5.6

There are 19 scores in that list. Therefore, the median will be the score that has nine scores below and nine above. That position in the distribution is occupied by 3.8, so that's our median.[6]

The **mean**, commonly known as the "average," is the result of adding up all the values and dividing the result by the total count. In other words:

Mean = Sum of all values / Total count of values

When describing a distribution, you can easily calculate the mode, the median, and the mean, but which one should you report, if you were to report just one? It depends. What you need to remember is that the mean is very sensitive to extreme values, while the median is not. The median is a **resistant statistic**.[7]

To understand the notion of resistant statistics, imagine that you're analyzing the historical starting salaries of people graduating from the University of North Carolina at Chapel Hill. You calculate the mean of all students, and you discover that geography alumni make a whopping average of nearly $740,000 a year. Now, *that's* interesting!

---

5 A brief note on terminology: a number that summarizes or describes an entire population is usually called a "parameter." If we then draw a sample of that population and calculate exactly the same number—its mean, for instance—we have a "statistic." For the sake of brevity, I will use just the word "statistic" in this chapter.

6 A note of caution is needed: the Brazilian Ministry of Education doesn't calculate the mode, median, or mean for all scores together. They first divide the schools into grades and calculate measures of central tendency for each of them. If you find the 2009 data, you'll see that there are discrepancies between what's shown in this book and the official statistics. When in doubt, trust their figures, not mine.

7 John Tukey was an advocate for the use of resistant statistics in exploratory data analysis. I'll explain how to use resistant statistics (like the median and quantiles) and non-resistant ones (like the mean and the standard deviation).

But it'd be hardly a surprise if you knew that Michael Jordan, the basketball player, was a geography major at UNC decades ago.[8] His initial salary was probably in the millions of dollars, compared to the few tens of thousands that his peers made. That distorts the mean. Michael Jordan's salary is an **outlier**, a value that is so far from the norm—the level of our distribution—that it twists our understanding of the data if we aren't careful enough.

Imagine that these were the first-year annual salaries of all geography graduates from UNC-Chapel Hill, in 2015 U.S. dollars:

$20,000, $22,000, $25,000, $30,000, $32,000, $40,000, $5,000,000

The mean of the series is $738,428. On the other hand, the median, which is the value that divides the salary distribution in half ($30,000), is a much better summary. As B. H. Erickson and T. A. Nosanchuk wrote in their book *Understanding Data*, when exploring variables like salaries and incomes, you shouldn't focus on how much people earn on average but on *how much the average person earns*. If you read that sentence again, you'll notice that it isn't a pun.

We say that the median is resistant because even if we added one outrageous value at the lower end of the series of values—say, 10 bucks a year—or increased Michael Jordan's annual salary to 100 *billion* dollars, the median would remain untouched, while the mean would go bananas.

Comparing the median to the mean and noticing that they differ a lot is one of the first warning signs of a skewed distribution. In the case of the Ideb scores I'm playing with right now, the median of all schools is 3.8 and the mean is 3.78, so they are almost identical. If we round the mean up, the result will also be 3.8.

Weighting Means

Before we continue, let me make an aside about how careful we need to be when calculating these very simple measures and how important it is to understand our data well before we manipulate them.

Imagine that the Ideb wasn't an index assigned to each school by one of the branches of the Ministry of Education, based on weighing different factors.

---

8 I was a professor at UNC-Chapel Hill between 2005 and 2009. Someone told me a story similar to this one, although I don't remember the exact figures. Apparently, this calculation was done once, to the amusement of students and administrators alike.

Instead, let's suppose that the score for each school is the result of calculating the mean of the grades that all students in that school get in a certain test. If we wanted to obtain the national mean (a mean of means, also called a **grand mean**), it would be risky to average the school scores.

To understand why, see **Figure 6.2**, where we are comparing four schools of different sizes.

	SCHOOL 1	SCHOOL 2	SCHOOL 3	SCHOOL 4
Student 1	3.6	5.4	2.3	4.6
Student 2	2.5	8.7	4.5	3.2
Student 3	4.5	5.6	2.3	5.5
Student 4	2.3	6.5	3.1	
Student 5	1.8	4.5	6.5	
Student 6	2.5	3.2		
Student 7	2.8	1.6		
Student 8	2.8			
Student 9	2.4			
Student 10	2.7			
Mean of each school	**2.79**	**5.07**	**3.74**	**4.43**
Mean of SCHOOLS	**4.01**			
Mean of STUDENTS	**3.82**			

Figure 6.2 Averaging averages of groups of different sizes is rarely a good idea.

School 1 is the largest (10 students), and School 4 is the smallest, with just three students. We can first obtain the mean for each school. Then we calculate the mean of school means. The result is 4.01.

If, instead, we calculate the mean of all students together, regardless of the school they attend, the result is 3.82.

Why do we get this discrepancy? There are a lot of students in School 1, and most of them performed rather poorly in the test. By calculating the mean of each school and then the grand mean of all schools, *rather than the mean of all students*, small schools are given the same weight as bigger schools. Calculating a grand mean—a mean of school means—would be appropriate only if all schools had a similar number of students.

But what if it's impossible to access the entire data set of millions and millions of test grades, one per student? In that case, we need to take school size into consideration to calculate a **weighted mean**. The formula for this is shown in **Figure 6.3**. Remember it the next time you need to calculate mean scores of groups of different sizes—schools, cities, counties, states, countries, or whatever. And be aware that this is one of the many techniques used by people who are fond of lying with statistics.

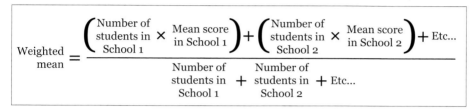

Figure 6.3 How to calculate a weighted mean.

Range

Calculating the median, mean, and mode is a good place to start when exploring data. Sometimes, they alone will lead you to interesting stories. But they won't be enough in most cases.

The challenge we face if we just rely on measures of central tendency to summarize our data is that we don't really know if most values in our data set are close to them or if they are widely spread apart. This is critical information.

In the case of the Ideb, we could first look at the highest and the lowest values. The difference between the maximum and the minimum value of a distribution is called the **range**. **Figure 6.4** shows it, along with all other statistics we have found so far, and a new one: the 6.0 minimum goal that the Brazilian government wants most schools to achieve in the future.

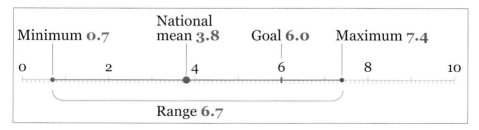

Figure 6.4 The center and the spread of our distribution.

We now know that there are some terrible schools (0.7!) and some very good ones. But how many bad and good schools are there, really? How many are clustered around the national mean? And how many are close to the 6.0 goal or even surpass it?

To find out, we need to take a more detailed look at our data. Let's create a plot that shows how many schools have obtained good and bad scores. It will also reveal the **shape** of our distribution. We call this a **histogram (Figure 6.5)**. In a histogram, values are aggregated into bins—ranges of Ideb scores, in this case. In Figure 6.5, the bins have a range of 0.1 score-points.

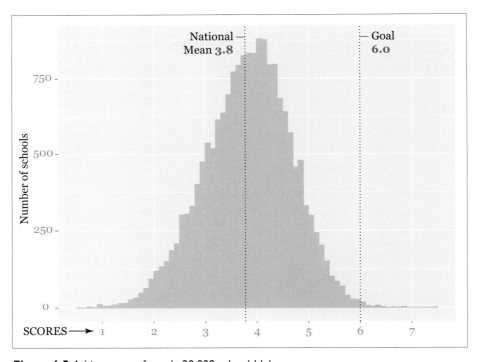

Figure 6.5 A histogram of nearly 20,000 school Ideb scores.

In a histogram, the height of each bar corresponds to the number of records or scores (school counts here) within each bin. A histogram is intended to show the **frequency** of each value, or of groups of values, within a data set. The higher the bar, the higher the frequency of the values aggregated in each bin.

When doing exploratory work, it's usually a good idea to design not just one histogram but many, changing the bin size just to get a clearer picture of the

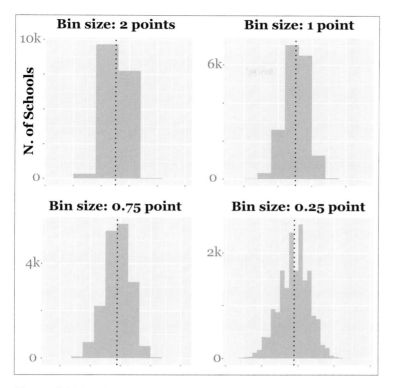

Figure 6.6 Multiple histograms of different bin sizes.

relative densities of the distribution. You can see several histograms of different bin sizes on **Figure 6.6**.

Histograms can cast light on features of the data that we may have overlooked. To begin with, we can see that most schools are close to the national mean, but just a tiny fraction of them are above the 6.0 threshold. Our distribution is almost symmetrical, and it's close to being normal (more about this later).

Our distribution could well have been asymmetrical. For instance, income levels don't usually follow a normal distribution but a highly skewed one, with a lot of people on the lower end of the curve and just a few individuals or families on the rightmost end of the long tail (**Figure 6.7**). The skew of a distribution can be a fruitful source for further exploration.[9]

---

9 Statisticians use many other measures to describe the shape of data. For instance, the peakedness of a distribution is called **kurtosis**, a word that, for some reason, I have always thought could be a great name for an ancient Greek hero.

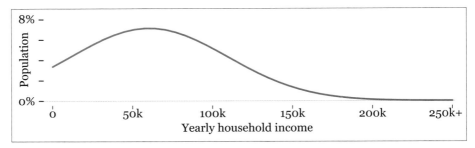

Figure 6.7 A smoothed histogram based on fictional data: the X-axis is household income, and the Y-axis is the percentage of households.

Some Fun with Ranges

Finding stories is sometimes a matter of repeatedly asking ourselves what would happen if we plot our data in a different way. We have learned about some important terms in data exploration, so let's pause to catch our breath and play for a bit. What if we design multiple range and frequency plots, one for each of the 27 states of Brazil, and see what they tell us? Many software tools will let us do this quite quickly.

In case you're not familiar with Brazil's geography, I've designed a handy map of all 27 states and the five regions the country is divided into (**Figure 6.8**).

Now, let's roll up our sleeves and get our hands dirty.

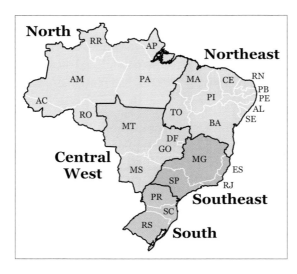

Figure 6.8 Map of Brazil. States in the north and the northeast are much poorer than those in the south and southeast.

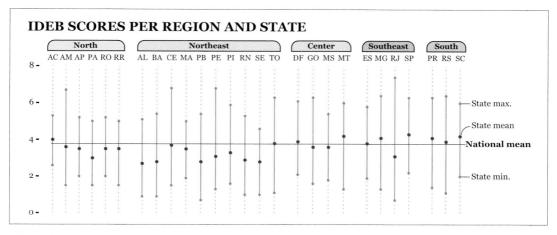

Figure 6.9 Summary data, state by state.

Let's begin with a very simple range chart (**Figure 6.9**) which divides our original distribution into 27, one per state in Brazil. I have arranged the states by region. Each vertical line shows the maximum, minimum, and mean score of each distribution.

Immediately, I can start writing down ideas for potential stories and infographics. There are clear differences between poor states (those in the north and the northeast) and rich states (the ones in the southeast and the south of the country).

If we focus on certain states, we'll also notice striking facts. For instance, what's going on in Rio de Janeiro (RJ)? It has the widest range: bad schools are among the worst overall, and its best schools are the best in the country. After consulting with experts in education, you may learn that Rio de Janeiro has the most unequal school system in Brazil, by far. We have just uncovered the evidence for that assertion.

We could go much further. Any visualization hides as much as it shows. This is certainly true of my range chart. We cannot really see any detail in it, just a crude summary of each of the 27 distributions. To understand our data well, we may want to explore them in all its glorious detail.

What if we design a chart plotting the score of each of the nearly 20,000 schools? How about a **strip plot** (**Figure 6.10**). It looks cool, I know, but don't give me credit. Thank R, the software that I used. It took a single line of code and 10 seconds of computer processing to generate that. Then I styled it a bit in Adobe Illustrator.

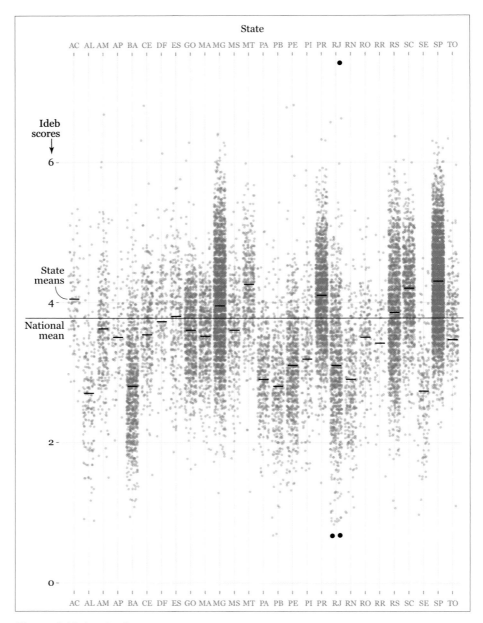

Figure 6.10 A strip plot.

I arranged the states alphabetically because I wanted to focus on individual cases. Organizing the states in different ways (alphabetically, by region, from highest to lowest mean, and so on) could lead us to more insights, more questions to ask of our data set, and more potential stories to tell, after we corroborate them.

The black dots in the chart are the schools I highlighted for additional reporting. Perhaps I could send someone to interview the principals, or consult with the Ministry of Education about why that school at the top of the scale in Rio de Janeiro is performing so well, or what is going on with the ones at the bottom.

And this is just if I'm interested in Rio de Janeiro. I may be a citizen in the state of Ceará (CE), in which case I could zoom in on the chart to analyze its outliers. There are quite a few very visible ones. The strip plot works well when we want to compare schools at the extremes of the distribution with the norm, those schools close to the national or state means.

The histogram, the lollipop chart, and the strip plot are three ways of visualizing the spread and shape of the same distributions **at different levels of detail**. This is usually the best strategy: **a visualization designer should never rely on a single statistic or a single chart or map** when doing exploratory work.

That's why, as you can see in **Figure 6.11**, I also created a histogram and a violin plot (also called a "bean plot") for each state. These two charts may be clearer than the strip plot if our goal was to get a clear sense of frequencies, instead of visualizing each single school.

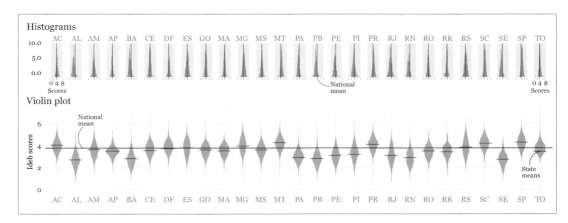

Figure 6.11 Two ways of visualizing distributions: histograms and violin plots. A violin plot is like a two-sided vertical histogram: the thickness of the color strips is proportional to counts.

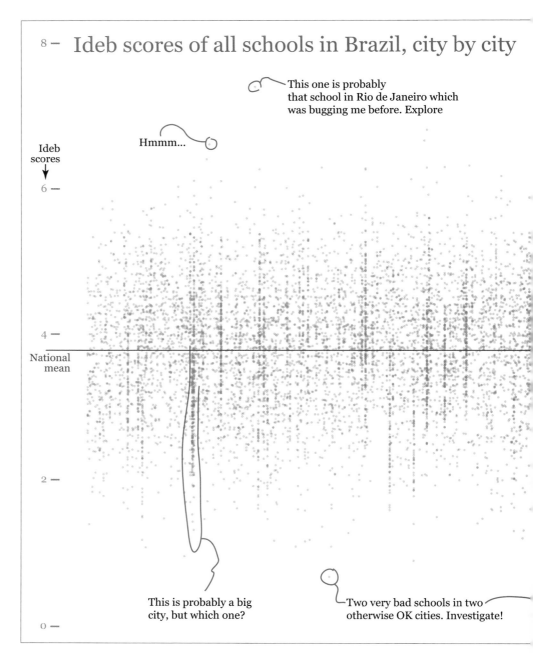

Figure 6.12 A strip plot of all schools in Brazil. Each dot represents one school, and each column of dots is a city. The annotations mimic what I do in a real project, which is to write down reminders of things that look promising in the data.

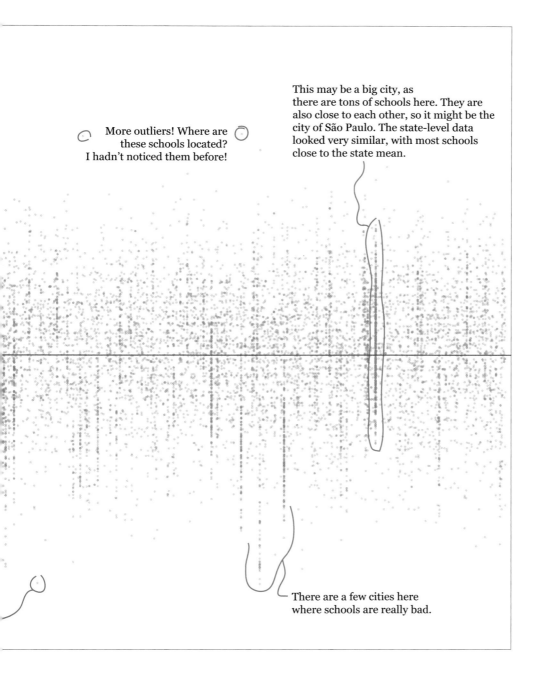

This may be a big city, as there are tons of schools here. They are also close to each other, so it might be the city of São Paulo. The state-level data looked very similar, with most schools close to the state mean.

More outliers! Where are these schools located? I hadn't noticed them before!

There are a few cities here where schools are really bad.

Which one of these charts is better? There's no "better." It all depends on what we want to see. For instance, if I had to visualize the number of schools above or below the national mean on each state, I'd choose the histograms, although I'd make them much bigger. But the violin plot works great as an overview, in my opinion (besides being really pretty!). The distributions of the more equal states are very fat in the middle, as many schools are clustered around the state mean; the skinnier distributions correspond to the most unequal states, as there are few schools in the middle and more on the extremes.

Finally—and just to see what would happen—I made R generate a second strip plot of all schools in each Brazilian city. This is completely unreadable, but it certainly looks curious (**Figure 6.12**). It would be much more useful if we kept just a few cities and we compared them to their state or national means. Still, I have noticed some interesting facts in this mess, so I have added notes to the chart, just as a reminder to myself. They might be worth examining, who knows?

To Learn More

- Caldwell, Sally. *Statistics Unplugged, 4th ed.* New York, NY: Cengage Learning, 2013. If I had to recommend just one introduction to statistics book, it'd be this one.

- Hartwig, Frederick, and Brian E. Dearing. *Exploratory Data Analysis.* Newbury Park, CA: SAGE Publications, 1979. A concise introduction to the techniques favored by John W. Tukey.

- Wheelan, Charles. *Naked Statistics: Stripping the Dread from the Data.* New York, NY: W. W. Norton & Company, 2013. A pain-free overview of the core principles of statistics.

7

Visualizing Distributions

I couldn't claim that I was smarter than 65 other guys—but the average
of 65 other guys, certainly!

—Richard P. Feynman, *Surely You're Joking, Mr. Feynman!:*
Adventures of a Curious Character

My favorite data-driven stories are those that reveal something funny about the
human condition. Christian Rudder, one of the founders of the dating website
OKCupid and author of *Dataclysm: Who We Are (When We Think No One's Looking)*,
has plenty of them.

Creating a profile in OKCupid involves filling out some surveys to give the website clues to find the people you may be most interested in dating. Based on your
answers, OKCupid soon begins sending you recommendations. By analyzing your
navigation patterns (see photo, click it, spend some time reading the profile), the
data folks at OKCupid can estimate the preferences of their users. In **Figure 7.1**,
I'm presenting the two charts I found most amusing in Rudder's book.

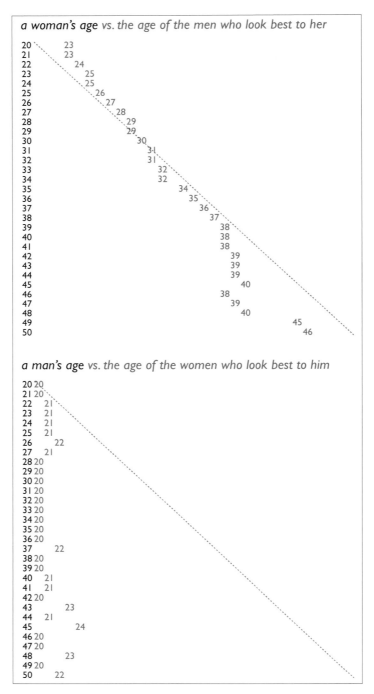

Figure 7.1 Chart by Christian Rudder.

The one on top shows the age of women compared to the average age of men they find most attractive. Women who are 20 like men who are 23, women who are 30 like men who are their own age, women of 40 like men of 38. The diagonal line is the age parity line.

The second chart shows that men of *all* ages invariably find women in their early twenties attractive. This isn't that surprising, is it? I guess that we all already knew that most men like the looks of younger women, even if we end up dating and marrying women who are close to our own age.[1] Well, here you have the data to confirm that hunch.

I like to show Rudder's elegant charts in my classes. My students are usually thrilled. These graphics are just so persuasive and clear, they say. Dangerously so, I reply. As we saw in the previous chapter, a single statistic—the mode, the mean, the median, etc.—may not be a model that represents the entire data set correctly. In his book, Rudder acknowledges this problem and explains caveats in his data.

I wish journalists and designers were that careful. How many times have you read news stories that report just averages, with no mention whatsoever of ranges, distributions, frequencies, or outliers? Sometimes it may be appropriate to mention just a simple average, but that doesn't happen often. The age of the women who most men my age (40) find most good-looking is 21. Now, imagine that we don't show just that figure to our readers. Instead, we plot all preferences of all men of 40 on a histogram.

I've designed five fictitious histograms (**Figure 7.2**) that share the same mode, 21. Each little red rectangle represents 1 percent of 40-year-olds, so there are 100 rectangles on each chart. Ask yourself on which of these cases you would report just an average.

I'd say that it'd be appropriate to do so just in the first case—and I still have my doubts—because all scores are clustered around the mode, at the lower end of the distribution, and the range is relatively narrow. All the other distributions would force you to show readers not just the average, but the very relevant details that hide behind them.

---

1 When asked directly, both men and women say they would like to date people who are roughly their same age.

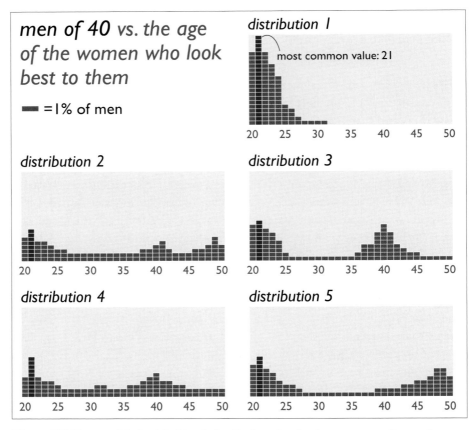

Figure 7.2 Five possible (and fictitious) distributions for the data corresponding to the preferences of men of 40. All of them have the same mode: 21.

On distributions 3 and 4, for instance, a good amount of 40-year-old men like women who are their age. On 5, many 40-year-old men find women who are *older* than they are attractive.

This is another example of why we should always design visualizations of our data. To supplement them, we can also calculate **numerical summaries of spread.** We'll learn about two methods in this chapter: first, the **standard deviation** and, then, the one that is preferred in exploratory data analysis, **percentiles.**

The Variance and the Standard Deviation

Any data analysis software can calculate a standard deviation for you faster than a frog zaps a fly with its tongue, but it's important to understand where that statistic comes from. So let's take a look at a handful of simple formulas.

To calculate the standard deviation, we first need to find the **variance**, a statistic that is quite useful for confirmatory tests.[2] **Figure 7.3** shows the formula for the variance with some explainers to clarify its elements.

$$\underset{\textbf{①}}{variance} = \frac{\overset{\textbf{④}}{\sum} (\overset{\textbf{②}}{Each\ score\ -\ mean})^{\overset{\textbf{③}}{2}}}{\underset{\textbf{⑤}}{Number\ of\ scores}}$$

❶ The variance of a distribution of scores can be obtained by
❷ subtracting the mean of your distribution from each score
❸ squaring each result
❹ adding all results up ($\sum$)
❺ and dividing that sum by the total number of scores you have

Figure 7.3 How to calculate the variance.

To calculate the variance, first you need to have the mean of your distribution. Remember that the mean is the result of adding up all your scores or values and then dividing the result by the number of scores. Once you have the mean, get all your scores, subtract the mean from each of them, and square each result. Then add up all the results.

After that, divide this sum by the total number of scores.

Two important side notes: First, **why the squaring portion of the formula?** The reason is that there are scores/values that are smaller than the mean. Therefore, when you do the subtractions, some results will be negative numbers. If you add up the results of all subtractions without squaring them first, negative values will cancel out positive ones, and the final sum will be zero. If you don't believe

---

2 You may have heard of ANOVA, which means "analysis of variance." This test is useful to analyze if the differences between the means of several groups of scores (say, test scores from several schools) are noticeable enough.

me, see the small data set in **Figure 7.4** and compare the non-squared deviations from the mean (each score minus the mean) to the squared ones.

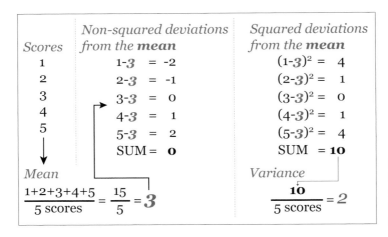

Figure 7.4
Non-squared versus squared deviations from the mean.

Second: At the end of the formula, we divided by the number of scores. However, most statistics and data analysis books recommend to do that only if you're calculating the variance of a *population*. If it's a *sample* from that population you're analyzing, they recommend to divide by the mean minus one.

Why minus one? The answer is a bit complicated, so I'm going to give you just the short version: it's a correction to remove possible distortions. When dealing with smallish samples, if you just divide the sum of squared deviations by the number of scores in the sample, the variance may be quite different from the real variance of the population. Subtracting 1 from the number of scores before making the division will result in a variance that may be closer to the variance of the population our sample is intended to represent. Let's leave it there.

Now that we know how to calculate the variance, the standard deviation will be as easy as 1+1. Here's the formula:

Standard deviation = Square root of the variance

The full version of the formula is on **Figure 7.5**. If you compare it to Figure 7.3, you will see that the only addition is the square root symbol. Now, let's learn what the standard deviation is useful for.

$$\text{standard deviation} = \sqrt{\frac{\Sigma(\text{Each score - mean})^2}{\text{Number of scores}}}$$

Figure 7.5 How to calculate the standard deviation of a population or of a sample of a population.

Standard Deviation and Standard Scores

Imagine that you are studying the gross annual salaries of the Information Technology (IT) employees of a company that operates in two countries, the United States and Nigeria. There are 100 IT workers in each country. **Figure 7.6** shows the first few rows of our data set, corresponding to the highest salaries.

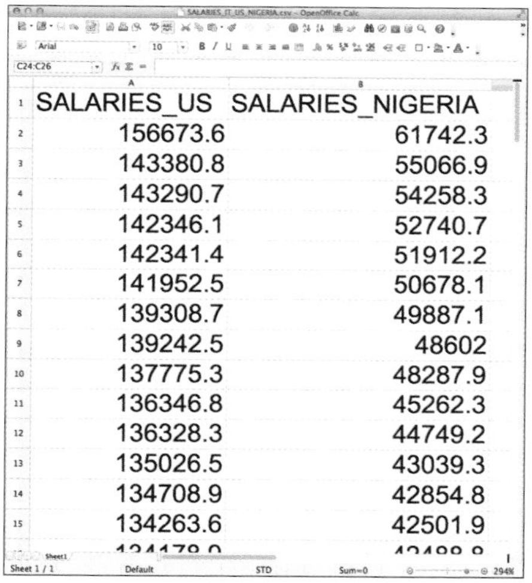

	SALARIES_US	SALARIES_NIGERIA
2	156673.6	61742.3
3	143380.8	55066.9
4	143290.7	54258.3
5	142346.1	52740.7
6	142341.4	51912.2
7	141952.5	50678.1
8	139308.7	49887.1
9	139242.5	48602
10	137775.3	48287.9
11	136346.8	45262.3
12	136328.3	44749.2
13	135026.5	43039.3
14	134708.9	42854.8
15	134263.6	42501.9

Figure 7.6 See the entire data set at www.thefunctionalart.com.

We want to run some comparisons based on these distributions. For instance, we may wish to know, roughly, in which country salaries are more or less equal or how salaries in both countries compare to each other. First, we calculate the mean and the standard deviation. I'm not even going to use the formulas explained before. I'll make the software do the heavy lifting for me:

U.S. salaries. Mean: 122,400; Standard deviation: 10,746

Nigerian salaries. Mean: 29,170; Standard deviation: 12,589

In the case of the United States, the standard deviation is roughly 8.8 percent of the mean salary. In Nigeria, the standard deviation is a whopping 43.2 percent of the mean salary! This may suggest that U.S. salaries have a reasonable range, while Nigerian ones tend to deviate a lot from their mean. Let's write a note about it and continue working.

Read the histograms on **Figure 7.7**. I designed two for each distribution, changing bin sizes to avoid being misled by any single graphic. I also overlaid density curves. These are lines that software can calculate for you and that may be helpful to spot patterns when a distribution is very messy.

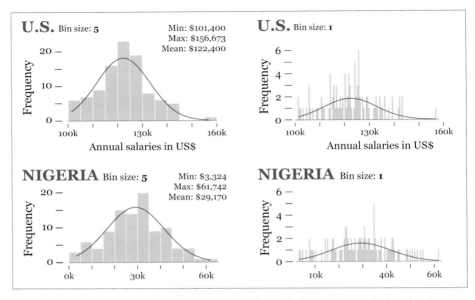

Figure 7.7 Two histograms of different bin sizes for each distribution, including density curves.

Next, suppose that we want to see what the equivalences are between U.S. and Nigerian salaries. Say that an IT employee makes $125,335 a year in the United States. What would be a similar salary in Nigeria?

When discussing where a specific score stands in its distribution and how it compares to others, we can transform it into a **standard score** (or **z-score**). A standard score is simply an indication of how far a raw score deviates from the mean, measured in number of standard deviations.

To better understand this idea, I'm plotting the standard deviation over our histograms (**Figure 7.8**). How far is the highest U.S. salary ($156,673) from the mean? Roughly, it's 3.2 standard deviations. This number is the standard score of that salary. And the lowest salary, $101,400? It's around –2.0 standard deviations from the mean. That's the standard score that corresponds to that raw score.

Notice something interesting in the distribution of salaries in Nigeria? The lowest salary there, $3,324, is just a bit below -2.0 standard deviations from the mean, similar to what happens in the United States. What about the highest salary in Nigeria, $61,742? It's 2.6 standard deviations from the mean. The highest salary

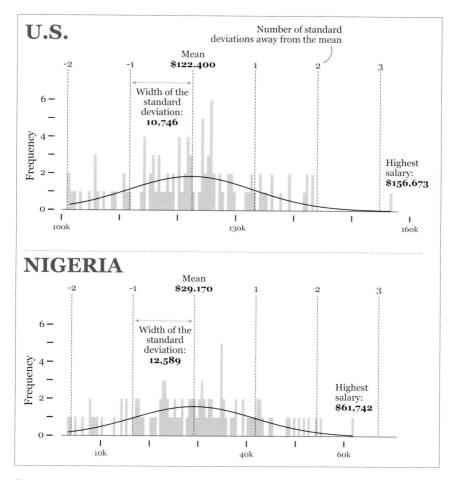

Figure 7.8 Measuring distances from the mean using the standard deviation.

in the United States. ($156,673), on the other hand, is 3.2 standard deviations from the mean of its distribution.

Does this mean that we have suddenly proved that U.S. salaries are more unequal than Nigerian ones? Not so fast. Read the charts again. In the U.S. distribution, if we ignore the highest salary, which is an unusual case, all the other ones lie within 2 and -2 standard deviations from the mean. In the Nigerian distribution, three values are beyond the –2 and 2 boundaries: the lowest salary and the two highest ones.

Lesson learned, again: Never trust just one statistic. Always plot your data.

Let's go back to standard scores. Here's how to calculate them:

z-score of a raw score = (Raw score-mean)/standard deviation

Let's apply this formula to some U.S. salaries. Remember that the mean is $122,400 and the standard deviation is 10,746:

$156,673 -> z-score = (156,673-122,400)/10,746 = **3.2** (I'm rounding these)

$125,335 -> z-score = (125,335-122,400)/10,746 = **0.3**

$101,400 -> z-score = (101,400-122,400)/10,746 = **-2.0**

Now, Nigeria. The mean is $29,170 and the standard deviation, 12,589:

$61,742 -> z-score = ($61,742-29,170)/12,589 = **2.6**

$31,074 -> z-score = ($31,074-29,170)/12,589 = **0.2**

$4,879 -> z-score = ($4,879-29,170)/12,589 = **-1.9**

Back to the question I posed before: If an IT employee is making $125,335 in the United States, what would a person in a similar position make in Nigeria? We know that the standard score of $125,335 is 0.3 (see above). Which salary in Nigeria has a standard score of 0.3?

To do this, we need to reverse our previous formula.

From **z-score of a score = (Raw score – mean)/standard deviation**

We derive **Raw score = (z-score × standard deviation) + mean**

Therefore: **Raw score = (0.3 × 12,589) + 29,170 = $32,947**

Standard scores can come in handy when comparing different distributions, mainly when these distributions are normal (more about this in a minute). Say that you are a student and that you have done two final exams, graded on a scale from 0 to 100. On the math exam you got 68. On the English one you hit a mark of 83.

Can you say that you did better in English than in math? Nope. To be sure, you need the grades of your peers to calculate the mean and the standard deviation of both exams. Suppose that the mean grade of the math exam was 59 and the mean grade of the English exam was 79. The standard deviation was 5 in the math exam and 7 in the English exam. Therefore:

Your grade in the math exam: **68** -> z-score = (68-59)/5 = **1.8**

Your grade in the English exam: **83** -> z-score = (83-79)/7 = **0.6**

So you did proportionally *better* in the math exam, as your grade was 1.8 standard deviations above the mean!

The name "standard score" to refer to z-scores may be a bit misleading, in the sense that it suggests that they are the only way of standardizing raw scores. **In reality, when you control one variable for another variable or factor, you are also *standardizing* the original variable. The very word "standardize" means "to compare with a standard," after all.**

A few chapters ago, I wrote about comparing motor vehicle fatalities in two cities that have widely different populations, Chicago, Illinois, and Lincoln, Nebraska. You'd never compare just the *total* accident counts. You'd also need to compare *rates*, which are standardized scores—for instance, the number of fatalities per 100,000 vehicles. Similarly, when you analyze salaries or prices of products across the years, you must adjust for inflation. This adjustment is a form of standardization.

We could explore our data set of salaries of IT workers in the United States and Nigeria by standardizing the scores in a different way. For instance, we know that the minimum salary in the U.S. headquarters is $101,400, whereas in Nigeria it's $3,324, and they are both around -2.0 standard deviations away from the means of their distributions. But this tells us nothing of how high or low these salaries are *in comparison to the income of the population in those countries*.

We can try to express all salaries as a function of the average national salary or of the Gross National Income (GNI) per capita. The 2013 GNI per capita was $53,470 in the United States and $2,710 in Nigeria. We could do the following operation:

Salary of each IT worker in the company/ GNI per capita of her country

Therefore, in the United States:

Minimum salary of IT worker: $101,400/$54,470 = **1.9 times** the U.S. GNI per capita.

Maximum salary: $156,673/$54,470 = **2.9 times** the U.S. GNI per capita.

And in Nigeria:

Minimum salary of IT worker: $3,324/$2,710 = **1.2 times** the Nigerian GNI per capita.

Maximum salary: $61,742 /$2,710 = **22.8 times** the Nigerian GNI per capita!

We could then re-create our histograms (**Figure 7.9**). After reading them, ask yourself again where IT workers are *really* better paid in relative terms.

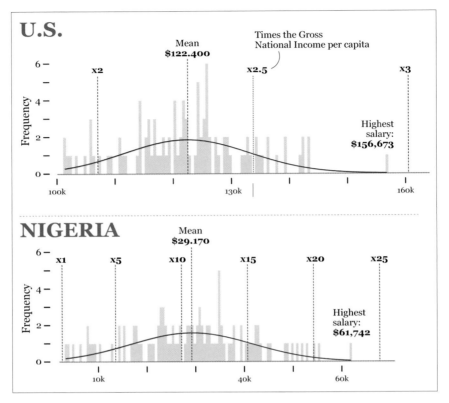

Figure 7.9 Standardizing values using the GNI per capita on each country.

Presenting Stories with Frequency Charts

Let's catch some breath after all that math. Frequency charts can be useful not just to explore the shape of your data but also to reveal it to your readers. And the histogram isn't the only graphic form you can use.

Take the presidential approval chart by *The Washington Post* on **Figure 7.10**. The darker the shade, the more common a particular approval rating was in Gallup polls for each president.

This lovely little graphic reveals that the range of approval ratings for presidents like Obama and Clinton is pretty narrow, particularly compared to George W. Bush and George H. W. Bush. However, Obama's approval ratings tend to concentrate at the lower end of the range, while Clinton's are a bit closer to the upper one.

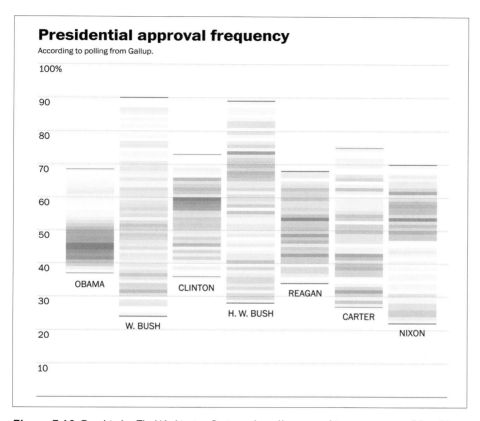

Figure 7.10 Graphic by *The Washington Post*; see http://www.washingtonpost.com/blogs/the-fix/wp/2015/01/02/barack-obamas-presidency-has-been-remarkably-steady-at-least-in-his-approval-rating/.

Figure 7.11 comes from Spain's elespanol.com, a news website that was launched right before the 2015 presidential election, so much of its initial coverage was related to this event. Each of these histograms compares the ideologies of people who intend to vote for each party with the ideology of the Spanish population in general. Data came from the Centro de Investigaciones Sociológicas (Center for Sociological Research), a governmental organization.

Citizens who declare themselves as voters for Partido Popular (PP) tend to lean to the right, while Podemos' and Izquierda Unida's (IU) sympathizers are mostly leftist. Ciudadanos' fans are centrists, for the most part.

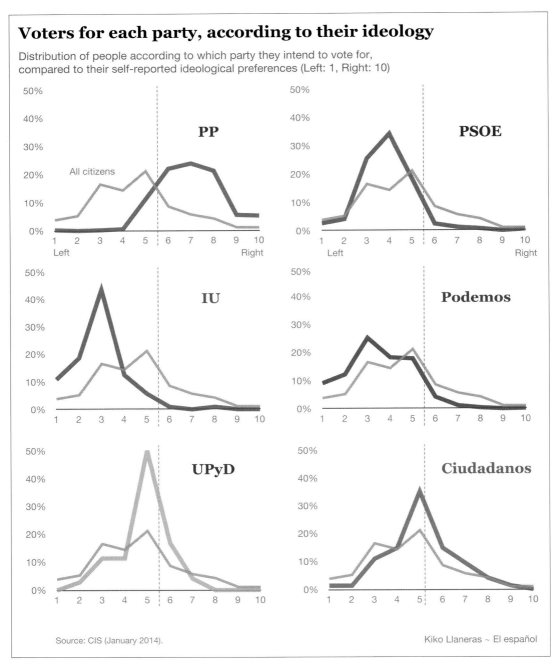

Voters for each party, according to their ideology

Distribution of people according to which party they intend to vote for,
compared to their self-reported ideological preferences (Left: 1, Right: 10)

Figure 7.11 Graphics by Kiko Llaneras for elespanol.com, http://www.elespanol.com/actualidad/
asi-es-la-ideologia-de-los-votantes-de-cada-partido-segun-el-cis/.

Besides the histograms, elespanol.com's **Kiko Llaneras** also designed vertically oriented charts (**Figure 7.12**) with a different distribution. In this case, potential voters weren't asked to position themselves on a scale from 0 (hard-left) to 10 (hard-right), but to choose the label that better defines their ideological stance—communist, conservative, ecologist, and so on. (Note for U.S. readers: In Europe, a "liberal" is a person on the center-right, usually progressive in cultural issues but conservative in economic ones.)

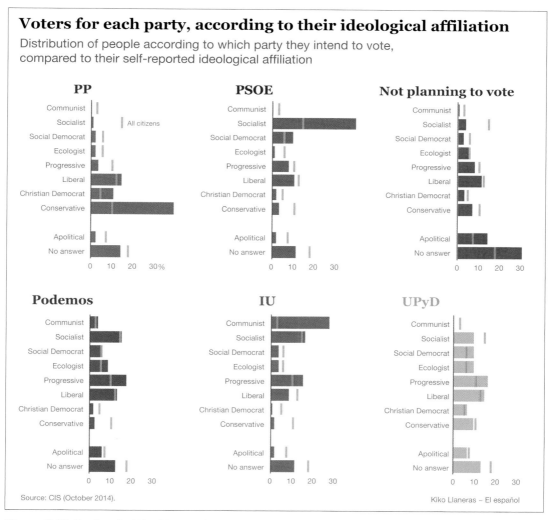

Figure 7.12 Graphics by Kiko Llaneras for elespanol.com: http://www.elespanol.com/actualidad/asi-es-la-ideologia-de-los-votantes-de-cada-partido-segun-el-cis/.

Exploring and presenting data may require multiple graphic forms shown simultaneously on screen. In 2013, Ukraine's Texty.org.ua published an interactive visualization of student performance in the largest cities (**Figure 7.13**). The GPA scores of each school is presented on a strip plot, as well as on hexagon-based maps. The drop-down menu lets readers choose subjects: math, English, etc. One critical feature that aids exploration in this case is that chart and maps are linked: when you hover over one hexagon, schools in that area are highlighted on the strip plot.

Finally, see the sequence of histograms and network diagrams in **Figure 7.14**. They represent the growing partisan divide in the United States between 1949 and 2011 by visualizing patterns of cooperation between pairs of representatives in Congress. The math behind these graphics requires some explanation, but I

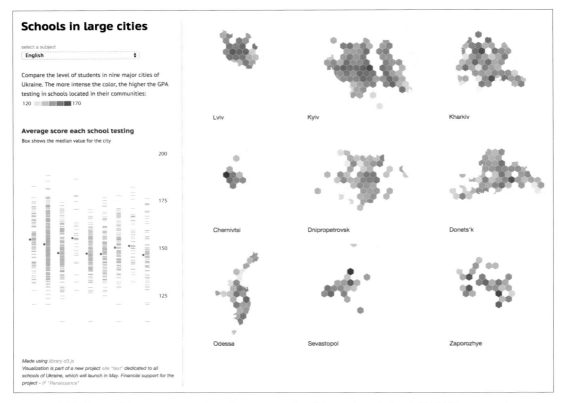

Figure 7.13 Graphic Texty.org.ua; see http://texty.org.ua/mod/datavis/apps/schools2013/. Use a translation tool if you don't read Ukrainian. That's what I did!

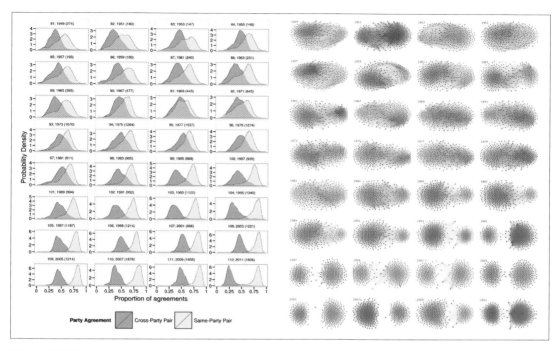

Figure 7.14 For an explanation on how to interpret these graphics, see "The Rise of Partisanship and Super-Cooperators in the U.S. House of Representatives." Clio Andris, David Lee, Marcus J. Hamilton, Mauro Martino, Christian E. Gunning, John Armistead Selden, at http://journals.plos.org/plosone/article?id=10.1371/journal.pone.0123507#abstract0.

think that they make it evident that since 1949, intra-party collaborations have become much more common than inter-party ones.[3]

How Standardized Scores Mislead Us

After praising standardized scores of all kinds, let me offer you a mystery: if you get a data set of cancer rates in the United States, you may observe that rural, sparsely populated counties have the lowest figures.

If you're similar to most journalists I know—including me—you'll quickly begin making conjectures about the causes: this surely has to do with environmental

---

3 Read the paper: http://journals.plos.org/plosone/article?id=10.1371/journal.pone.0123507 #abstract0. Politico.com published some comments about it: http://www.politico.com/ story/2015/04/graphic-data-america-partisan-divide-growth-117312.html.

factors, such as lack of pollution, tons of exercise, and a healthy diet based on homegrown vegetables and antibiotic-free meat. This will make for such a good story! Let's write it right away! I can even suggest a headline: "Want to Avoid Cancer? Move to Clark County, Idaho (Population: 867)!"[4]

Sorry to be a killjoy, but let me suggest that we plot all our data. The maps on **Figure 7.15** show the counties with the lowest *and highest* kidney cancer death rates. The main features of the counties with the highest rates? They are rural and sparsely populated, too. Oops!

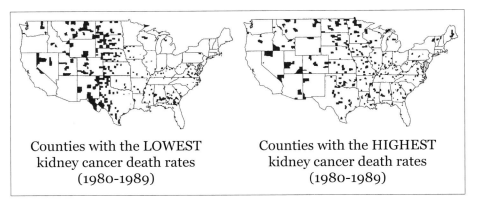

Counties with the LOWEST
kidney cancer death rates
(1980-1989)

Counties with the HIGHEST
kidney cancer death rates
(1980-1989)

Figure 7.15 Maps by Deborah Nolan and Andrew Gelman. See the "To Learn More" section at the end of this chapter.

What's going on? Could the age of the population be related to this? That might be a lurking factor. Imagine that you compare the cancer death rates of Santa Clara and Laguna Woods, two counties in California. Santa Clara, where Silicon Valley is, has lots of young people. Much more than half of the population of Laguna Woods is older than 65. It wouldn't be surprising to see more cancer cases in the latter than in the former (I haven't checked these numbers).

But age isn't the problem here. Our figures were age-adjusted beforehand. The problem that will shred my beautifully crafted headline is *population size*. Always keep this in mind: **estimates based on small populations (or samples) tend to show more variation**—to include proportionally more extreme scores relative to the number of scores that are closer to the mean—**than estimates based on large populations.**

---

4 I've chosen that county from this list: http://tinyurl.com/jru6xjw.

This is an unfortunate result of how probability works, and you can see it plotted in **Figure 7.16**. The X-axis is population, measured on a logarithmic scale; each tick mark identifies a value 10 times larger than the previous one. The Y-axis is age-adjusted cancer rates.

Each dot is a county. Notice that many counties with small populations—those on the left side—show both very high and very low cancer rates. The more we move to the right, the larger the population of each county is, and the narrower the variation of cancer death rates becomes. This kind of chart, which plots a variable against population or sample size, is called a **funnel plot**.

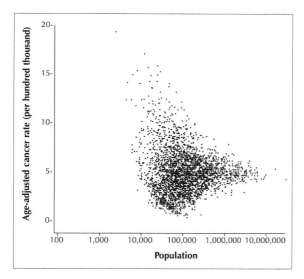

Figure 7.16 Funnel plot by Howard Wainer. Source: http://press.princeton.edu/ chapters/s8863.pdf.

To understand why this happens, you can try a woodworking exercise at home. You'll need a sturdy box, some pieces of wood or cardboard, and a good number of pins and marble balls. You're going to build something similar to **Figure 7.17**. This is called a **Galton probability box**, or *Galton quincunx*, in honor of Sir Francis Galton, the famous polymath we met chapters ago.[5]

Even if you haven't built the box, you may imagine what would happen if we send a marble rolling through the opening on top.

---

5 I learned about Galton's box in a lecture by statistician Stephen Stigler, back in 2013. Stigler's writings about the history of statistics are a delight. I'm saying this just in case you don't have enough reading materials already.

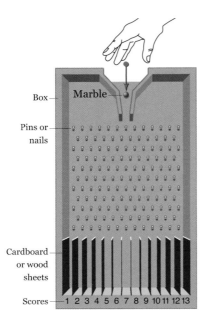

Figure 7.17 The Galton probability box.

See illustration A on **Figure 7.18**. Every time that the marble hits a pin, there's a 50-50 chance that it will continue rolling down at either side of it. If we built our Galton box with care, with the pins evenly spaced, any combination of left and right is equally likely. Our first marble can end up falling inside any of the spaces at the bottom of the box, either one close to the center or one at the extremes.

Imagine now that this single marble is a sample extracted from a population whose average score is 7. As our sample size is 1 (one marble), the score we'll obtain when letting the marble go will also be the mean of the sample. As illustration A on Figure 7.18 shows, our marble lands on space 12. That's quite far from the true mean, isn't it?

Now, let's suppose that we draw two samples of three scores each. We throw two sets of three marbles (illustrations B and C.) Just by chance, we have obtained two very different means. On illustration B, the mean of the scores is (5+7+12)/3 = 8, and the one for C is (2+3+7)/3 = 4. These are closer to the real mean.

Now comes the magic: **the more marbles you send rolling, the more of them will end up in the middle portion of the box,** as you can see in illustrations D, E, and F. And the larger our sample, the more likely it will be that its mean is

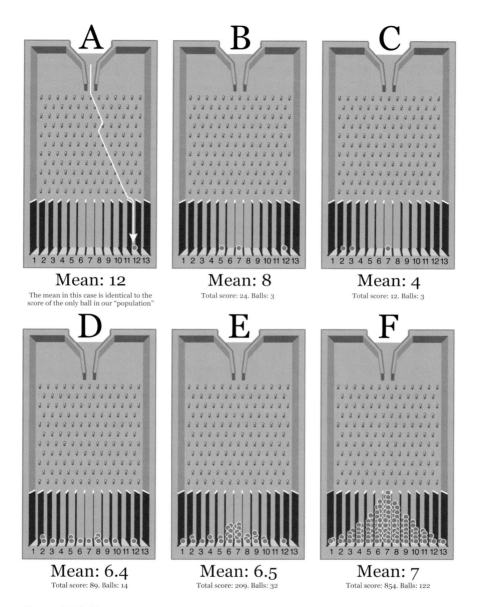

Figure 7.18 The more marbles we throw, the more the distribution will look like a bell shape.

close to the mean of the population it was drawn from.[6] Why? Because *cumulative* probability isn't the same as *individual* probability.

Just think about it: the probability of falling at either side of a pin is 50 percent. To fall on the bottom space corresponding to a score of 1, a marble would need to bounce left-left-left-left, etc., tons of times. Getting that result with just one marble is possible, but when you throw a large number of marbles—122 in illustration F—combinations closer to the 50 percent, left-right split will be more likely.

This is cumulative probability at work: your marbles will start forming a very peculiar bell shape, and the mean of all scores will approximate 7 more and more. If we could somehow throw millions of marbles, this curve would be very smooth, and the number of marbles at either side of the mean would be exactly the same. Congratulations. You've made a **normal distribution** out of marbles.

The Galton probability box helps us understand what happened with our erratic kidney death cancer rates before: small counties are like illustrations A, B, and C.[7] They have small populations and, therefore, their rates vary a lot, with many of them being at the highest and lowest extremes. **If a county has a population of 10 and one person dies of kidney cancer, which is possible just out of bad luck, suddenly its rate will be higher than the one of a county of 10,000 where 900 people die of the same cause. On the first county, 10 percent of the population died of cancer. On the second one, it'd be 9 percent.**

The Galton box also explains why researchers conducting any study (a survey, an experiment, etc.) always try to increase the size of their random samples as much as possible. A study based on a sample of 10 randomly chosen individuals won't be as reliable as another in which the sample size is 1,000. **Very small samples are living bait for the demons of chance.**

Peculiarities of the Normal Distribution

No phenomenon in nature follows a perfect normal distribution, but many of them approximate it enough as to make it one of the main tools of statistics: the distribution curves of heights, weights, life expectancy at birth, exam scores, and so on, all are usually close to normal.

---

6 I should add: in a real experiment, this is true only if the samples are randomly chosen. This is an important caveat.

7 There are some cool simulations of Galton probability boxes on YouTube. See this one, for instance: https://www.youtube.com/watch?v=3m4bxse2JEQ.

Normal distributions can be fatter and thinner than the one depicted in **Figure 7.19**, but this is a common one, called the standard normal distribution. It has the following properties:

1. Its mean, median, and mode are the same.

2. The distribution is symmetrical: 50 percent of scores are above the mean, and 50 percent are below it.

3. We know what percentage of scores lay in between certain ranges: 68.2 percent of cases in the data are 1 standard deviation (sd) away from the mean, 95.4 percent are within 2 sd, and 99.8 percent are within 3.

4. We can do some arithmetic with those figures. They can be halved to calculate, for instance, what percentage of cases lie between the mean and 1 sd above it: 34.1 percent. They can also be added or subtracted, to calculate the probability of finding a particular score between any others. What percentage of cases are between 1 and 2 sd above the mean and 1 and 2 sd below the mean? The answer is 27.2 percent (13.6+13.6.)

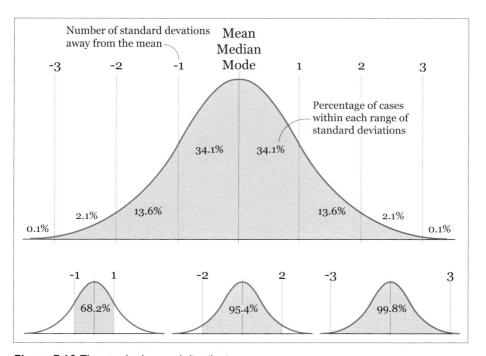

Figure 7.19 The standard normal distribution.

If you know that the phenomenon you're studying is normally distributed, even if not perfectly, you can estimate the probability of *any* case or score with reasonable accuracy.

For instance, say that you are analyzing the science test scores of a large population of students and that you know that they are close to being normally distributed. The mean is 54 and the standard deviation is 14. How likely would it be to find a student with a score of 82 or higher if we chose one randomly?

I've done the calculations for you in **Figure 7.20**. This example is easy, as 82 is exactly 2 standard deviations above the mean, but any software tool for data analysis should let you calculate the probability of finding scores above or below any threshold, or within two other scores.

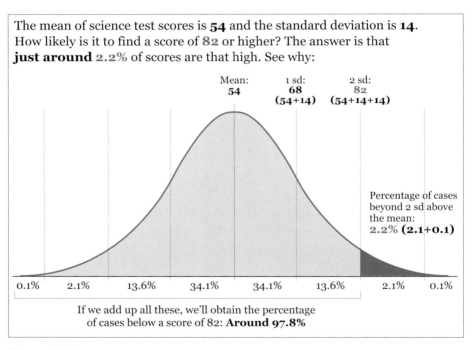

Figure 7.20 Some simple arithmetic can take you a long way.

Percentiles, Quartiles, and the Box Plot

So far we've explored distributions using non-resistant statistics, like the mean and the standard deviation, which are very sensitive to extreme values. Following John W. Tukey, it is advisable to also summarize and visualize our data using resistant statistics, which are not distorted by outliers. The fictional example about U.S. and Nigerian salaries we saw pages ago is one case in which calculating resistant statistics would be essential.

We have already learned about the **median**, the score or case that divides a distribution in half. If your scores are 1, 4, 7, 9, 11, 13, 15, 16, and 19, the median is 11. The median is resistant because if the scores at the lower and higher end of that distribution were 0.1 and 10,000, instead of 1 and 19, the median would be as imperturbable as an Egyptian sphinx.

We can measure the spread of the data beginning with the median using percentiles. A percentile (let's call it p) is a value that splits up your distribution in a way that (p) percent of the other values lie below it. The median is always the 50th percentile, as it's the score lying in the middle of the distribution.

Percentiles divide your distribution into hundredths, and they work as a rank: whenever you learn that you're at the 90th percentile in some sort of measure or test, you can be certain that you are equal or better than 90 percent of the rest.

Certain percentiles receive specific names. For instance, the 10th, 20th, 30th, and so on, continuing to the 90th percentile are called **deciles**. They divide your distribution into tenths. The 20th, 40th, 60th, and 80th percentiles are called **quintiles**. Quintiles divide your distribution into fifths.

When exploring data, Tukey recommends **quartiles**. The quartiles are the 25th, 50th (median), and 75th percentiles. They divide your distribution into—yes, you guessed right—quarters!

Let's visualize all this. Imagine that you're analyzing the household annual income of a neighborhood. You randomly sample 100 families, and you visualize them on a strip plot (**Figure 7.21**).

We can represent quartiles using a **box plot**, a graphic form devised by John W. Tukey himself. To learn how to read the most common kind of box plot, pay attention to the middle figure in **Figure 7.22**. This kind of graphic, sometimes also called a box-and-whisker plot, is a simplified representation of a distribution, less detailed than other charts like the histogram or the strip plot.

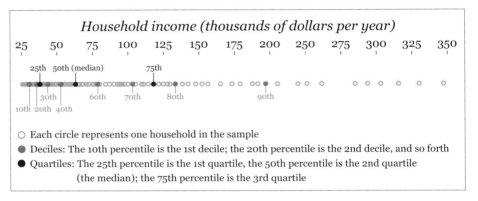

Figure 7.21 Percentiles—deciles and quartiles.

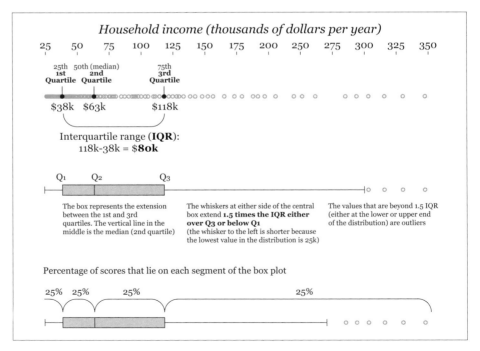

Figure 7.22 How to read a box plot (or box-and-whisker plot).

Notice that I calculated the **Interquartile Range (IQR)**. This is the difference between the first and the third quartiles. As the scores that correspond to those are \$38,000 and \$118,000, the IQR is 80,000 (118,000-38,000).

The whiskers represent the range of scores that lie within 1.5 times the IQR either below the first quartile or above the third quartile. Scores beyond these thresholds are considered outliers and are displayed as individual dots. Why 1.5 times the IQR? According to my friend **Diego Kuonen**, a statistician at Statoo Consulting in Switzerland, Tukey was once asked by a student and he replied, "Because 1 is too small and 2 is too large!" Remember this next time someone suggests that statistics is an exact science.

Why would we use a box plot next to histograms and strip plots? There are several reasons: first, histograms and especially strip plots sometimes show so much detail that important information may get obscured. Second, the box plot emphasizes the boundaries of segments of equal size in our distribution (that's what percentiles are for, after all) and it stresses outliers. Good luck seeing them clearly on a histogram, particularly if the distribution is very pointy and has very flat tails. Outliers will always stand out on a box plot.

Third, box plots are excellent when you are analyzing not just one distribution but comparing several of them. **Figure 7.23** shows the distribution of Ideb scores I described in Chapter 6. Compare this figure to any histogram or strip plot in that chapter.

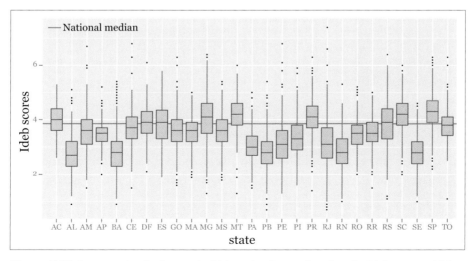

Figure 7.23 An example of a box-and-whisker plot. Remember that the Ideb score, which we discussed in Chapter 6, is an index (1–10) that measures school quality in Brazil.

Manipulating Data

Remember that doing exploratory data analysis consists of observing trends and patterns (the **norm**, or smooth), and then identifying deviations or exceptions from them. You have just learned the basics of what that means.

The operations we've learned so far created abstract models that summarized the essential nature of our data sets. This "essential nature" is the norm, which is made of three main features: the **level** (measures of central tendency, such as the mean), the **spread**, and the **shape** of our data.

But there are always departures from the elements of our models, values that don't fit our density curves perfectly or that lie so far from the mean or median that they can be considered outliers, as we've just seen. Exploring both the norm and the exceptions is crucial for finding insights and, subsequently, designing visualizations to explain them to our readers.

Exploring exceptions often involves transforming our data to **set aside one of the elements of the norm**, with the goal of discovering features that might remain unseen otherwise. We'll return to this idea in the following chapter, so let's just see a simple example.

We transformed data a bit already when we calculated standard scores (z-scores) to compare two distributions that had very different ranges. Transforming the original data sets into standard scores set aside the real measure of spread of the data and substituted it with a standardized one, based on the number of standard deviations away from the mean.

Using the previous box plot as a starting point, we can try to set aside another element of the norm: the level. Doing it is quite simple. It just requires doing a series of subtractions:

New score = Each original score – Any measure of central tendency

See an example in **Figure 7.24**. To create that plot, I did this:

Difference between a school's Ideb quality score and the mean score of the state where that school is = **Each school's Ideb score – Mean Ideb score of the state**.

Why choose the state means, rather than the national mean? No particular reason. I could have done either or both. I could have used the median, too. Seeing our data from multiple angles, through the lenses of as many visualizations as

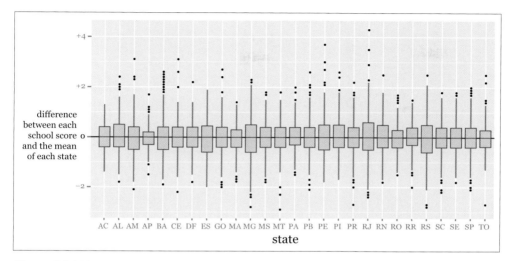

difference
between each
school score
and the mean
of each state

state

Figure 7.24 Plotting departures from the mean—that's each individual value minus the state mean.

possible, is arguably the wisest choice at these early stages of our exploration. You'll never know what you can find.

In Figure 7.23 we saw all schools against the same baseline, the national mean. Figure 7.24 helps a bit in finding schools that are unusually good or bad compared to their in-state neighbors, which are probably subject to the same policies and rules.

Frequency Over Time

To end this chapter on a high note (no pun intended), see the strip plots in **Figure 7.25**, by the *Los Angeles Times*. Those dots are 17,000 songs that made it to the U.S. Billboard Hot 100 between 1960 and 2010. **Len DeGroot**, director of data visualization at the *LA Times*, told me that this project was produced *in just one day,* using a tool called CartoDB, which was originally designed to create interactive maps. This is real breaking-news visualization.

The X-axis is time, and the Y-axis is the prevalence of specific qualities of the music, such as rhythm, harmony, instrumentation, style, and so on. The higher a song is on the Y-axis, the more prevalent that quality is in it. Green bubbles are either on the yearly average or above it. Gray bubbles are below the average.

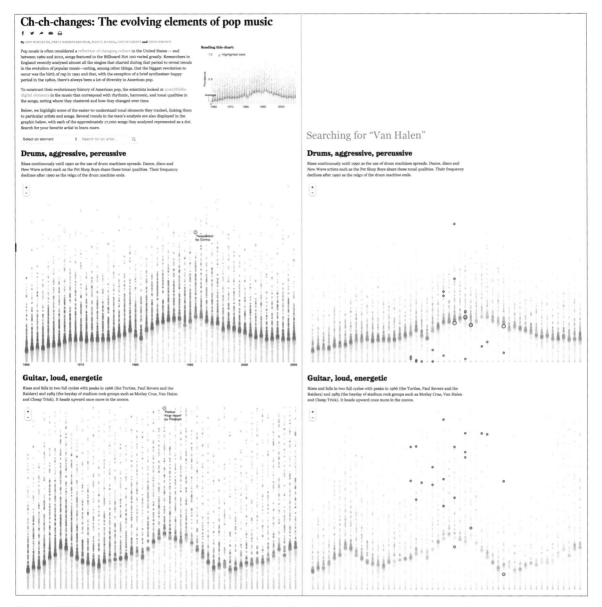

Figure 7.25 Visualization by the *Los Angeles Times*: http://graphics.latimes.com/pop-music-evolution.

Bubble size represents proximity to the mean.

When you visit this series of visualizations online, notice how well-thought-out they are. They don't just show the yearly distributions, but you can also search for specific bands—I chose Van Halen as I'm an old-fashioned rocker.

The page where the graphics are inserted includes links to YouTube videos of songs that ranked high or low on each category, which is a nice aid for readers. Moreover, the titles of each section are catchy and, in some cases, even funny: "Manilow couldn't keep the orchestra alive." Poor Barry!

To Learn More

- Behrens, John. T. "Principles and Procedures of Exploratory Data Analysis." Psychological Methods, 1997, Vol. 2, No. 2, 131–160. Available online: http://cll.stanford.edu/~langley/cogsys/behrens97pm.pdf.

- Erickson, B.H. and Nosanchuk, T.A. *Understanding Data*, 2nd ed. Toronto, Canada: University of Toronto Press, 1992. A very readable introduction to the principles of exploratory analysis.

- Gelman, Andrew, and Ann Nolan, Deborah. *Teaching Statistics: A Bag of Tricks*. Oxford: Oxford UP, 2002.

- Wainer, Howard. *Picturing the Uncertain World: How to Understand, Communicate, and Control Uncertainty through Graphical Display*. Princeton: Princeton UP, 2009.

8

Revealing Change

In statistics, you can't win arguments by invoking the truth… if the truth is knowable, statisticians would all be unemployed.

—Kaiser Fung, "Numbersense and true lies"

On a sluggish August 2013 afternoon, the national public television channel in Spain, Televisión Española (TVE), delivered some cheery news. After enduring five years of economic crisis, unemployment in the country experienced a noticeable drop, from 5.0 million people to 4.7. TVE's audience was exposed to a chart similar to **Figure 8.1** for a few short seconds. Uncork the champagne!

Critics of TVE, whose content is "inspired" (ahem) by whoever governs Spain at each moment, were quick to point out that the chart was flawed. It not only exaggerated the downward slope but, more importantly, its horizontal axis was truncated in a disingenuous manner.

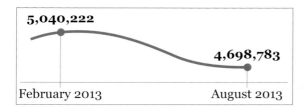

Figure 8.1 Unemployed workers in Spain. Do you notice something fishy?

Nearly 12 percent of Spain's jobs are related to tourism, so unemployment in my country of origin is highly *seasonal*: it regularly goes up during the fall and winter—except in December—and shrinks during the summer. Therefore, to get a truthful depiction of how much unemployment has varied, it's necessary to go back in time at least 12 months.

When we do that (see the first chart in **Figure 8.2**), we see that unemployment didn't get better in August 2013. Actually, there were *more* unemployed people in August 2013 than in August 2012, something that becomes even clearer when you compare the figures of both months with the yearly average (second chart) Where did I put the cork? The champagne is going to lose its fizz.

Quoting economist **Ronald H. Coase** "If you torture your data long enough, nature will always confess." To get a confession in this case, we don't even need

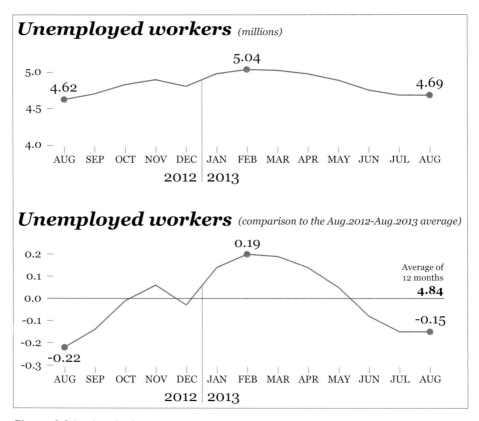

Figure 8.2 Looking back in time.

to be very thorough or smart, as trimming the axes in the right places yields a message our apparatchik-in-chief will find palatable: we can fabricate change where there's barely any.

Trend, Seasonality, and Noise

The change in one or more continuous variables is usually—not always—visualized with **time series line charts.** The X-axis (horizontal) in this kind of chart represents equally spaced time intervals, and the Y-axis (vertical) corresponds to the magnitude of the variables we wish to explore or present.

Thanks to the tricky example we've just seen, we have identified two of the features we need to pay attention to when reading a time series chart:

- The **trend**. Do the variables go up, down, or stay the same during the time segment we chose to explore?

- The **seasonality**. Do the variables show consistent and periodic fluctuations that may muddle our understanding?

We can add a third one: the **noise**. Are some of the variations we observe simply random changes?

It's usually hard to see those three features at once in a single chart. They need to be separated. As Spanish book publisher **Jacobo Siruela** said in a 2015 interview in *El País* daily newspaper, **"We must move away from the noise to be able to hear the melodies."** He was referring to life in general, but the dictum applies to the melodies data frequently hide.

Decomposing a Time Series

I began this chapter writing about unemployment in Spain. TVE's chart got me curious about long-term trends. The unemployment rate is just one of the variables we could use to analyze the health of a country's workforce. Another one, at least in Spain, is the amount of people who make contributions to Social Security (SS) to get unemployment and retirement benefits later.

Figure 8.3 is a small portion of a data set downloaded from Spain's Instituto Nacional de Estadística (INE). The first column is the total number of SS affiliates— or enrollees—between January 2002 and December 2014.

MONTH	SSAFFILIATES	POPULATION16_64	PERCENTAGE
Jan2002	15727566	27649100	56.9
Feb2002	15822158	27649100	57.2
Mar2002	15912352	27649100	57.6
Apr2002	16023487	27794900	57.6
May2002	16154714	27794900	58.1
Jun2002	16290434	27794900	58.6
Jul2002	16326631	27929200	58.5
Aug2002	16276570	27929200	58.3
Sep2002	16187368	27929200	58.0
Oct2002	16236870	28073200	57.8
Nov2002	16369029	28073200	58.3
Dec2002	16188390	28073200	57.7
Jan2003	16215761	28211300	57.5
Feb2003	16335717	28211300	57.9
Mar2003	16455090	28211300	58.3

Figure 8.3 The first few rows of our data set of Social Security affiliates in Spain.

You can see this variable on the top chart in **Figure 8.4**. There were 1 million more people enrolled in SS at the end of 2014 than at the beginning of 2002, which seems to be good news. However, if we ask our analysis software to overlay a straight trend line, news gets somber: the line goes down.[1] Spain plunged into a deep crisis at the beginning of 2008. By 2014, the country had not fully recovered.

We face another challenge: we are not taking population size into account. One of the most confusing paradoxes of unemployment figures, if they aren't correctly adjusted, is that they tell you how many people *want to work but can't*, but not how many people *could work but have given up looking for a job*. This is very difficult to measure, so in our exercise we'll use an imperfect proxy variable.

The second column in Figure 8.3 is the working age population in Spain, those folks between 16 and 64 years of age.[2] This is visualized on the second chart of

---

1 Displaying a trend line in a time series chart is not very orthodox in most cases; smoothed curves are much more useful, as you'll soon see. I am using R for the following charts, but you can get similar results with Excel or most other data analysis tools.

2 This is a variable suggested by INE itself. I wrote that it's imperfect because it may well happen that a considerable chunk of its fluctuations is due to lurking factors, such as how many of those people are still studying.

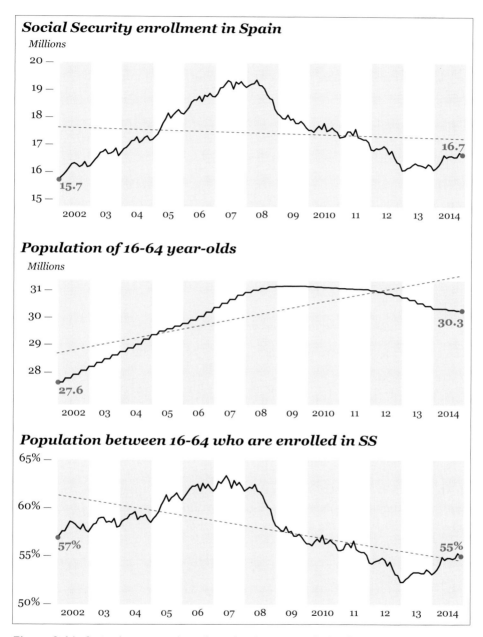

Social Security enrollment in Spain

Millions

Population of 16-64 year-olds

Millions

Population between 16-64 who are enrolled in SS

Figure 8.4 In Spain, the raw number of people who are enrolled in Social Security increased (although the trend line suggests otherwise) between 2002 and 2014 (chart 1), but the population ages between 16 and 64 also grew quite rapidly (chart 2), so the percentage of people who could work and actually do has decreased (chart 3).

Figure 8.4, which shows that Spain's working age population increased until 2008 and then started shrinking after the crisis that hit that year. Spain's population is getting older, and large swaths of Latin American immigrants have returned to their countries, unable to get jobs. Moreover, a good number of young and well-educated Spaniards have also left.

The third column in Figure 8.3 is the result of calculating the percentage of people of working age who are enrolled in SS. Or, mathematically put, this equals (SS enrollees/Population between 16 and 64) × 100.

This is displayed on the third chart in Figure 8.4. Compare it to the first one: the raw counts got higher (16.7 in 2014, versus 15.7 in 2002), but the percentage got lower. This is another example of why visualizing your data in multiple ways is so important.

Next, I am going to compare each percentage score with the average percentage of SS affiliates between January 2002 and December 2014. This average is 57.9 percent.

Each value – Average (57.9 percent) = Difference

The results are on **Figure 8.5**, which is really boring. The chart is identical to the third one on Figure 8.4 on everything but its scale. Besides, is a straight line a good descriptor of our variable? It isn't. The shape of the raw data doesn't resemble a straight line, not even close. Rather, it looks like an ocean wave with a bump in the middle. Therefore, a linear model is not adequate in this case. It doesn't really help us put the trend (or smooth) aside to explore the other relevant features of our data, its seasonality, and noise.

With the aid of software, we can generate a new trend line, a model that better fits our data. You can see it on **Figure 8.6**. This curve is based on a **moving average**. Without getting overly technical, what the computer has done for us is to divide our time series into small chunks of, say, 4, 6, or 8 months each (you decide that) and calculate the average of each chunk, rather than the average of the entire period, as I did before.[3]

---

3 There are many kinds of moving averages (simple or arithmetic, weighted, exponential, etc.), but it's beyond the scope of this book to explain them. If you're interested in learning about them, see the references at the end of this chapter.

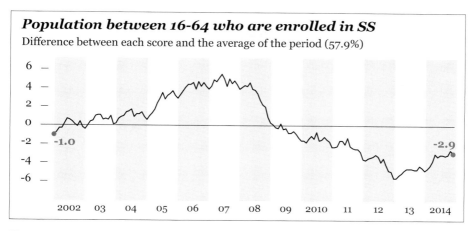

Figure 8.5 Comparing each percentage score to the average of the period between January 2002 and December 2014. This isn't that revealing!

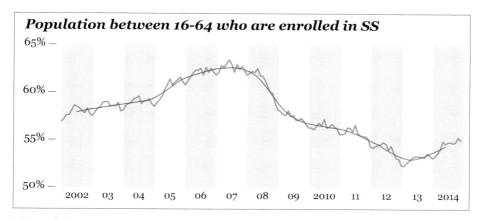

Figure 8.6 In red, a much better model for our data, based on a moving average.

Now we can subtract the moving average scores from all scores to design a new chart (**Figure 8.7**). What we get is a comparison between the moving average and the actual raw scores.

This strategy of comparing raw scores and expected or smoothed ones has many applications. Imagine that you are analyzing data from your company and that you want to compare your actual daily sales with your target sales per day. You can plot the actual scores, as in the first chart of **Figure 8.8**, or you can plot the *difference*, as in the second one. Which one of them is better? As usual, it depends on what you want to emphasize: sales and goals as separate entities, or the difference between the two. The first chart can be misleading, as both lines in it are shifting.

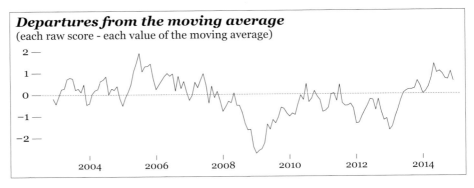

Figure 8.7 Plotting residuals.

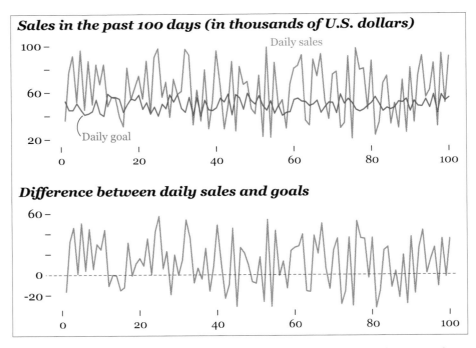

Figure 8.8 Daily sales versus daily goals. These charts are based on randomly generated scores.

Let's go back to our Spanish Social Security exercise. We have a decent smooth plot, but we haven't studied how much of the variation is due to a pattern of periodic oscillations or to randomness. This is something we could do by hand, but a computer will handle it much more quickly. A few lines of code or mouse clicks in a data analysis software may yield something like **Figure 8.9**, a summary of our time series: the observed values, the underlying trend, the seasonality, and the remaining noise that isn't part of the preceding charts.

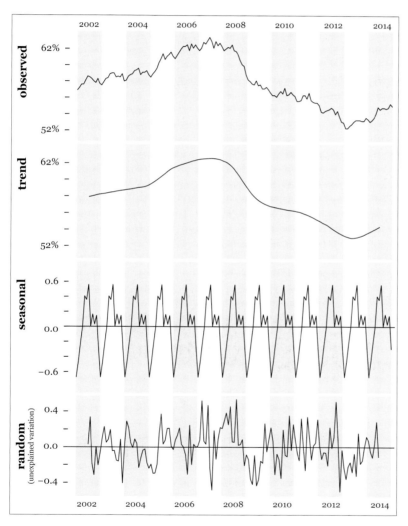

Figure 8.9 Our time series, decomposed with the help of R.

Focus on the seasonality chart and notice that the number of SS affiliates goes up sharply in the middle of each year, and then it drops in the fall and winter. This is impossible to detect on the first chart, the one encoding the raw scores.

Seasonality varies from roughly –0.6 to 0.6, while the noise in the data (the "random" plot in Figure 8.9) goes from less than –0.4 to more than 0.4. As long as the computer has extracted these two features from the original data set for us, we can plot them directly. **Figure 8.10** is a chart of the monthly variation in our data that can be explained by seasonality and noise combined. This variation can obscure the real one. You may want to consider it for your exploration by subtracting it from the raw scores, like in **Figure 8.11**, which looks very much like the trend in Figure 8.9.

Adjusted variation = Each raw score - (Each score of the seasonal chart + Each score of the Random chart)

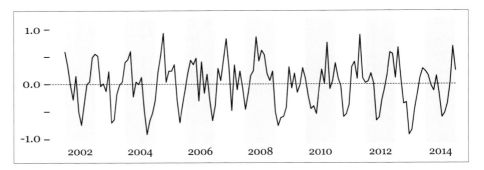

Figure 8.10 This chart is the result of adding the seasonality scores and the random scores from Figure 8.9.

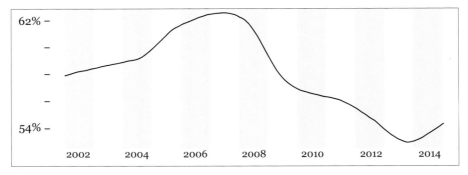

Figure 8.11 This is the result of subtracting the scores shown on Figure 8.10 from our original data of affiliates to the Spanish Social Security.

Before we move on, we should play around with our SS data a bit more. Let's suppose that what you want to see is not the year-by-year variation, but month-by-month. In other words, you intend to compare January to January, February to February, March to March, and so forth, between 2002 and 2014. You could design something like **Figure 8.12**, in which we overlay the observed values and the average score of each year.

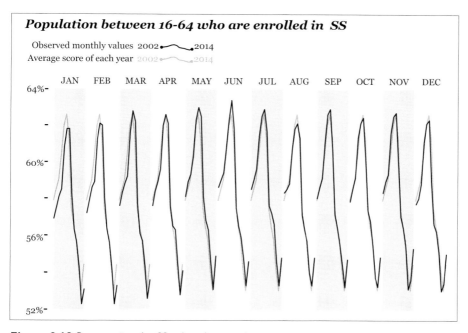

Figure 8.12 Rearranging the SS values by month.

The differences in this chart are so tiny, though, that they are barely visible, so it might be better to plot things directly, as in **Figure 8.13**. Here, we can immediately spot some interesting facts. For instance, June and July vary little year by year; July is among the months that depart the most from each year's average. November, December, and January show the widest changes. All these tidbits got obscured in our previous chart.

This kind of **seasonal subseries chart** can be very powerful. In climate science, for instance, it may be used as in **Figure 8.14** to visualize concentrations of carbon dioxide and other greenhouse gases. Companies may choose this graphic form to compare their month-by-month performance with both monthly and yearly averages.

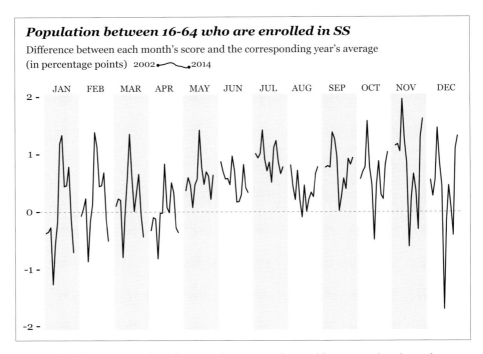

Figure 8.13 Emphasizing the differences between each month's score and each year's average.

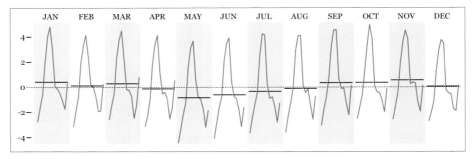

Figure 8.14 An example of seasonal subseries plot, comparing the average of all years (dotted line) with the average of every month throughout those years (horizontal black lines) and the variation within a certain month (red line).

Visualizing Indexes

Another way of exploring and presenting time series data to readers is to calculate indexes. I recently bought a single-family house in Miami, so I got curious about how the market for this kind of house has changed in the past few years, both before and after the real estate bubble exploded, roughly between 2006 and 2008.

I downloaded a data set from the U.S. Census Bureau. I visualized the total number of houses sold and then the inflation-adjusted price range breakdown (**Figure 8.15**). We can immediately spot some promising patterns: sales of cheap houses declined steadily even before the crisis hit and didn't increase at all later. More expensive houses also suffered mightily between 2006 and 2008 but picked up a bit in 2013.

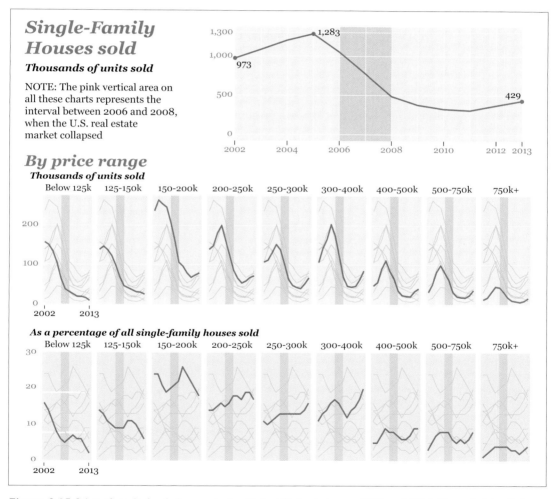

Figure 8.15 Sales of single-family houses in the United States between 2002 and 2013. Biostatistician Rafe Donahue calls this idea of plotting all values (gray lines) in comparison to one specific subset of the values (red lines) "You-are-here" plots. He describes this technique and many others in a free book: http://biostat.mc.vanderbilt.edu/wiki/pub/Main/RafeDonahue/fscipdpfcbg_currentversion.pdf.

We can better represent the relative change using a zero-based index. On **Figure 8.16**, the first row of charts compares the sales of single-family houses to the average score of the 2006–2008 period, when the crisis hit. This is called the **index origin**, the 0 percent in the charts. On the second row of charts, the index origin is the sales in 2002. The Y-axis is the difference between each year's sales and the index origin I chose on each case.

Calculating zero-based indexes is quite easy. Just tell your favorite software tool to follow the universal formula to obtain percentage change:

Percentage change = ((Each score – Index origin) / Index origin) × 100

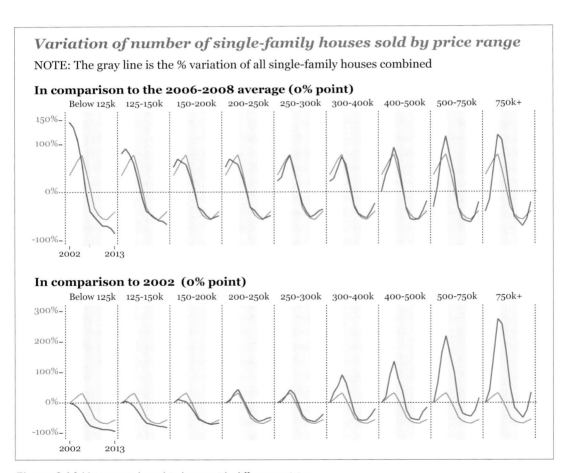

Figure 8.16 Using zero-based indexes with different origins.

To illustrate this with an example, the average number of houses that sold for less than $125,000 per year between 2002 and 2013 was **63,750**. This is going to be our origin. I know that the number of cheap houses sold in 2002 was **157,000**. What is the percentage difference? Formula!

$$((157{,}000 - 63{,}750) / 63{,}750) \times 100 = \textbf{146.3}$$

So sales of cheap houses in 2002 were 146.3 percent higher than the average sales between 2002 and 2013. If you go to the first chart on the first row of Figure 8.16, you'll see that number plotted. It's the first data point of the red line, which is close to 150 percent.

Let's do the same, but using the sales of 2002 as the origin. This year, as we've just seen, **157,000** houses priced $125,000 or under were sold. In 2013, that number was just **14,100**. Let's calculate the percentage difference:

$$((14{,}100 - 157{,}000) / 157{,}000) \times 100 = \textbf{-94.3}$$

That's a 94.3 percent decrease, meaning that sales of very cheap single-family houses have almost vanished in the United States. Again, if you wish to see that number represented, go to the first chart on the second row of Figure 8.16. It's the end point of the red line.

By the way, the first time I designed these charts they didn't look great (**Figure 8.17**). If there were just three or four lines on each, they would be fine, but whenever a graphic gets as cluttered as these, it's better to opt for small multiples.

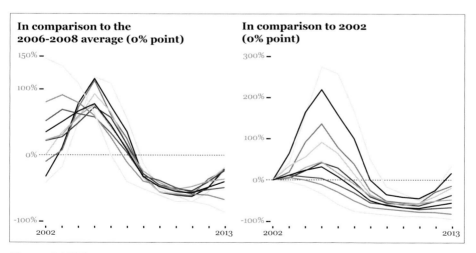

Figure 8.17 There are so many lines in this first version of my zero-based indexed charts that I didn't even bother styling them further.

From Ratios to Logs

We've just learned how to compare all values in our time series to a single index value, a data point in the data set such as the one for 2002, or the average of several years. But what if we are interested in the rate of change of each time period in comparison to the previous one?

The first chart on **Figure 8.18** shows the growth of the U.S. population between 1776 and 2010. This upward, regular-looking line, based on estimates with varying margins of error, looks nice, but it might hide important facts. For instance, were there noticeable changes in certain historical periods? If so, they are hard to detect. Let's transform our data a bit.

To calculate the change rate between two time periods (consecutive years, in this case) and generate the second chart in Figure 8.18, use this formula:

Change rate = New period / Previous period

For instance, the estimated U.S. population in 1800 was 5,308,483 people. In 1801, it was 5,475,787. Therefore:

Change rate between 1800 and 1801 = 5,475,787 / 5,308,483 = **1.03**

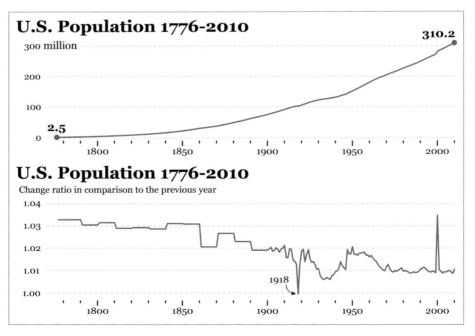

Figure 8.18 Data from the U.S. Census Bureau.

This 1.03 can be read as 103 percent, which means that the population in 1801 was roughly (I've rounded the figures) 103 percent the population of 1800. In other words, for each 100 people in 1800, there were 103 in 1801.

On the second chart in Figure 8.18, we can spot the only year when the U.S. population was estimated to shrink slightly: 1918. The change rate between 1917 and 1918 is 0.9994, which should be rounded to 1.0. That means that the population in 1918 was basically the same as it was in 1917, or a tiny bit smaller. We can't tell, as we don't know the margin of error—which is likely to be greater than this 0.0006 difference, anyway!

Another way to visualize change rate is to use a **logarithmic scale**. Imagine that you are studying the growth patterns of a bacterial culture of 5,000 bacteria over 50 days. Most bacteria reproduce by binary fission: after a certain period of time, a bacterium grows to a size that allows it to divide into two new bacteria.

Each day, a random percentage of our bacteria, from none (0 percent) to all of them (100 percent) may reproduce. We have the data for all days, so we can obtain the daily percentage change, as in **Figure 8.19**.

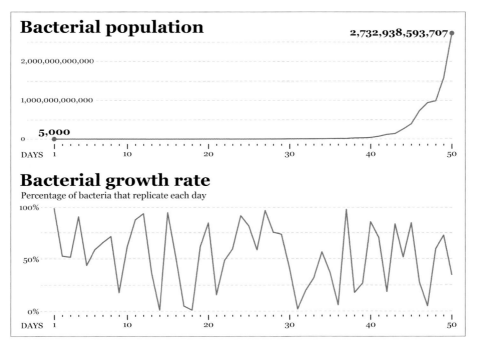

Figure 8.19 Growth of bacterial population: Raw increase and percentage of bacteria that replicate each day.

None of these charts give us a clear idea of the overall change rate, though. The first one, in fact, is almost useless, as the growth rate in our bacterial culture is exponential. The population may double in just a single day or in a few days: we began with 5,000 specimens, and after 50 days we ended up with 2,732,938,593,707, so changes on the line chart become noticeable only after day 40 or so.

What to do? A **log transformation** may come in handy. All logarithmic calculations start by deciding on a "base," which in visualization is commonly 10 but could be any other number. In a log10 scale, each increment of 1 unit of magnitude doesn't really represent an increment of 1, but a tenfold increase. Similarly, in a log2 scale, each increment of 1 on the scale means "double the size of the figure right below me."[4]

Get ready for a mouthful: the logarithm of each number in a data set is the power to which the base (we chose 10) should be raised in order to obtain that number. This sounds much more confusing than it really is, so let's illustrate it with a couple of values from our data set:

Day 20: **14,193,517** bacteria; Day 50: **2,732,938,593,707** bacteria

The log10 of 14,193,517 and 2,732,938,593,707 are the powers our base number 10 should be raised to obtain each of those numbers. We can express it this way:

Log10 (14,193,517) = **7.15**. This means that $10^{7.15}$ = 14,193,517

Log10 (2,732,938,593,707) = **12.44**. This means that $10^{12.44}$ = 2,732,938,593,707

(Note: Don't think I'm a genius. Google's online calculator is a good friend.)

Now see **Figure 8.20** and notice that on day 20 our line is a bit above the 7.0 point on the Y-scale (day 20's log is 7.15). On day 50, it rises beyond the 12.0 point (that day's log is 12.44.)

This new chart lets us see facts that remained invisible before, such as that the growth rate of our bacterial population is nearly constant, becoming 10 times larger roughly every 5 to 7 days.

If you are still having trouble reading the base-10 scale, think about it this way: the figures on the Y-axis are actually a number of zeroes following a 1. In other words, if you see an 8 on the Y-axis, change it for a 1 followed by 8 zeroes: 100,000,000.

---

4 Logs are much more common than you may think. The Richter scale, used to measure the magnitude of earthquakes, is a log10 scale: an 8.0 earthquake is 10 times more powerful than a 7.0 earthquake.

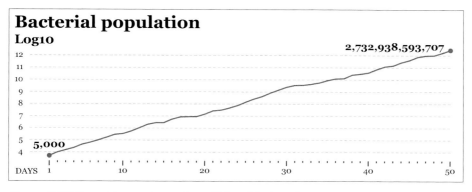

Figure 8.20 Bacterial growth on a base-10 logarithmic scale.

How Time Series Charts Mislead

Badly designed time series line charts may be as misleading as any other kind of visualization. The first chart in **Figure 8.21** is lousy because gaps in the data (we don't have scores for April and May) are ignored and so time intervals on the X-axis are not equally spaced. Charts two and three are much better.

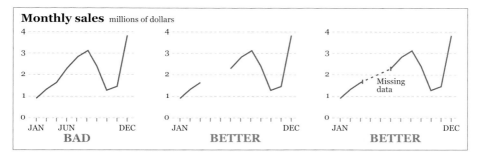

Figure 8.21 Always use equal intervals on the X-axis and emphasize missing scores.

Another way a line chart may be deceptive is by not displaying an appropriate level of detail or depth. On April 24, 2015, the famous economist and Nobel prize-winner Paul Krugman lambasted conservative candidates for the Republican presidential nomination for proposing that the age of eligibility for Social Security and Medicare be raised to 69.[5]

---

5 "Zombies of 2016." http://www.nytimes.com/2015/04/24/opinion/ paul-krugman-zombies-of-2016.html

"Doesn't this make sense now that Americans are living longer?" asked Krugman rhetorically, and he proceeded to reply to himself: "No, it doesn't (...) The bottom half of workers, who are precisely the Americans who rely on Social Security most, have seen their life expectancy at age 65 rise only a bit more than a year since the 1970s."

Krugman was quoting a 2007 Social Security Administration report that includes charts like **Figure 8.22**.[6] According to this, a man born in 1941 who reached the age of 65 being on the top half of the earnings distribution could expect to live an average of nearly 22 years more. That same number for a 1941 male in the bottom half of the earnings distribution was 16 years.

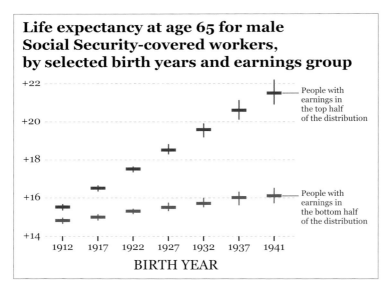

Figure 8.22 The thin vertical lines represent the 95 percent confidence intervals.

People with different political leanings will disagree on how to interpret these data, but I think that this chart is a bit more useful for an informed discussion than one displaying just the average life expectancy. Of course, we could think of dividing the data further, perhaps by income quintiles or deciles.

6 "Trends in Mortality Differentials and Life Expectancy for Male Social Security-Covered Workers, by Average Relative Earnings." http://www.ssa.gov/policy/docs/workingpapers/wp108.html

Exploring multiple levels of aggregation—not just when dealing with time series data—is critical to avoid **paradoxes** and **mix effects**. In a 2015 paper on how to visualize them, **Zan Armstrong** and **Martin Wattenberg** defined mix effects as "the fact that aggregate numbers can be affected by changes in the relative size of the subpopulations as well as the relative values within those subpopulations."[7] We discussed mix effects a bit (without naming them) in previous chapters, when we learned how to calculate weighted averages.

Most famous among mix effects is the **Simpson's Paradox**, named after statistician E. H. Simpson, who described it in 1951. Here's what Armstrong and Wattenberg say about it:

> Mix effects are ubiquitous. Experienced analysts encounter (paradoxes and mix effects) frequently, and it's easy to find examples across domains. A famous example of a Simpson's-like reversal is a Berkeley Graduate Admissions study in which 44% of males were accepted but only 35% of females. The discrepancy seemed to be clear evidence of discrimination, yet disappeared once analyzed at the per-department level: it turned out that departments with lower acceptance rates had proportionally more female applicants.

Mix effects don't appear just when examining time series data, but their consequences when displaying change in charts can be spectacular. On **Figure 8.23**, I am posing a mystery mentioned by Armstrong and Wattenberg: between 2000 and 2013, the inflation-adjusted change in median wage in the United States was 0.9 percent. However, when you disaggregate the data by educational attainment, you'll observe that all groups are making less money than they did in the past!

Change in median wage 2000-2013

	Total U.S.	+0.9%	
Degree attainment (highest degree achieved)	No degree	-7.9%	
	High school	-4.7%	
	Some college	-7.6%	
	Bachelor's or higher	-1.2%	

Figure 8.23 Isn't there a contradiction in this chart?

7 "Visualizing Statistical Mix Effects and Simpson's Paradox."
http://static.googleusercontent.com/media/research.google.com/en/us/pubs/archive/42901.pdf

Armstrong and Wattenberg offer the explanation, "Although median wages went down in each segment, something else happened as well: the number of jobs increased for higher-educated groups and declined for lower. Thus, the higher-educated, and therefore higher-earning, group had more weight in the 2013 data. The summary number of +0.9 percent depends not just on the change within population segments, but on the change in the relative sizes of those segments."

Situations like this are as counterintuitive as they are common, so, again, never trust just an amalgamated figure. Always look beyond it.

Communicating Change

We've covered a lot of pretty dense material in this chapter, so it's time for some creative inspiration. Let's begin with **Jorge Camões**, author of the indispensable *Data at Work: Best practices for creating effective charts and information graphics in Microsoft Excel* (2016) and www.excelcharts.com. Jorge is able to achieve wonders with Microsoft Excel and forces it to create graphics it was not designed for, like horizon charts.

The **horizon chart** is a novel graphic form invented by **Hannes Reijner** of Panopticon Software,[8] and later tested by Jeffrey Heer, Nicholas Kong, and Maneesh Agrawala.[9]

Here's how to design and read horizon charts: say you need to display dozens of line charts like the first example in **Figure 8.24** simultaneously. To make a chart like this more space-efficient we can (1) subdivide its vertical scale evenly, and color code positive and negative values, (2) mirror the color bands corresponding to negative values, and then (3) collapse the color bands. Following these steps results in a much shorter chart.

---

8 "The Development of the Horizon Graph."
http://www.stonesc.com/Vis08_Workshop/DVD/Reijner_submission.pdf
9 "Sizing the Horizon: The Effects of Chart Size and Layering on the Graphical Perception of Time Series Visualizations." http://vis.berkeley.edu/papers/horizon/2009-TimeSeries-CHI.pdf

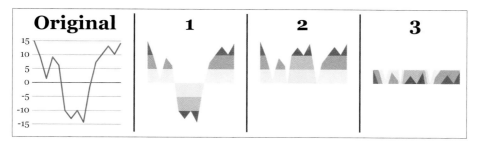

Figure 8.24 How to design and read horizon charts.

Now you are ready to be wowed by Jorge's graphic in **Figure 8.25**.

Jorge's graphics prove that business charts and maps don't need to be dull and ungracious and that even tools with dubious default options—Excel is great, but its base charts are notoriously ugly—can be forced to create elegant figures. **Aesthetics, playfulness, and the exquisite care for typography, color, and composition are as important in artistic visualization as they are in the presentation of analytic results.**

Figure 8.26 is compelling and minimalistic. The eye navigates these patterns effortlessly, aided by the highest-lowest arrangement, with the best teams on top and the worst performers at the bottom. Incidentally, I'm listening to Chopin's Nocturnes while writing these lines and, in a brief glimpse of synesthetic insight, I thought that we could imagine this chart as a piano tune: high tones for victories, low ones for defeats, silences for gaps. Data sonification could be the next frontier in communication.

By showing that winter months are a slow period for maternities, **Figure 8.27** also reveals that human beings mostly prefer the summer and the early fall to devote time to the labors of love—just focus on months with a high proportion of births and count nine months back. I wonder if the pattern would be reversed were the countries depicted in the Southern Hemisphere, rather than in the Northern one.

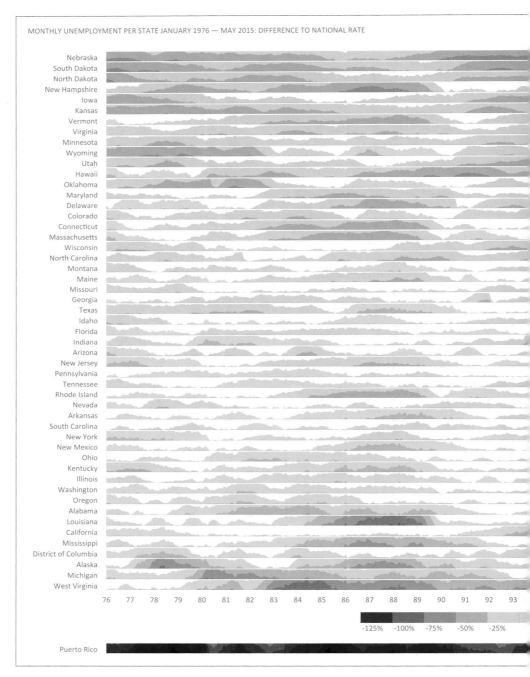

Figure 8.25 Horizon chart by Jorge Camões.

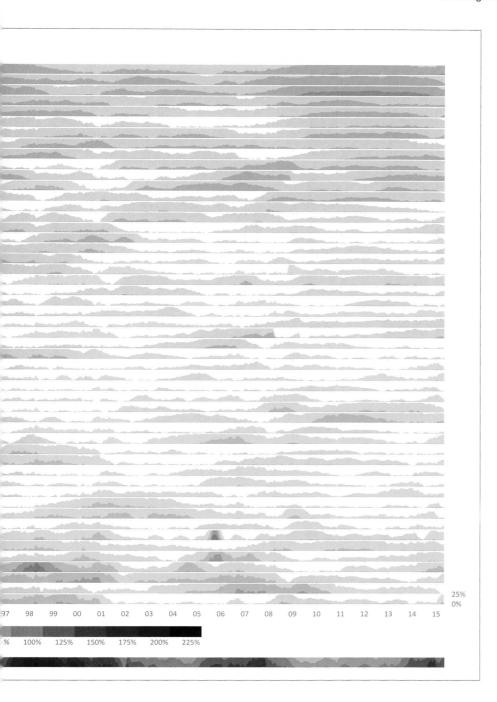

25%
0%

97   98   99   00   01   02   03   04   05   06   07   08   09   10   11   12   13   14   15

%   100%   125%   150%   175%   200%   225%

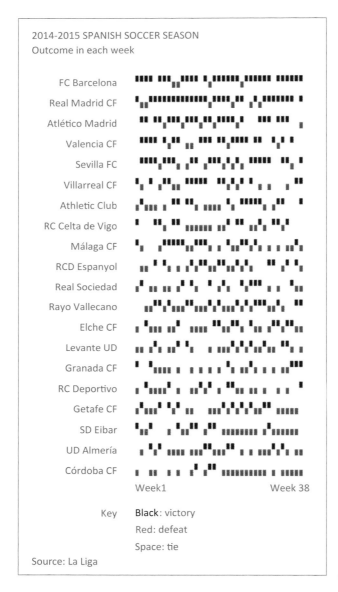

Figure 8.26 Graphic by Jorge Camões.

Hue and shade lie at the bottom of William Cleveland's and Robert McGill's scale of methods of visual encoding, described in Chapter 5, but as **Figure 8.28** attests, they can be priceless when precision matters less than the unearthing of general patterns and trends. Here, the specifics of each country's ups and downs are secondary in comparison to the simpler less-versus-more message that this tapestry-like heat map avows.

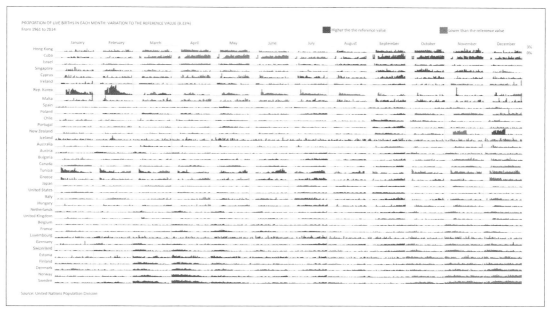

Figure 8.27 Time series bar chart by Jorge Camões.

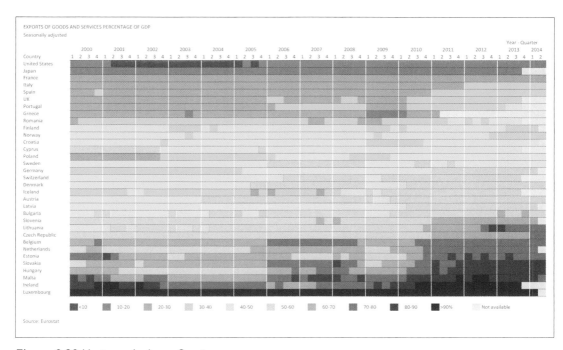

Figure 8.28 Heat map by Jorge Camões.

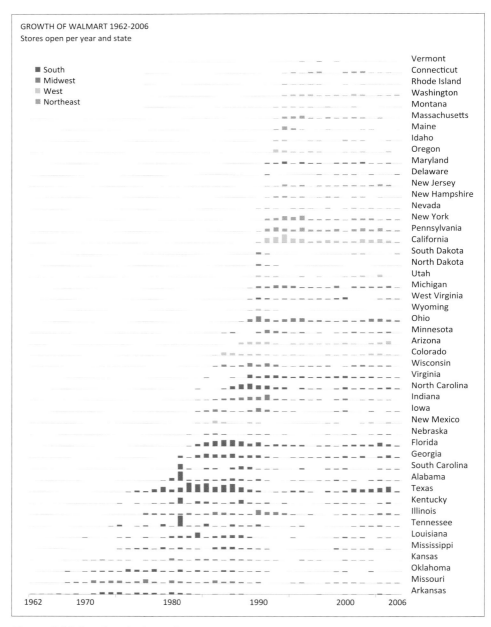

Figure 8.29 Bar chart by Jorge Camões.

Something similar occurs in **Figure 8.29** and **Figure 8.30**, which strengthen each other when presented side by side, in an example of a whole being greater than the sum of its parts.

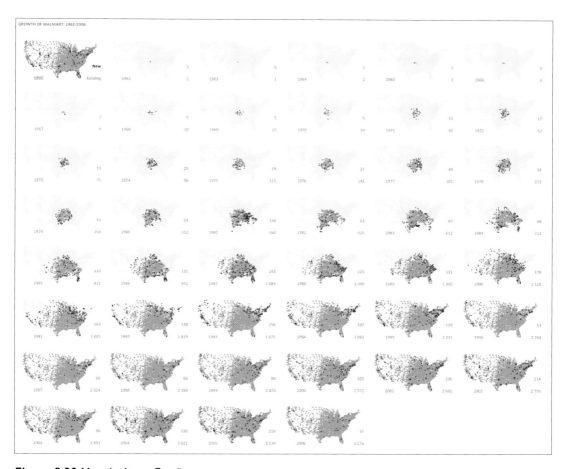

Figure 8.30 Maps by Jorge Camões.

Most unusual among graphic forms to present data to the public is the **connected scatter plot**, which works best when turns and swirls don't obscure the data, as in **Figure 8.31**. Each dot is a year, the Y-axis is the U.S. Defense budget, and the X-axis represents military personnel. Begin reading the chart from the bottom right and follow the line as if it were a path (it is) toward a much smaller army, but also much higher expenditures during the presidencies of George W. Bush and Barack Obama.

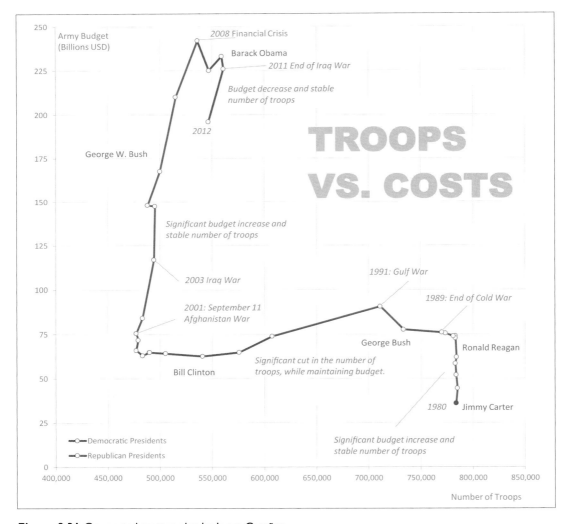

Figure 8.31 Connected scatter plot by Jorge Camões.

Max Roser is also fond of connected scatter plots. He is an economist at the University of Oxford's Institute of New Economic Thinking and author of the popular www.ourworldindata.org project, which is devoted to visualizing publicly available data about living standards, health, poverty, and other topics.

OurWorldInData showcases plenty of traditional time series line charts (**Figure 8.32**) but also strives to depict the historical change in factors such as GDP per capita and life expectancy at birth (**Figure 8.33**) or infant survival rates versus birth rates (**Figure 8.34**). These charts anticipate the topic we're about to have fun with: the visualization of relationships.

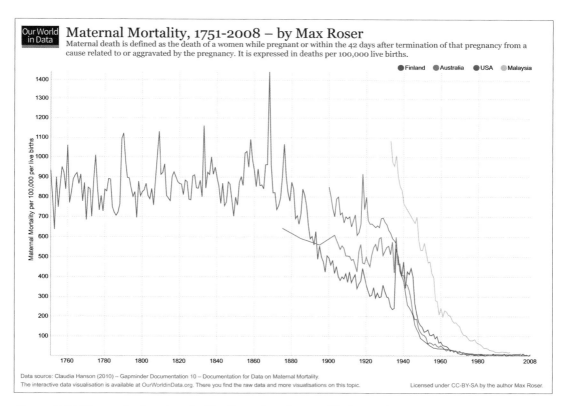

Figure 8.32 Time series line chart by Max Roser, http://ourworldindata.org/.

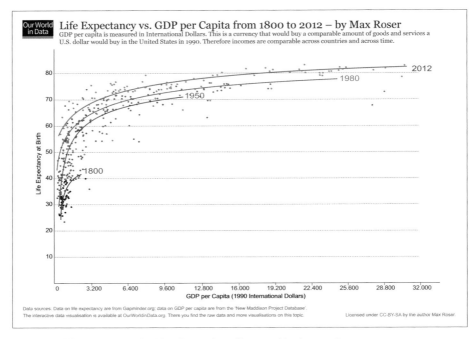

Figure 8.33 Scatter plot by Max Roser, http://ourworldindata.org/.

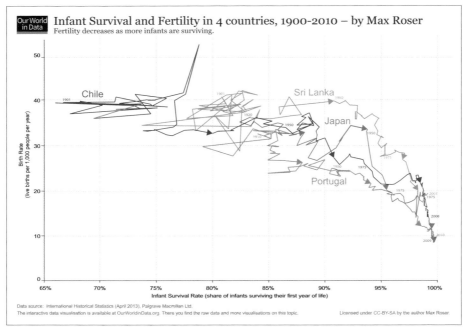

Figure 8.34 Connected scatter plot by Max Roser, http://ourworldindata.org/.

To Learn More

- Behrens, John. T. "Principles and Procedures of Exploratory Data Analysis." Psychological Methods, 1997, Vol. 2, No. 2, 131-160. Available online: http://cll.stanford.edu/.

- Camões, Jorge. *Data at Work: Creating effective charts and information graphics.* Berkeley, CA: Peachpit Press, 2016. One of the best business visualization books in the market.

- Coghlan, Avril. T. *A Little Book of R For Time Series.* Available online: https://a-little-book-of-r-for-time-series.readthedocs.org/en/latest/.

- Donahue, Rafe M.J. *Fundamental Statistical Concepts in Presenting Data: Principles for Constructing Better Graphics.* A free book available online: http://biostat.mc.vanderbilt.edu/wiki/pub/Main/RafeDonahue/ fscipdpfcbg_currentversion.pdf.

9

Seeing Relationships

Guy: "I used to think correlation implied causation. Then I took a statistics class. Now I don't."

Girl: "Sounds like the class helped."

Guy: "Well, maybe."

—Dialogue in an XKCD.com cartoon: https://xkcd.com/552/

There are certain headlines that are impossible for any journalist to resist. I'll give you one: "Eat More Chocolate, Become Smarter!" You may think that I'm joking, but here's a real 2012 headline from Reuters: "Eat chocolate, win the Nobel Prize?"

The story—written tongue-in-cheek, or so it seems—was based on a "study" by Dr. Franz H. Messerli, director of the Hypertension Program at New York City's St. Luke's-Roosevelt Hospital, published in the well-respected *New England Journal of Medicine*. Reuters wasn't the only news organization that picked up Dr. Messerli's results.[1]

---

1 Dr. Messerli's article is "Chocolate Consumption, Cognitive Function, and Nobel Laureates," http://tinyurl.com/bh3eeea, and the story by Reuters is here: http://tinyurl.com/8bbweav. For comments about this case, read: "Chocolate consumption and Nobel Prizes: A bizarre juxtaposition if there ever was one," http://tinyurl.com/pzlbuf6.

Dr. Messerli's "study" didn't truly qualify as such. It was just a short piece in a section called "Occasional Notes," and it was based on data downloaded from Wikipedia: the chocolate consumption per capita for each country (kilograms per year) and the number of Nobel Prize winners per 10 million people.

Throw those two variables together in a scatter plot, and you'll get **Figure 9.1**. You can see an $r = 0.79$ in there. We'll get to what that means in a minute. For now, just keep in mind that r measures the strength of the linear relationship between two quantitative variables. The highest value that r can adopt is 1.0, so 0.79 denotes a pretty strong linear relationship.

Dr. Messerli told Reuters, "I started plotting this in a hotel room in Kathmandu, because I had nothing else to do, and I could not believe my eyes." Well, it's better to believe them. **Figure 9.2** exposes the even stronger relationship ($r = 0.87$) that exists between the age of Miss America and the number of murders by steam, hot vapors, or hot objects in the United States I may have just proved that the Miss America jury has a grave responsibility in reducing murder rates by picking younger winners.

As demonstrated by the website this example came from, **Spurious Correlations** (http://tylervigen.com/spurious-correlations), you don't need to look into data too hard to find stirring, but utterly absurd, associations between disparate variables.

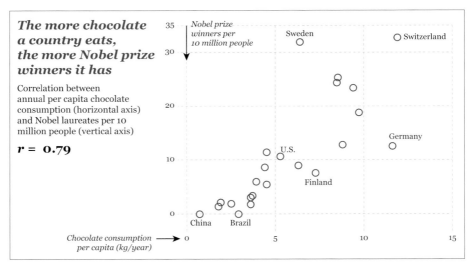

Figure 9.1 Chocolate and Nobel prizes.

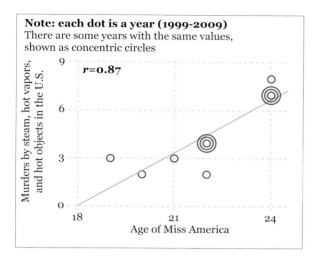

Note: each dot is a year (1999-2009)
There are some years with the same values,
shown as concentric circles

$r=0.87$

Murders by steam, hot vapors, and hot objects in the U.S.

Age of Miss America

Figure 9.2 The older Miss America gets, the more people are murdered with steam, hot vapors, or hot objects. Who said that it's hard to find joy in numbers?

As goofy as these examples look, we find them every day in the media. We all have taken stories like this seriously at some point. I dare you to deny it.

Some researchers devoted time to write rebuttals to Dr. Messerli's meditation.[2] The most amusing one was published in *The Journal of Nutrition*,[3] and it stated the obvious: chocolate consumption is indeed correlated with the number of Nobel laureates in a country. But so is wine consumption—and the number of IKEA stores (**Figure 9.3**).

What all these variables have in common is that they are related to each country's wealth. That's the lurking variable we're overlooking. The higher the median income is in a country, the more money citizens have to invest in education, wine and chocolate, or impossible-to-assemble furniture from IKEA.

---

2   To be fair to Dr. Messerli, his article has plenty of caveats: it's based on a known fact—chocolate improves cognitive function—and it's written in a cheeky, half-serious tone. When observing that Sweden is an outlier, Dr. Messerli wrote, "Either the Nobel committee in Stockholm has some inherent patriotic bias when assessing the candidates for these awards or, perhaps, the Swedes are particularly sensitive to chocolate, and even minuscule amounts greatly enhance their cognition." At the end of the article, he adds, "Dr. Messerli reports regular daily chocolate consumption, mostly but not exclusively in the form of Lindt's dark varieties."

3   "Does Chocolate Consumption Really Boost Nobel Award Chances? The Peril of Over-Interpreting Correlations in Health Studies," http://jn.nutrition.org/content/143/6/931.full.

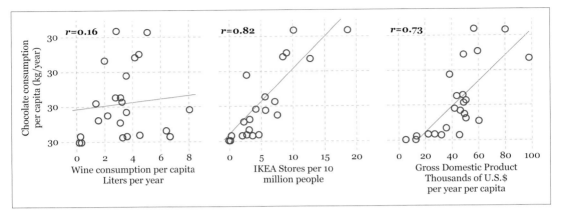

Figure 9.3 The relationship between chocolate consumption—and IKEA stores!

If dealing with a single variable is tricky, exploring how different variables influence each other is even worse. In this chapter, we're going to enter the world of quantitative relationships, correlation, regression, and the multiple ways we can display them visually. We'll also address a big elephant that has made a home of our tiny living room (packed with IKEA furniture, of course): is it possible to make the leap between correlation and causation?

From Association to Correlation

We say that two variables are related when changes in one of them are accompanied by variations on the other one. Take the small data set of student scores on **Figure 9.4**. You can represent the positive linear relationship between the variables with a scatter plot and a trend line.

Students	Math scores	English scores
Maria	10	16
Helen	11	17.5
Alice	14	22
Jorge	15	23.5
Lucius	16	25
Finn	18	28
Ricky	21	32.5
Alisha	22	34
Joe	23	35.5
Liz	24	37

Figure 9.4 A perfect correlation.

In a scatter plot, the closer the data points are to this trend line, the stronger the association between our variables is. In our current data set, all points are sitting on the line, meaning that the association is perfect. The line is an excellent model for our data. We can express it with an equation or function. Let's call math scores X and English scores Y. Here's the function:

$$Y = (X \times 1.5) + 1$$

You can double-check the function yourself. When the English score is 14, the math score is 22, which is the result of (14 times 1.5) + 1.

Our function doesn't just take actual values into account, but it can also predict missing or inexistent ones. For instance, not a single student got a score of 20 in the English exam. If that were the case, we could estimate her math score: (20 × 1.5) + 1 = 31. With some minimal effort, just by reversing the previous formula, we can also estimate English scores based on math scores.

Unfortunately, the world is far messier than made-up examples. Associations between variables are rarely perfect. Just check the relationship between IKEA stores and chocolate consumption in Figure 9.3 again. There's a trend line in there, too, but it doesn't fit the data perfectly. The points aren't sitting on the trend line but cluster close to it.

If the relationship between two quantitative variables is linear, we can talk about a **correlation** between them. Its strength can be expressed with that puzzling *r* we saw before. That's the **correlation coefficient**.[4] The formula for *r* is pretty straightforward, but not relevant for this discussion.[5] Here are a few important things to remember about it:

- *r* may adopt any value between –1.0 and 1.0.

- Correlation has a direction. If *r* is a negative number, each increment of X will result in a consistent decrease of Y. If *r* is a positive number, X and Y increase and decrease together. In both cases, the ratio of change is constant.

---

4 As per usual in this book, I'm just giving you an overview, so refer to the recommendations at the end of the chapter for more information.

5 In case you're interested in how to do this manually, here we go: first, remember z scores, discussed in previous chapters? You need to calculate all z scores for X and Y values. Then, multiply each z score of X by each z score of Y and add up all products. Then, divide the result by the number of X-Y pairs.

- The closer r is to 1.0, the stronger the positive correlation between X and Y is. The closer r is to -1.0, the stronger the negative correlation between X and Y is.

- Authors disagree on what constitutes a weak or a strong correlation, but here's a useful scale: 0.1–0.3 is modest; 0.3–0.5 is moderate; 0.5–0.8 is strong; and 0.8–0.9 is very strong. The same applies to negative correlations: just put a minus symbol in front of those figures.

- Let's mention this again, just in case: in any scatter plot, the closer most of the data points are to the trend line, the greater r will be, and vice versa.

- Correlation is very sensitive to outliers. It's a non-resistant statistic. A single outlier may distort r badly. There are methods to deal with this challenge. You can refer to the bibliography and learn, for instance, about Spearman's resistant correlation coefficient or the Kendall rank correlation coefficient.

I'll reiterate that **correlation applies only when the relationship between variables is linear**. This isn't always the case. Sometimes, the association between two variables is better described as a curve.

I have an old data set of fuel efficiency with two variables: speed and miles per gallon consumed by 15 cars tested in 1984. I calculated the correlation between speed and average mileage and got: r = -0.27. Should I move on? First, let's see the data on a connected scatter plot. **Figure 9.5** shows the average of the 1984 cars compared to the average of nine cars tested in 1997.

It is clear to me that a simple linear association is inadequate in this case: both 1984 and 1997 cars are inefficient at low speeds and at high speeds. The high-efficiency peak is reached at medium speeds.

An interesting pattern I spotted was that the curve for the 1997 cars has a distinctive two-peak shape, and it is flatter than the one of 1984 cars. Newer cars are more efficient at low and high speeds but slightly less efficient at medium speeds. This might mean nothing, as I don't know if the models tested in 1984 and 1997 were the same. We cannot assess if this comparison makes sense.

Out of curiosity I decided to plot all nine models tested in 1997 to see if the two-peak pattern is common. It is (**Figure 9.6**). Several models show a sudden drop

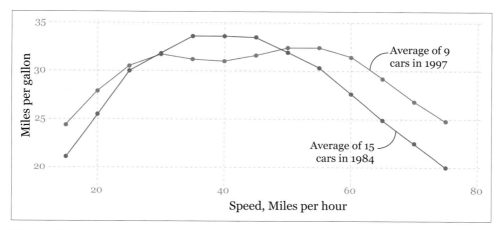

Figure 9.5 A non-linear relationship. (Source: Transportation Energy Data Book Edition 3: http://tinyurl.com/oaevnrx.)

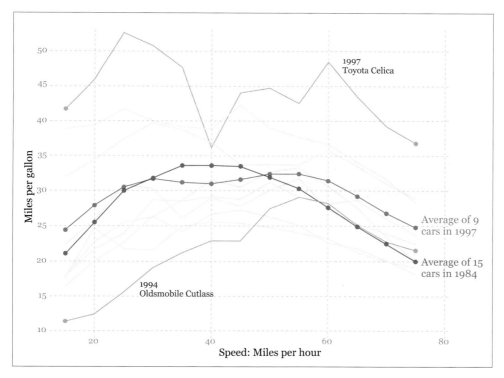

Figure 9.6 Comparing the average of 15 cars tested in 1984 to the average of nine cars in 1997 and to the models tested that year (light blue).

in efficiency in the middle of the curve. Call me a dummy—my ignorance about cars is as epic as my ignorance about sports, and I'm not proud of either—but this was surprising. I had always thought that fuel efficiency invariably follows a smooth up-and-down curve, like the one for 1984 cars. I've learned something new, thanks to a chart (again).

Smoothers

Data puzzles are often the best starting point to spot potential stories, so here's another one: I once read that the best-performing U.S. state in the SAT (Scholastic Aptitude Test) is North Dakota. That sounded interesting. Inspired by an exercise devised by statisticians **David S. Moore** and **George P. McCabe**, I searched the Internet and downloaded the average state-level 2014 SAT scores and the participation rate and designed a scatter plot with a straight trend line (first chart on **Figure 9.7**).

There are several intriguing patterns in that chart. I can see at least three data clusters and a few exceptions (second chart on Figure 9.7):

1. States with very low participation rates and very high average scores,

2. States with high participation and lower scores, and

3. States with full participation and even lower scores.

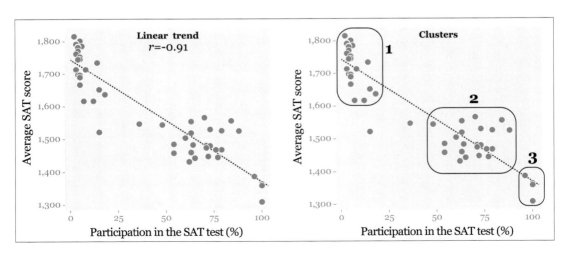

Figure 9.7 Straight trend line and data clusters.

A single linear association, then, isn't a good summary of these data, and r alone, even being high, can mislead us. A solution could be to divide the data into groups of identical size and then calculate trend lines for each.

This is, roughly speaking, the idea behind **locally weighted scatter plot smoothing**. That's quite a mouthful, so let's use the acronym LOWESS instead. Many tools and programming languages for visualization can calculate a LOWESS model and curve for us. After that, we may color-code the states by region (**Figure 9.8**).

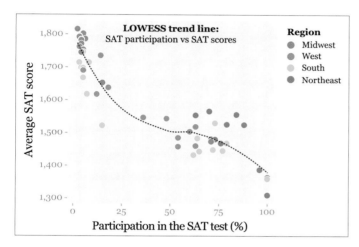

Figure 9.8 SAT participation versus average score with a LOWESS line.

Imagine that someone were to report just the average SAT scores. The resulting bar chart would be distorted by the fact that in states with low participation rates, probably just the best high schoolers take the SAT.[6] North Dakota, for instance, has a participation rate of just 2 percent and a score of 1,816, while Washington D.C., where all students take the exam, the average score is just 1,309. Our scatter plot is a much better depiction of the situation.

When I first learned about this participation-score mismatch, I felt so curious that I did some digging. If high schoolers don't take the SAT, what do they do? I read that most students in Midwestern states take the ACT (American College Testing,) so I decided to see if the inverse relationship between participation and average scores still held.

6 This is just a guess. Read "Why The Midwest Dominates the SAT," http://www.forbes.com/sites/bentaylor/2014/07/17/why-the-midwest-dominates-the-sat/.

I downloaded data from www.act.org and designed **Figure 9.9**. It's like the mirror image of Figure 9.8, with a handful of exceptions: states in the Midwest have higher participation rates this time, but their average scores don't drop as dramatically as I was expecting. It would hardly be possible to discover such quirky morsels of information without these color-coded scatter plots.

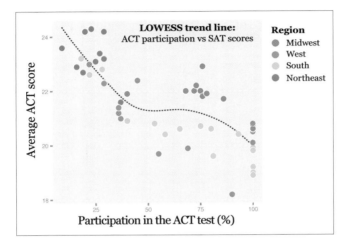

Figure 9.9 ACT participation versus average score.

Matrices and Parallel Coordinate Plots

A single scatter plot displays the relationship between two variables. But what if we wish to compare more?

The data set of SAT scores I've been playing with doesn't just include the average state scores, but also the scores for each test: critical reading, math, and writing. **Figure 9.10** is a series of scatter plots that share the same Y-axis (score) and X-axis (participation). If this graphic were interactive, whenever a reader selects a state or group of states in one of the scatter plots, they'd be also highlighted on the other charts, enabling the identification of patterns of similitude and difference. Math scores seem to be higher than writing ones. Interesting, isn't it?

The limitation of this kind of graphic is that you can compare participation to any other score, but you can't see the correlation between individual tests (math versus writing, for instance).

Enter the scatter plot matrix (**Figure 9.11**), a common tool in scientific research that unfortunately doesn't get much attention from news organizations. Scatter

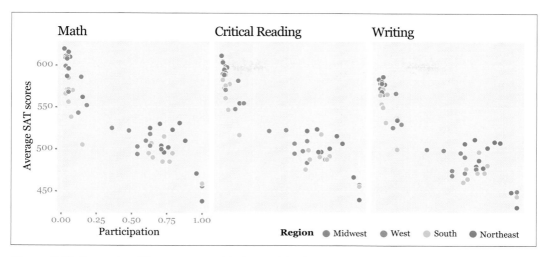

Figure 9.10 Comparing different scores with the participation rate.

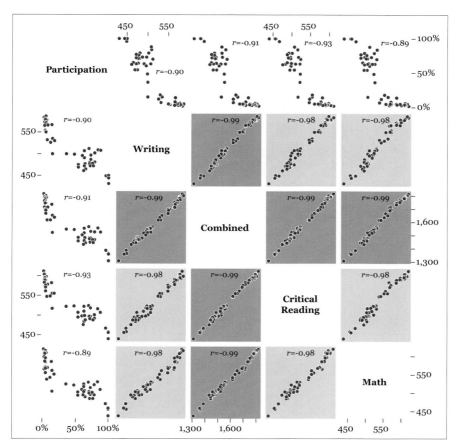

Figure 9.11
A scatter plot matrix. Even if I have calculated *r* for each of the panels, always be aware that outliers can greatly influence this statistic.

plot matrices are tailored to explore multivariate data. They can provide a very rich big-picture view of the relationships between numerous variables.

If you've never seen a matrix like this before, it will take you a minute to learn how to read it, so I have designed a little infographic guide (**Figure 9.12**). As you can notice, scatter plot matrices can be color-coded according to the strength of the correlations and even simplified as heat maps (**Figure 9.13**).

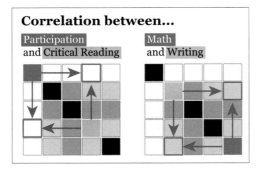

Figure 9.12 How to read a scatter plot matrix.

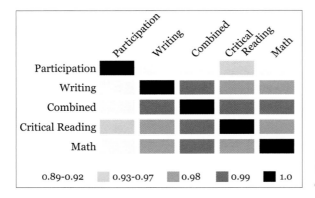

Figure 9.13 A simple heat map based on a correlation matrix.

My data set of SAT scores isn't particularly interesting, as correlation coefficients are barely distinguishable from 1.0, so I designed another example of scatter plot matrix and heat map (**Figure 9.14**) where I compared several state-level metrics, such as poverty, food stamp recipients, obesity rates, educational attainment, and so on.

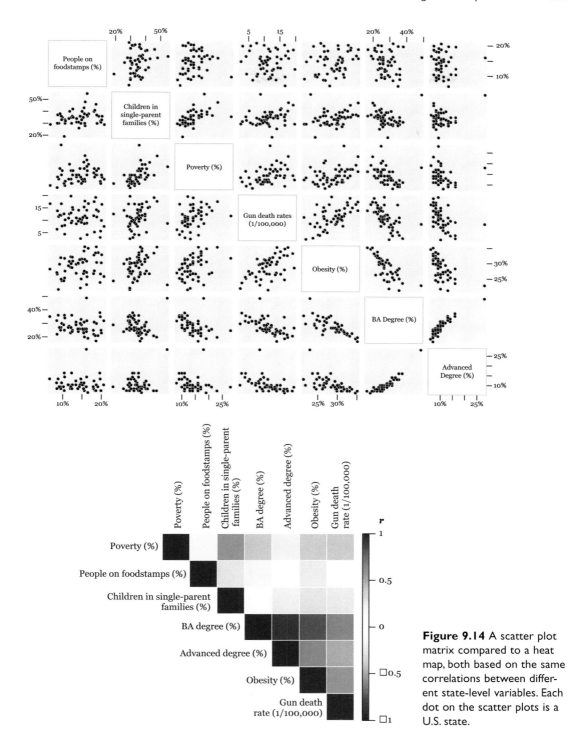

Figure 9.14 A scatter plot matrix compared to a heat map, both based on the same correlations between different state-level variables. Each dot on the scatter plots is a U.S. state.

Deciding between a scatter plot matrix and a heat map depends on many factors. For instance, heat maps alone are not appropriate when the relationship between variables isn't always clearly linear, as in the example before. However, a heat map can be a concise summary of large data sets. When in doubt, always do a detailed scatter plot first.

Another powerful way to visualize multivariate data, which we saw briefly in Chapter 5, is the **parallel coordinates plot**, invented by mathematician **Al Inselberg** in 1959. A strength of parallel coordinates plots is that they can be used to show relationships between any kind of data, categorical or quantitative, as shown in **Figure 9.15**, designed by **Stephen Few** for his book *Signal*. It shows the performance of 10 products (divided into three groups) in four different regions.

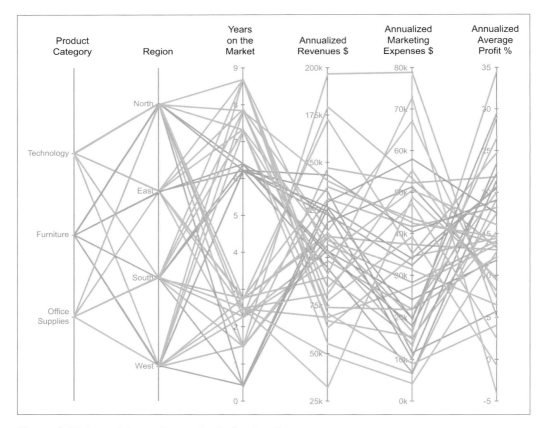

Figure 9.15 A parallel coordinates plot by Stephen Few.

Steve writes:

> At first glance, what we have here looks like a cluttered mess, but suspend your disbelief in its potential until I've explained a bit more about (the insights we can gain). Here are a few that stand out:
>
> - No technology products have been on the market for more than three years.
>
> - All products have either been on the market for less than three years or for more than six years.
>
> - The four top-grossing items are all technology products.
>
> - The top-grossing item is probably doing well because of a major investment in marketing in a particular region, resulting in a fairly low profit margin.
>
> - The lowest-grossing items are all office supplies.
>
> - The products that have been on the market for the shortest time are all furniture products that earn better than average annualized revenues.
>
> - Four of the top five profit margins are associated with technology products.
>
> - Two office supply products are losing money in particular regions, which in one case appears to be tied to an expensive marketing campaign.[7]

Not bad for what we initially thought to be a hopelessly busy chart, I'd say.

Two features are critical in the design of parallel coordinates plots. First, ordering variables in different ways helps identify relevant patterns. Second, adding interactivity helps readers. Parallel coordinates with many lines are usually more effective when people can highlight the portions they're interested in, while graying out the rest.

---

7 Few, Stephen. *Signal: Understanding What Matters in a World of Noise.* Analytics Press, 2015.

Correlation for Communication

The SAT data I explored before reminded me of an interactive visualization I made with my colleagues **Gerardo Rodríguez** and **Camila Guimarães** when I was the head of infographics and visualization at *Época* magazine, in Brazil. In September 2010, the Ministry of Education released the results of the ENEM, the Brazilian equivalent of the SAT.

We designed an online tool that first let parents search the entire database to find any school in the country. But we also wanted to play with visualizations a bit. One of our sources, a statistician who specializes in educational data, suggested that we look into the relationship between average school scores and participation rates.

The reason, according to him, was that ENEM scores are distorted because a large percentage of students from good schools take the test, but a much smaller proportion from bad schools do so. Some bad schools allegedly try to look better by discouraging their low-performing students from participating.

Our source also suggested to color-code public and private schools. Brazil's educational system is very unequal: most public schools are much worse than most private schools. Curious about the results? See **Figure 9.16**. Each dot is a school. The X-axis is the average ENEM scores. The Y-axis encodes participation rate (as a percentage). The vertical and horizontal lines are the averages of those variables, and they divide the plot into quadrants. Most public schools are on the lower-left quadrant (bad scores, low participation), while most private schools are on the upper right (good scores, high participation). There are plenty of exceptions, but the pattern is clear.

|||❚❚❚❚❚||||

In the past five years, data teams have flourished in Brazilian media. The most active one is Estadão Dados, from *O Estado de S. Paulo*, one of the main national newspapers in the country. **Figure 9.17** is, in my opinion, one of its finest projects. Its title reads, "How the Bolsa Família influenced voting for Dilma Rousseff." It was designed by **Rodrigo Burdarelli** and **José Roberto de Toledo**.

The Bolsa Família is a welfare program that aids poor families in exchange for keeping their kids in school and vaccinated. Dilma Rousseff was elected president of Brazil twice, in 2010 and in 2014, when this graphic was published.

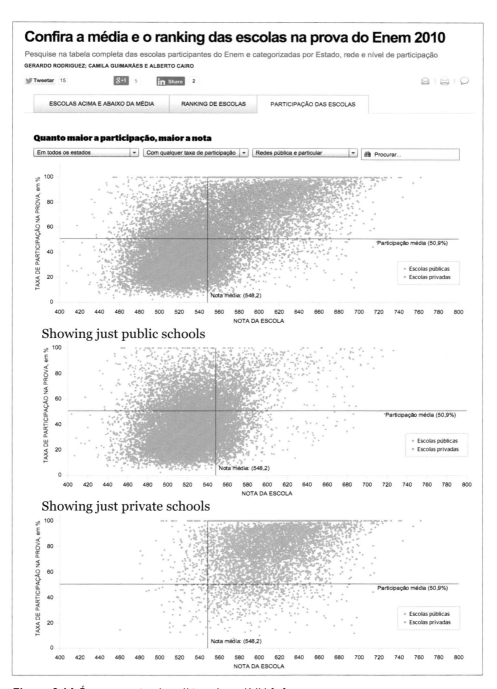

Figure 9.16 *Época* magazine, http://tinyurl.com/64kbfwf.

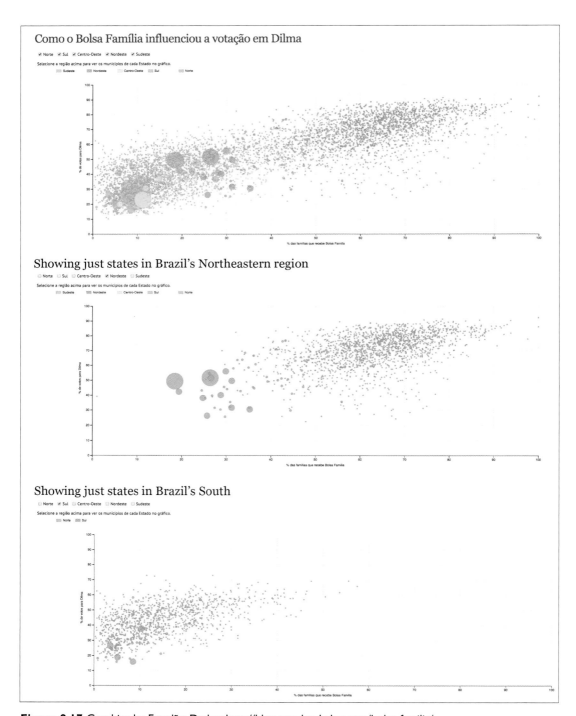

Figure 9.17 Graphics by Estadão Dados; http://blog.estadaodados.com/bolsa-familia/.

Rousseff belongs to a leftist party (the PT, Partido dos Trabalhadores). Estadão Dados' goal was to show that there's a clear relationship between percentage of families who receive help from Bolsa Família (X-axis) and vote for Rousseff (Y-axis).

In the graphic, each circle is a municipal district. Bubble size represents population. The association is solid, and it becomes even clearer when you only show northeastern districts or southern ones. Brazil's northeast is very poor; southern cities and towns are much richer, on average.

I really liked this visualization the first time I saw it, but its title made me feel uneasy. Scatter plots can be deceptive: the relationship between Bolsa Família and votes for Rousseff exists, but does that mean that benefitting from this welfare program leads to an increase in votes for leftist candidates? We could be getting the sequence of events wrong: it may be that voting for leftist candidates in poor regions was already strong when Bolsa Família was launched in 2003. Longitudinal analyses are always more illuminating than cross-sectional ones.

I asked Estadão Dados about my misgivings, and its members told me that the headline was based on studies published in 1989, 1994, and 1998, which showed that before Bolsa Família, poorer areas didn't vote massively for PT candidates. Moreover, a 2010 analysis by the Brazilian Institute of Public Opinion and Statistics (Ibope) revealed that the factor that better explained voting for the PT presidential candidate was Bolsa Família.

From Mexico's *El Financiero* comes an elegant example of an interactive scatter plot (**Figure 9.18**). Designer-developers **Hugo López** and **Jhasua Razo** were interested in analyzing if the surface area of houses and apartments in Mexico City is proportional to their price. The relationship between the two variables is robust, but there are some curious outliers.

The visualization lets readers select which neighborhoods to show, and the X- and Y-axis vary accordingly. When you visit the graphic, notice how beautifully animation effects are used here, not just to make the presentation flashier but easier to understand as well.

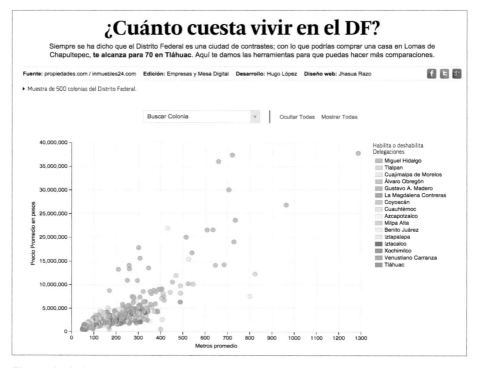

Figure 9.18 Graphic by *El Financiero* http://tinyurl.com/of4p6mu.

|||▮▮▮▮▮||||

In the years that I've been a *New York Times* subscriber (since 2012), its enormous graphics desk—around 30 people at the time of this writing—has produced plenty of fine relationship charts. Two of them have remained in my memory to this day. The first one, by **Hannah Fairfield** and **Graham Roberts** (**Figure 9.19**), is visualization expert **Robert Kosara**'s favorite chart ever:

> It shows men's versus women's weekly earnings, with men on the horizontal axis and women on the vertical. A heavy black diagonal line shows equal wages, three additional lines show where women make 10%, 20%, and 30% less. Any point to the bottom right of the line means that women make less money than men. The diagonal lines are a stroke of genius (pun fully intended). When you see a line in a scatterplot, it's usually a regression line that models the data; i.e., a line that follows the points. But such a line only helps reinforce the difficulty of judging the differences between the two axes, which is something we're not good at, and which is not typically

something you do in a scatterplot anyway. But the diagonal line, as simple as it is, makes it not just possible, but effortless. It's such a simple device and yet so clear and effective. All the points on the line indicate occupations where men and women make the same amount of money. To the top left of the line is the area where women make more money than men, and to the bottom right where women make less.[8]

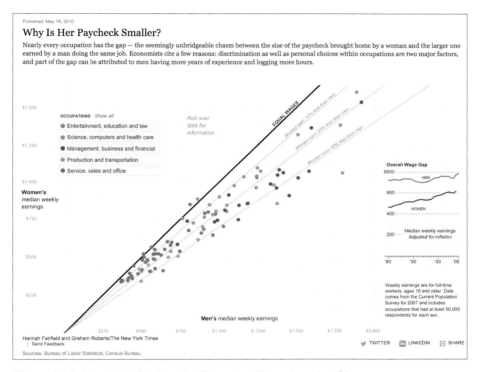

Figure 9.19 Graphic by *The New York Times*, http://tinyurl.com/cnrj2f.

Amen to that. My other personal favorite is the heat map in **Figure 9.20**, designed by **Jon Huang** and **Aron Pilhofer** and launched the day after Osama bin Laden was killed in Pakistan. The *New York Times* asked readers to send their opinions about the event: was it significant or not? Was their view positive or negative? Readers were also prompted to plot their responses on the chart. The result gives you an idea of how nearly 14,000 *NYT*'s readers reacted to this news: most of them are on the upper-right quadrant, that is, positive and significant.

8 "My Favorite Charts," https://eagereyes.org/blog/2014/my-favorite-charts.

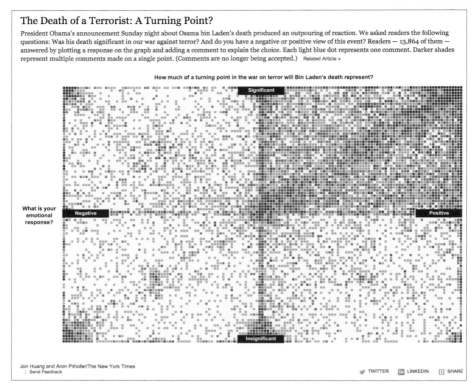

Figure 9.20 Graphic by *The New York Times*, http://tinyurl.com/43skv8s.

||||❙❙❚❙❚❙|||||

On Monday, October 27, 2014, **John Tory** was elected mayor of Toronto by a comfortable margin of 6 percentage points. His main opponent was **Doug Ford**, the seedy older brother of the even seedier ex-mayor Rob Ford, who couldn't run for re-election because he was diagnosed with cancer. Rob Ford's tenure as a mayor had been punctuated by repeated incidents related to substance abuse, anything from alcohol to crack.

In a long story published by *Global News*, investigative reporter **Patrick Cain** asked "Who is Ford nation?"[9] As he explained in the methodology section of the story, he first gathered the results of several polls. Then he found the center

9 "Ford Nation 2014: 14 things demographics tell us about Toronto voters," http://tinyurl.com/qeeezoj.

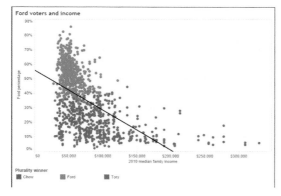

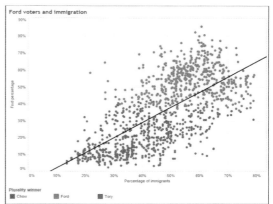

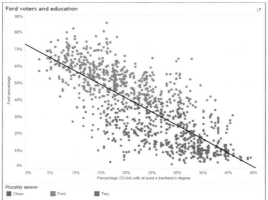

Figure 9.21 Charts by Patrick Cain (*Global News*).

geographic point of where each poll had taken place with the help of a mapping program. He placed that point in, or as close as possible to, its corresponding electoral track. That way, he could compare polling estimates to indicators such as unemployment and income.

The plots are striking. **Figure 9.21** shows just three of them: even as right-wingers, the Ford brothers found strong support in old areas of Toronto, where many citizens have low income, only a high school education, weren't born in Canada, and English is not their primary language.

|||▮▮▮▮▮|||

The connection between poverty and educational success, which is bidirectional and confounded by many factors, has been explored by social scientists and journalists for decades. However, it is rare to find a narrative as convincing as the one that ties together a 2015 series of articles and visualizations by the *Daily*

Herald, a newspaper that serves Chicago's suburbs, in collaboration with WBEZ (Chicago Public Radio).[10]

Reporters and designers at both organizations looked at a decade of test scores and neighborhood-level poverty rates and revealed a very strong connection between low income and kids' performance at school. See the scatter plots on **Figure 9.22**, created by **Tim Broderick**.

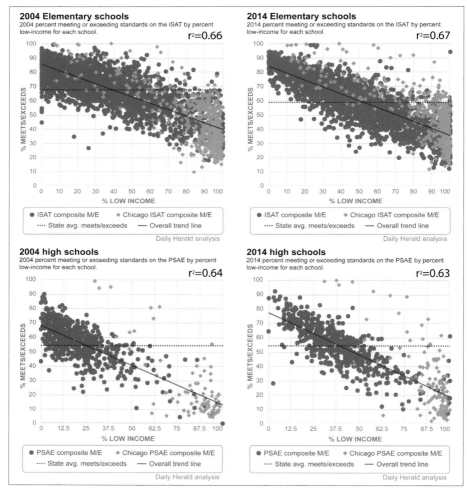

Figure 9.22 Charts by the Tim Broderick (*Daily Herald*). Don't worry about that r squared on the upper-right corner of each chart. We'll learn about that a few pages from now.

10 First story: http://www.dailyherald.com/article/20150622/news/150629873/. All data and the methodology used: http://reportcards.dailyherald.com/lowincome/.

Journalists also looked into the past and discovered that a variation in the proportion of poor students in a school is a very good predictor of test scores in the following time period. They also explored data at the district level, and the same relationships exist. In some of the counties that encompass the Chicago urban sprawl, correlation is very close to being 1.0.

Moreover, the stories written by the *Herald* and WBEZ are inspiring examples of how to present complex data: not as charts alone—which may open the door for misinterpretation—but by putting the data in context by interviewing experts, school officials, politicians, parents, and children, and explaining the many nuances, caveats, exceptions, and gray areas in the analysis.

Regression

There is a difference between the scatter plots I designed at the beginning of this chapter and the ones coming from *Global News* and, above all, the *Daily Herald*. In the charts I used to explain correlation, it didn't matter much which variable went into the X-axis and which into the Y-axis: they were interchangeable. In the charts from the *Daily Herald*, they aren't: X (low income) is an **explanatory variable**, and Y (performance in tests) is a **response variable** (a variation in low-income rates can explain variations in test scores, at least in part).[11] This isn't just a correlational chart. It's a called a **regression** model.

In regression, X has some limited predictive value. If you anticipate a future value of X, you'll also be able to roughly predict the corresponding Y value. How? I'm going to explain just the most simple kind of regression, **univariate linear least squares regression**. To learn about other kinds (logistic regression, Bayesian regression, etc., both univariate and multivariate), please go to the recommended readings at the end of the chapter.

Remember what we learned about scatter plots: the linear relationship between two quantitative variables can be expressed as an equation, a function of the form.

$$Y = X \text{ modified in some way}$$

---

11 In many books, explanatory variables are called "independent" variables, and response variables are called "dependent" variables. I find that nomenclature needlessly confusing. Some statisticians prefer the terms "input" and "output" variables.

The formula for simple linear regression will look bewildering for a second, but don't worry. I am including it just for you to understand the results you'll get when you ask a software tool to calculate it:

Y = Intercept + X × Slope

When you calculate regression in a computer, you'll usually get at least four estimated values: the intercept, the slope, a certain amount of error, and a confidence level. (We'll get to the latter two soon.) What are the intercept and the slope? Look at **Figure 9.23**, which displays the relationship between SAT participation rates and scores.

The **intercept** is the value of Y at which the regression line crosses the 0 point on the X-axis.

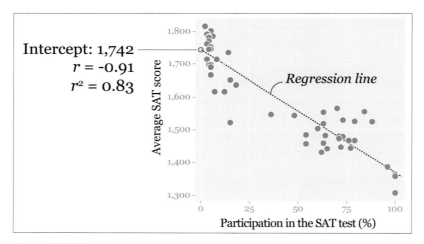

Figure 9.23 The intercept.

The **slope** is the rate at which values of Y vary when values of X change. In our data set, this value is -3.68. That means that for each increment of 1 in the participation rate, there's very roughly a 3.68 decrease in average SAT scores. This "very roughly" is an indispensable qualifier. In the scatter plot, many states are far from the regression line. Still, we can predict what the average score might be for a participation rate of 25 percent, for instance:

Intercept + X × Slope = Y

Therefore:

1,742 + 25 × (-3.68) = Average score of 1,650

You can check this value on the chart itself. Just put your finger on the 25 point on the horizontal scale and see at what point on the Y-axis the vertical gridline crosses the regression line: exactly at the 1,650 point. This is not considering the error in the model, though. As you can see in the chart, the actual SAT scores close to the 25-percent participation rate differ from that estimate quite a bit. No model is ever perfect.

A couple of warnings are relevant at this point: first, visualization designers and journalists regularly deal with high-level aggregated data, such as country or state averages. Be aware that association between variables is usually much stronger in this kind of data than it is at lower levels of analysis—by city block, for instance.

Second, it is absolutely crucial to keep in mind that **inferences from data should be done only at the same level of aggregation as the data**. Group-level data can't be used to analyze individual-level phenomenon.[12] In the current case, we're dealing with state-level data. Our model would not work well to predict the average SAT score of a single school based on its rate of participation.

Let's go back to Figure 9.23. Besides r, the correlation coefficient, there's also an r^2 by the chart. This is the **coefficient of determination**, which is simply the result of squaring the correlation coefficient. If $r = -0.91$, as in this example, then $r^2 = (-0.91) \times (-0.91) = 0.83$.

The coefficient of determination is a pretty useful statistic. It is a measure of how much of the variation in a response variable (Y) depends on the explanatory variable (X). You can think of it as a percentage. If $r^2 = 0.83$, you can say that 83 percent of the variation in SAT scores can be explained by the participation rate. We saw r^2 in the *Global Herald* charts before (Figure 9.22), with values such as 0.63. Therefore, the proportion of students from low-income households (X-axis, explanation variable) explains 63 percent of the variation in school test results.

From Correlation to Causation

There's a difference between using one or more explanatory variables to estimate the variation of a response variable, and assuming that our explanatory

---

12 This is called the ecological fallacy. Read "Ecological Inference and the Ecological Fallacy," http://web.stanford.edu/class/ed260/freedman549.pdf.

variables are the *causes* for the changes on the response variables. Neither correlation nor regression imply causation, although they can be used as first clues when they are solid enough.

Ultimately, the only way to determine causation with reasonable certainty is to run randomized controlled experiments that can rule out extraneous factors. However, running experiments is difficult or isn't even an option in many cases. If you wish to determine if poverty really causes worse performance in school, you'd need, for instance, to test a group of middle-income kids one year, then make them poor for a few years, and test them again, comparing them to another group of students whose living conditions don't change (this is the control group). That's not something that an academic ethics committee would ever approve!

What happens, then, when an experiment is out of the question? It is still possible to make the case for a causal connection if some strict criteria are met. Statisticians David S. Moore and George P. McCabe (see the recommended readings section) suggest these:

- The strength of the association—a high coefficient of determination, for instance—between the variables you're studying.

- The association with other alternative explanatory variables is weaker.

- Several observational studies, using different data sets than yours, show a consistent strong connection between the variables.

- The explanatory variable precedes the response. For instance, to infer causation from a correlation between educational attainment and poverty levels, you need to examine if changes in education policies precede variations in poverty rates in a consistent manner.

- The cause makes logical sense and is rational. Remember Chapter 4, particularly the part about coming up with good explanations.

Moore and McCabe use the link between smoking and lung cancer as an example. The evidence we have is overwhelming, but is observational, not experimental.[13]

---

13 A more controversial case, at least in some parts of the United States, is that of the association between gun legislation and gun violence, which I believe fulfills all of Moore's and McCabe's criteria. To learn more, see Adam Gopnik's "Armed Correlations," http://www.newyorker.com/news/daily-comment/armed-correlations.

No sane person would dare put people at risk of getting lung cancer just to test if cigarette consumption is the cause.[14]

Data Transformation

Relationship charts can be transformed in a similar way as we did when exploring time series and other kinds of data in other chapters: we can separate the smooth from the rough and then study the residuals. Or we can transform the magnitudes of the axis to clarify the relationship.

A classic example to illustrate this idea in statistics and biology courses is the correlation between body weights and brain weights of several species of mammals (**Figure 9.24**). When you design a scatter plot with the raw scores, most dots lie at the lower-left end because of the three glaring outliers. Correlation is very strong (r = 0.93), but our scatter plot is hard to read. If we take the logs, as I did on the second chart, gaps in the data disappear, and our model becomes clearer and more effective.

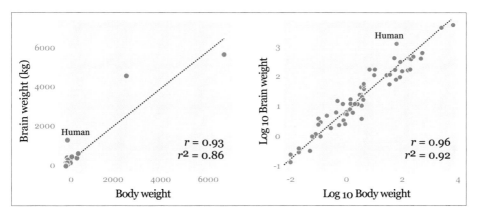

Figure 9.24 Correlation between body weight and brain weight for 62 mammal species. Raw data and logs. Data from Allison, T. and Cicchetti, D. V. (1976), "Sleep in mammals: ecological and constitutional correlates," *Science*, v. 194, pp. 732–34. Full data set at http://tinyurl.com/pbm9pzg.

---

14 This hasn't been the case in the past. The history of unethical medical experimentation on human subjects is long and painful to read. And its protagonists were usually quite sane, as books like *Dark Medicine: Rationalizing Unethical Medical Research* (2008) and *Against Their Will: The Secret History of Medical Experimentation on Children in Cold War America* prove. The discussion about if it is ethical to use data generated by unethical experiments has kept philosophers and bioethicists busy for ages. For a good introduction, see Jonathan Steinberg's "The Ethical Use of Unethical Human Research," at http://tinyurl.com/qhoe346.

To Learn More

- Few, Stephen. *Signal: Understanding What Matters in a World of Noise.* Burlingame, CA, 2015. Steve's fourth book is a concise and meaty overview of exploratory data analysis.

- Moore, David S., and George P. McCabe. *Introduction to the Practice of Statistics* (5th edition). New York, NY: W.H. Freeman and Company, 2005. Besides including a crystal-clear explanation of correlation and regression, this whole book is a treat.

10

Mapping Data

A map does not just chart, it unlocks and formulates meaning; it forms bridges between here and there, between disparate ideas that we did not know were previously connected.

—Reif Larsen, *The Selected Works of T. S. Spivet*

In a broad sense of the word, this entire book is about maps, as it deals with the spatial representation of information with the goal of revealing the unseen. In this chapter, I will be using a narrower meaning of "map" to refer just to visualizations that display attributes or variables over pictures of geographical areas.

As any of the other graphic forms we've learned about so far, maps can be used to communicate or to explore information. Maps are critical to many areas of inquiry, from epidemiology to climate science.

The main attributes of a map are its scale, its projection, and the symbols used to depict information.[1] The scale is a measure of the proportion between distances and sizes on the map and those on the area represented—that is, how big is the map compared to reality?

---

1 In the next few pages, I will be following Mark Monmonier's *How to Lie With Maps* (2nd ed., 1996.) For a complete list of books consulted, see the references at the end of this chapter.

There are many ways to express this ratio: as a verbal statement ("1 inch on this map represents 100 miles in the real world"); as a fraction (1:1,000, or, "One unit of measurement on the map is equivalent to 1,000 of those units in the real world"); or as a bar with a length that is equivalent to a rounded distance in reality (10, 100, 1,000 miles, etc.).

Maps can be classified according to their scale. A **large-scale map** (1:10,000, for example) will show a small area with higher detail than a **small-scale map** (1:100,000,000). When you represent Earth as a whole, you are using a small-scale map. A close-up of your hometown is a large-scale one.

The scale you choose for a map is closely related to your assumptions about how much most of your readers know about the area shown. A map like the first one on **Figure 10.1**, locating Ranau, in Malaysia, would be good for the International News section of a large American newspaper (therefore, the inset on the upper-left corner). The second map might be useful for South Asian readers, who are more familiar with these latitudes.

Figure 10.1 The same region of the world represented at two different scales.

Projection

I don't think that I'll reveal anything new if I tell you that Earth is a globe.[2] Transforming it into a two-dimensional representation is tricky. Imagine trying to wrap the peel of an orange over a flat surface without tearing it. That's similar to what we need to do when we create a map.

Projection is the process of making a globe, or a portion of it, fit into a flat picture. When you make that transformation, some features will always be distorted; some distances, shapes, and areas will be stretched, and others will be compressed. There's no 100 percent accurate representation of a globe other than a globe itself.

As a visualization designer, it is unlikely that you will ever have to deal with the nightmarish math involved in the creation of projections, but you'll often a) download copyright-free maps from the Internet to trace and modify, or b) generate maps with software tools like Geographic Information Systems (GIS). In both cases, it'll be useful to get acquainted with some terms.

In technical jargon, the geometrical objects where the globe can be projected to create a map are called **developable surfaces**. The most widely used developable surfaces are the cylinder, the cone, and the plane. **Figure 10.2** is an infographic that explains how elementary conical, planar, and cylindrical projections work.

The areas of the developable surface that are tangent to the globe during the projection process are called **standard lines**. As a general rule, the scale of a map is only accurate along those lines. The farther away we move from them, the greater the distortion. As many mapping tools let you choose standard lines, it's always a good idea to make sure that they are as close as possible to the area your story refers to.

Figure 10.3 is a map of western Europe that I generated with an old free tool, Versamap. I chose a conical projection. Notice that the standard lines are the 65th and the 40th parallels north. Those two parallels nicely frame the region in which I'm interested.

---

2 Some people disagree. See http://www.tfes.org/, which isn't a parody. These folks play on a higher league than those who still sustain that humans were created in their current form 6,000 years ago.

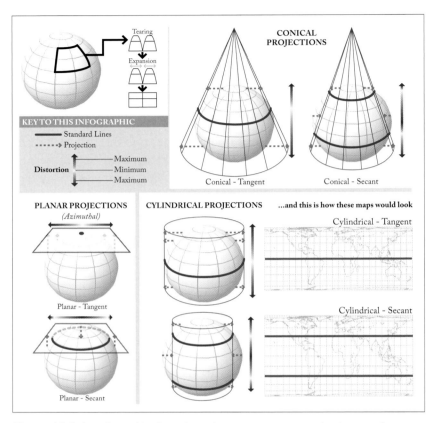

Figure 10.2 An infographic about how the most common projections work.

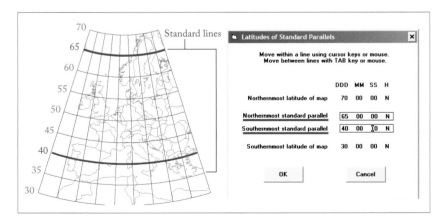

Figure 10.3 Choosing the standard lines (parallels) to generate a map.

There are five properties that can (and will) be distorted when you project a globe on a flat surface: **shape**, **area**, **angles**, **distance**, and **direction**. Any projection can respect one or two of those properties, but not more. At least three attributes will be sacrificed regardless of the projection you choose. Creating a flat map is always a trade-off.

Taking these properties as classifying criteria, we can identify two major map groups. Some maps preserve continental shapes—the overall look of landmasses—and local angles (any angle created by two intersecting lines will be the same on the map and on the globe). In software tools and cartography books, you'll see that these are called **conformal projections**. The most famous one is the Mercator, the first one on **Figure 10.4**.

Mercator

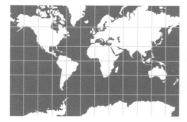

Lambert cylindrical

Goode's Homolosine

Mollweide

Figure 10.4
Four very popular map projections.

The Mercator projection was created for sea navigation, but it isn't a good choice for world maps because landmass area ratios are totally off.[3] As the standard line is placed on the Equator, the farther north or south you go, the larger the map regions will be in relation to reality. See Alaska, for instance, which looks as big as Brazil. It is a shame that the Mercator projection has become the standard in online tools like Google Maps.[4]

---

3 I like the Mercator projection, even if it's so often misused. See Mark Monmonier's *Rhumb Lines and Map Wars: A Social History of the Mercator Projection* (2004) for a forceful defense of it.

4 There's a reason for this: Mercator is a good choice for maps of small areas, as it preserves shapes and angles. But it sucks when used on world maps. What could be the solution for online map services? Perhaps it could be switching projections depending on the region of the world readers are exploring and on how much they zoom in or out.

A second family of projections available in mapping software, **equal-area projections**, preserve area ratios. That is, the sizes of the areas represented on the map are proportional to the areas on the Earth. The Lambert cylindrical projection, also shown on Figure 10.4, is a good example. Equal-area projections tend to distort shapes heavily: the farther the distance from the standard lines is, the greater this distortion becomes.

No map can be conformal and equal-area simultaneously. Those are mutually exclusive characteristics. However, there are some projections, like Goode's Homolosine, that are neither conformal, nor equal-area. They don't respect shapes or sizes completely, but they achieve a reasonable balance between the two, and so are called trade-off, or compromise projections. The Mollweide projection is another example.

So the million dollar question is: how do I choose the best projection? I usually say about projections what Ellen Lupton wrote about choosing typefaces in her graceful book *Thinking With Type* (2004): there are no good or bad typefaces. There are *appropriate* and *inappropriate* typefaces. It's the same for maps.

Imagine that you need to create a data map showing which areas of the world may be covered with ice for more than 90 percent of the year in 2020 (**Figure 10.5**). A Mercator projection would give you a different picture than a Goode map, as regions close to the poles look huge on the former and much smaller on the latter.

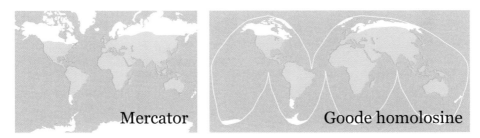

Mercator   Goode homolosine

Figure 10.5 The same story will look very different depending on the projection you choose.

Figure 10.6 is a summary of very popular projections and of the cases when it is advisable to use them. If you are planning to show a larger region, a country, or even the whole world, it should be clear at this point that as a general rule you should always use a projection that preserves areas without distorting shapes heavily. If you are going to show just a very small region, such as your neighborhood or town, try to stick to comformal projections, those that preserve shapes and angles.

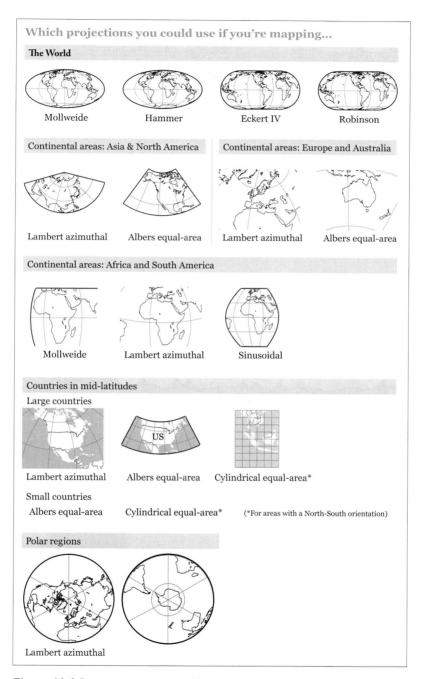

Figure 10.6 Projection suggestions. If you do maps for the Web, be aware that Mercator is the default projection many online tools use. Try to avoid it, using the recommendations above.

Playing with different projections can lead to beautiful visualizations. Back in 2012, **John Nelson**, a map designer, became interested in visualizing the paths of all hurricanes and tropical storms the National Oceanic and Atmospheric Administration has records for. Nelson first used some predictable projections (see one of his drafts on **Figure 10.7**). Then, he tried a projection centered on the South Pole, and the map became an unforgettable piece of art (**Figure 10.8**).

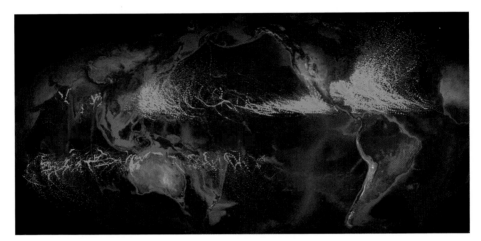

Figure 10.7 A draft for the map of hurricanes in Figure 10.8.

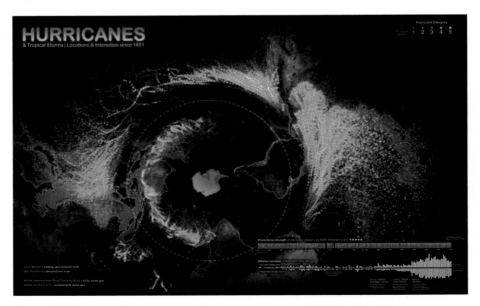

Figure 10.8 A map of hurricanes and tropical storms since 1851, by John Nelson: http://tinyurl.com/9y2axf4.

Data on Maps

In the literature about cartography, data maps are usually called **thematic maps**. Here's the definition of thematic maps from Axis Maps, a cartography visualization firm: "Thematic maps are meant not simply to show locations, but rather to show attributes or statistics about places, spatial patterns of those attributes, and relationships between places."[5]

Data on maps can be encoded by means of points, lines, areas, and volumes, as shown on **Figure 10.9**. Symbols can represent qualitative information (a location, the boundaries of an area) or quantitative information (magnitude or concentration of a variable or phenomenon in certain places).

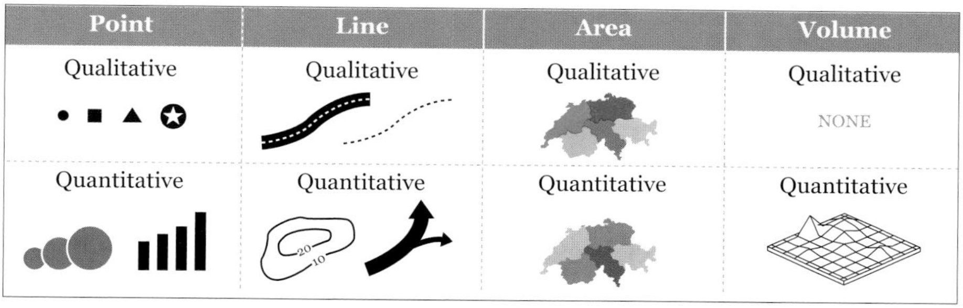

Figure 10.9 Symbols to encode data on maps.

Point Data Maps

The simplest way to put data on a map is by using dots representing either individuals or groups of a fixed size.

Figure 10.10 is a dot map of evergreen forests (green) and woody wetlands (blue). The data and the code behind this project comes from **Nathan Yau**, who regularly posts tutorials in his website (**flowingdata.com**) besides being the author of two books on data visualization. Each dot on the map doesn't represent a single tree or plant—that would only be feasible if we were mapping a tiny area—but a spot of land that is mostly covered by each kind of vegetation.

---

5 Axis Maps has a good and free introduction to thematic maps: http://axismaps.github.io/thematic-cartography/articles/thematic.html.

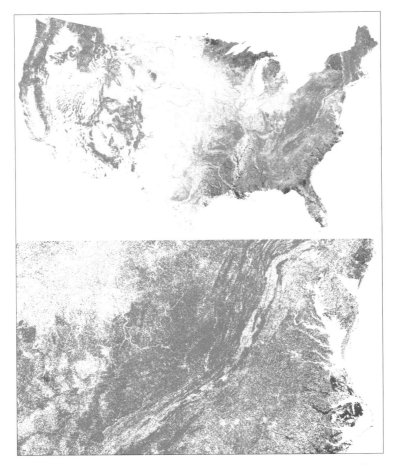

Figure 10.10 A dot map of evergreen forests (green) and woody wetlands (blue). The code used to create this map comes from www.flowingdata.com.

Another beautiful example of a dot map is **Figure 10.11**. This one was designed by ***The Baltimore Sun's*** five-person design and development team, which is responsible for creating visualizations, apps, and infographics. Dots are color-coded according to race, so readers can immediately envision the segregation that ails Baltimore, which unfortunately also exists in many other U.S. cities.

On a dot map, quantity is represented by the amount and concentration of dots, but there's another kind of point map that represents it through symbol size: the **proportional symbol map**. On a proportional symbol map, geometric objects (usually circles) or icons are scaled in proportion to quantitites. You can see an example on **Figure 10.12**, by *The Washington Post*.

Figure 10.11 Legacy of segregation lingers in Baltimore, a dot map by *The Baltimore Sun*: http://tinyurl.com/osxj37x

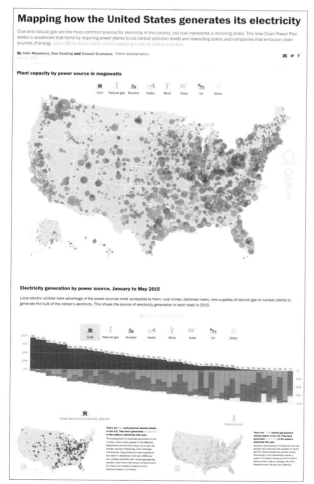

Figure 10.12 Proportional symbol maps and chart by *The Washington Post* https://www.washingtonpost.com/graphics/national/power-plants/.

There's a lot to like in this project. The main map represents all energy plants in the United States The size of the circles is proportional to megawatts. A bar chart shows the percentage of energy generated in each state that comes from each source. This chart is sortable, so if you click on Nuclear, the bars will rearrange themselves: states getting most of their energy from nuclear plants will be placed on the left side. Finally, the designers were very aware of one of the main challenges in proportional symbol maps, the fact that excessive overlap may obscure information. Therefore, they added six smaller maps at the bottom, one for each power source.

Many visualization tools let you design proportional symbol maps quite easily, but there might be a case in which you'll need to create them manually. Let's suppose that we're doing an income map with just three circles, corresponding to $100, $200, and $400. This should be easy, right? Just draw one circle to represent $100, duplicate it, and then scale it 200 percent to obtain the circle representing $200. The results are on the left side of **Figure 10.13**. They are horribly wrong.

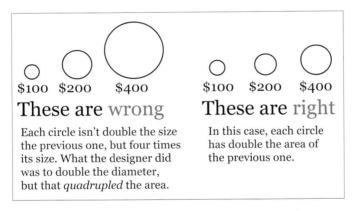

Figure 10.13 How to size circles incorrectly and correctly.

Just think about it: if you tell a software tool to scale something 200 percent, it will make it twice as tall and twice as wide. Therefore, you aren't doubling the size of your original circle. You are making it *four times larger*. You can just eyeball the evidence for this: you can insert four $100 circles inside the area of the $200 circle, and four $200 circles inside the $400 circle.

On the right side of Figure 10.13, circles are scaled correctly. How to size circles manually? Follow the formula on **Figure 10.14**.

Imagine that the largest circle on a map of monthly household income equals $2,600.
The radius of this circle (R1) is 1.1 inches. How to calculate the radius (R2) of a circle representing $1,100?

$$R2 = \sqrt{\frac{\text{New value (1,100)}}{\text{Largest value (2,600)}}} \times R1 \rightarrow R2 = \sqrt{0.42} \times 1.1 = 0.71 \text{ inches}$$

Figure 10.14 How to calculate the area of circles in proportional symbol maps.

This said, it's worth remembering that maps are priceless at offering an overview of your data, but they don't enable very accurate judgments. **Even if objects on a proportional symbol map are correctly sized, readers won't estimate their relative sizes well**. Remember that area was on the lower half of the scale of methods of encoding (devised by William Cleveland and Robert McGill) that we saw in Chapter 5.

Cartographers often refer to phenomena like the **Ebbinghaus illusion** to illustrate maps' shortcomings. An example of that illusion: If you surround two circles of the same size with larger or smaller circles, your perception of their size will change. (See **Figure 10.15**.)

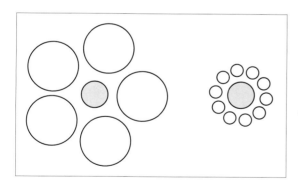

Figure 10.15 The Ebbinghaus illusion, named after German psychologist Hermann Ebbinghaus. The gray circle surrounded by large white circles looks smaller than the one surrounded by small white circles. In truth, they are the same size.

You also need to pay attention to **symbol placement**. Each symbol should be located where each value was observed. If the location is a point (a town, a city), this is quite easy: just center the symbol to the point. If the symbol represents a value associated with an area (a province, a state, a country), you should put it in the visual center of the region. There is an exception to this rule: when too much overlap occurs, it is acceptable to displace the symbols slightly off-center.

Overlaps can become problematic in proportional symbol maps: some areas may get so crowded that it becomes difficult to see what's going on. There are two ways of addressing this problem, as shown on **Figure 10.16**: make sure that smaller symbols are always in front of larger ones, or make all symbols semi-transparent. If this is not enough to reduce clutter, scale all the symbols down.

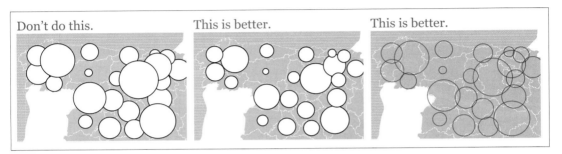

Figure 10.16 How to make proportional symbol maps clearer.

Although there are no fixed rules about how to design the legend of a proportional symbol map, two main styles have become popular (**Figure 10.17**): **nested** (the smaller symbols are placed within the larger ones) and **linear** (the symbols are placed next to each other).

Linear legends can have a vertical or horizontal orientation. The number of circles on a legend depends on the amount of detail you estimate readers will need to understand the map. As a general rule, though, try not to use more than four.

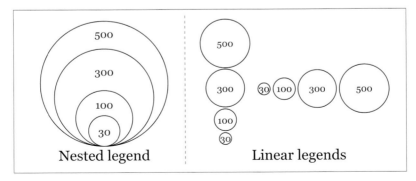

Figure 10.17 Legends for proportional symbol maps.

The scores to include in the legend may vary depending on the content and goals of your map but, as a general rule, first include two circles representing rounded values that are as close as possible to the highest and lowest values in your data set. This will help readers get an idea of the range of your data set. After that, you can include a couple of extra circles proportional to rounded scores in between the highest and the lowest ones.

Proportional symbol maps can be multivariate. Simply using a second method of encoding (shading, for example, as in **Figure 10.18**) may give readers a more nuanced understanding of the data.

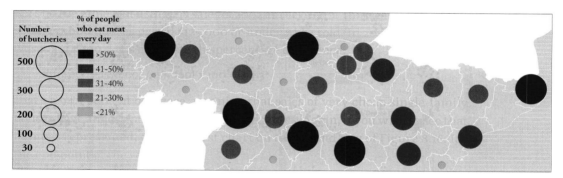

Figure 10.18 A made-up map of meat consumption in northern Spain.

Line Maps

The most common kind of data map based on the use of lines is the **flow map**, usually showing the movement of entities between geographic areas.

Figure 10.19 was designed by **Bestiario**, a Spanish data visualization firm. It's part of a huge project called "Commuting and Mobility Dynamics in the 73 Neighborhoods of Barcelona." Based on data from mobile companies, Bestiario plotted several maps in which line weight is proportional to the amount of people moving from the neighborhood where they live to the places where they study or work.

The maps are supplemented by bar charts on the right side. Here, neighborhoods are sorted according to how far they are from the point of origin. A black vertical line indicates time of commute. Bars are proportional to number of commuters.

On **treballen**
o **estudien** els
residents de
Raval

48.800
*Població Total
(desembre 2013).*

*Percentatge de desplaçaments
sobre total sortides.*

1 el Raval	*19* les Corts	*38* la Teixonera	*57* la Trinitat Vella
2 el Barri Gòtic	*20* la Maternitat i Sant Ramon	*39* Sant Genís dels Agudells	*58* Baró de Viver
3 la Barceloneta	*21* Pedralbes	*40* Montbau	*59* el Bon Pastor
4 Sant Pere, Santa Caterina i la Ribera	*22* Vallvidrera, el Tibidabo i les Planes	*41* la Vall d'Hebron	*60* Sant Andreu
5 el Fort Pienc	*23* Sarrià	*42* la Clota	*61* la Sagrera
6 la Sagrada Família	*24* les Tres Torres	*43* Horta	*62* el Congrés i els Indians
7 la Dreta de l'Eixample	*25* Sant Gervasi - la Bonanova	*44* Vilapicina i la Torre Llobeta	*63* Navas
8 l'Antiga Esquerra de l'Eixample	*26* Sant Gervasi - Galvany	*45* Porta	*64* el Camp de l'Arpa del Clot
9 la Nova Esquerra de l'Eixample	*27* el Putxet i el Farró	*46* el Turó de la Peira	*65* el Clot
10 Sant Antoni	*28* Vallcarca i els Penitents	*47* Can Peguera	*66* el Parc i la Llacuna del Poblenou
11 el Poble Sec - AEI Parc Montjuïc	*29* el Coll	*48* la Guineueta	*67* la Vila Olímpica del Poblenou
12 la Marina del Prat Vermell - AEI Zona Franca	*30* la Salut	*49* Canyelles	*68* el Poblenou
13 la Marina de Port	*31* la Vila de Gràcia	*50* les Roquetes	*69* Diagonal Mar i el Front Marítim del Poblenou
14 la Font de la Guatlla	*32* el Camp d'en Grassot i Gràcia Nova	*51* Verdun	*70* el Besòs i el Maresme
15 Hostafrancs	*33* el Baix Guinardó	*52* la Prosperitat	*71* Provençals del Poblenou
16 la Bordeta	*34* Can Baró	*53* la Trinitat Nova	*72* Sant Martí de Provençals
17 Sants - Badal	*35* el Guinardó	*54* Torre Baró	*73* la Verneda i la Pau
18 Sants	*36* la Font d'en Fargues	*55* Ciutat Meridiana	
	37 el Carmel	*56* Vallbona	

Figure 10.19 Graphic by Bestiario.org.

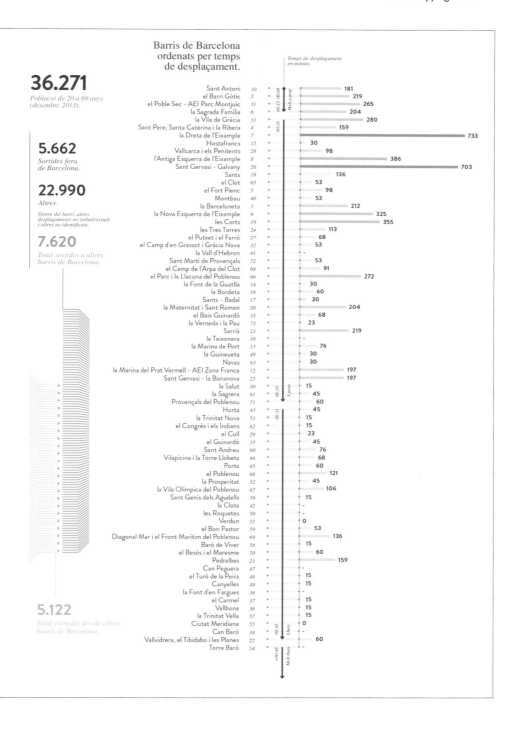

36.271

*Població de 20 a 69 anys
(desembre 2013).*

5.662

*Sortides fora
de Barcelona.*

22.990

Altres.

*Dintre del barri, altres
desplaçaments no treball/estudi
i altres no identificats.*

7.620

*Total sortides a altres
barris de Barcelona.*

5.122

*Total entrades des de altres
barris de Barcelona.*

Barris de Barcelona
ordenats per temps
de desplaçament.

*Temps de desplaçament
en minuts.*

Barri		Valor
Sant Antoni	10	181
el Barri Gòtic	2	219
el Poble Sec - AEI Parc Montjuïc	11	265
la Sagrada Família	6	204
la Vila de Gràcia	31	280
Sant Pere, Santa Caterina i la Ribera	4	159
la Dreta de l'Eixample	7	733
Hostafrancs	15	30
Vallcarca i els Penitents	28	98
l'Antiga Esquerra de l'Eixample	8	386
Sant Gervasi - Galvany	26	703
Sants	18	136
el Clot	65	53
el Fort Pienc	5	98
Montbau	40	53
la Barceloneta	3	212
la Nova Esquerra de l'Eixample	9	325
les Corts	19	355
les Tres Torres	24	113
el Putxet i el Farró	27	68
el Camp d'en Grassot i Gràcia Nova	32	53
la Vall d'Hebron	41	-
Sant Martí de Provençals	72	53
el Camp de l'Arpa del Clot	64	91
el Parc i la Llacuna del Poblenou	66	272
la Font de la Guatlla	14	30
la Bordeta	16	60
Sants - Badal	17	30
la Maternitat i Sant Ramon	20	204
el Baix Guinardó	33	68
la Verneda i la Pau	73	23
Sarrià	23	219
la Teixonera	38	-
la Marina de Port	13	76
la Guineueta	48	30
Navas	63	30
la Marina del Prat Vermell - AEI Zona Franca	12	197
Sant Gervasi - la Bonanova	25	197
la Salut	30	15
la Sagrera	61	45
Provençals del Poblenou	71	60
Horta	43	45
la Trinitat Nova	53	15
el Congrés i els Indians	62	15
el Coll	29	23
el Guinardó	35	45
Sant Andreu	60	76
Vilapicina i la Torre Llobeta	44	68
Porta	45	60
el Poblenou	68	121
la Prosperitat	52	45
la Vila Olímpica del Poblenou	67	106
Sant Genís dels Agudells	39	15
la Clota	42	-
les Roquetes	50	-
Verdun	51	0
el Bon Pastor	59	53
Diagonal Mar i el Front Marítim del Poblenou	69	136
Baró de Viver	58	15
el Besòs i el Maresme	70	60
Pedralbes	21	159
Can Peguera	47	-
el Turó de la Peira	46	15
Canyelles	49	15
la Font d'en Fargues	36	-
el Carmel	37	15
Vallbona	56	15
la Trinitat Vella	57	15
Ciutat Meridiana	55	0
Can Baró	34	-
Vallvidrera, el Tibidabo i les Planes	22	60
Torre Baró	54	-

The Basics of Choropleth Maps

A choropleth map encodes information by means of assigning shades of color to defined areas such as countries, provinces, states, counties, etc. A choropleth map can show different kinds of data (ordinal, interval, ratio, etc.), as **Figure 10.20** shows.

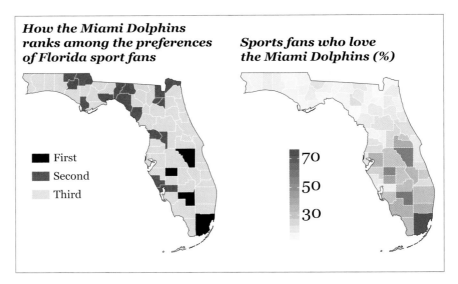

How the Miami Dolphins ranks among the preferences of Florida sport fans

Sports fans who love the Miami Dolphins (%)

First
Second
Third

70
50
30

Figure 10.20 If you are a Dolphins fan, be aware that these data are fake.

Choropleth maps can be used for quick data exploration. **Figure 10.21** is a set of maps that I put together recently to compare racial groups, per capita income, and median age in Florida.

These maps are OK for what they are (letting me see interesting things in the data), but they have many flaws. To begin with, the three on top should perhaps share the same continuous color scheme. But I let the program choose this for me, forgetting my own dictum, **never trust software defaults**. (This is valid advice for any tool, not just for mapping programs.)

Sticking to software defaults uncritically will lead you to maps like **Figure 10.22**. Notice the color scales. In principle, they aren't that bad: around 17 percent of the U.S. population is Hispanic, so these maps offer a quick "below average/ above average" portrait. However, the fact that most values above the national

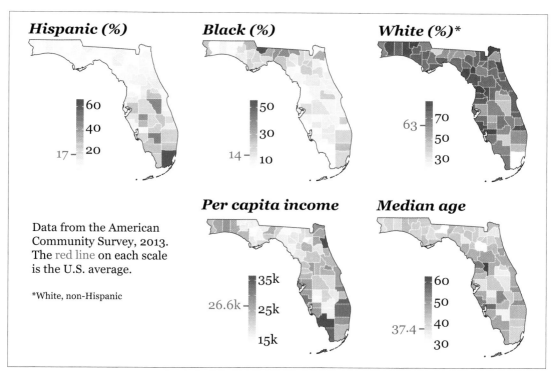

Figure 10.21 Exploring Florida with choropleth maps. Designed with code inspired by a tutorial by Ari Lamstein (www.arilamstein.com).

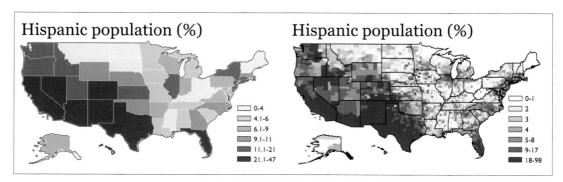

Figure 10.22 Two levels of data aggregation: state level and county level. If you paid attention to my words about projections at the beginning of this chapter, you may have noticed that these maps are based on a Web Mercator projection. That isn't a great choice, but I couldn't change the default projection in the software I was using!

average are grouped together exaggerates the amount of Hispanic people in the United States. To me, the county-level map suggests that in a large portion of the United States, more than half of the population is of Latino origin.

In a choropleth map, each interval of values associated with a shade of color is called a **class**. Grouping values in classes in a way that causes relevant patterns to become visible without exaggerating them much is quite a challenging task, one that shouldn't be left to a dumb algorithm to complete. Manual adjustments are often necessary.

In the current county-level example, I'd like to use a scale in which the higher values are shown with more detail, something like 0-8, 8.1-17, 17.1-50, 50.1-75, and 75.1-98 (**Figure 10.23**). Notice that I put one break at 17 percent (the U.S. average) and another at 50 percent (beyond that, the majority of the population is Hispanic).

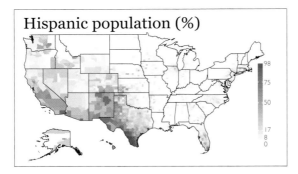

Figure 10.23 Adjusting the color scale to reveal more detail.

Classifying Data

Cartographers have developed multiple ways of choosing breaks and classes for choropleth maps. I'm going to explain how to design the most common ones. I'll also show how to calculate them, even if in most cases your computer can do the math for you. When designing maps, always try different intervals until you find the one that better represents the data.

I'll do this exercise using the percentage of Hispanic population at the state level. **Figure 10.24** shows a strip plot in which each circle is a state, and a histogram of frequencies. Before you create any choropleth map, always take a look at the shape of your data, as we did in Chapters 6 and 7.

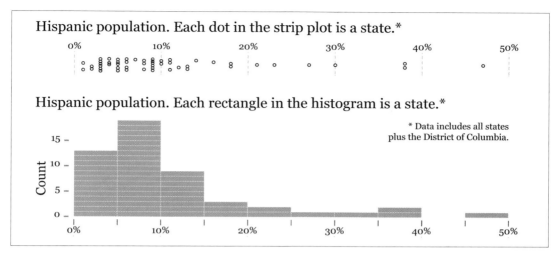

Figure 10.24 Visualizing the frequency of scores in our data.

Our distribution is pretty skewed: nearly two-thirds of the states are on the lower end of the spectrum (between 0 and 10 percent); in only 17 of them, more than 10 percent of the population is of Hispanic origin. The minimum value in our data set is 1 percent (Maine and West Virginia) and the highest is 47 percent (New Mexico.)

The first method to calculate breaks is to place them at **intervals of constant size**. Boundaries calculated according to this method will enclose equal ranges of data, such as 0–10, 11–20, 21–30, 31–40, and so on. This method usually works well when frequencies are constant, but let's give it a try. Here's how to calculate your breaks:

Get the maximum and the minimum scores: **47 percent** and **1 percent**

Subtract them: **47-1 = 46**

Divide the result by the number of classes (intervals) you want. Say you want 6:

46/6 = 7.7

This 7.7 is your class size. The lower boundary of your first class should be the minimum value, 1, and the upper boundary should be 8.7 (which is 1+7.7). The boundaries for the subsequent classes can be calculated just by adding 7.7 over and over again, as shown on **Figure 10.25**. For instance, the upper boundary of class two can be calculated with this formula:

Minimum value + $(2 \times$ Class size$)$; in other words: 1.0 + (2×7.7) = 16.4

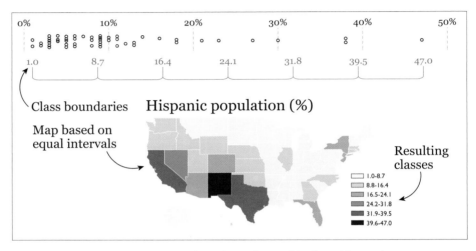

Figure 10.25 Choropleth map based on classes (intervals) of roughly equal size.

The choropleth map based on equal intervals isn't that bad, after all. New Mexico has a class of its own, and the states with the highest rates stand out nicely. But perhaps we are losing some important details at the lower end of the spectrum, as so many states lie within the 1.0 to 8.7 range. To reveal it, we may want to try something different.

Remember percentiles, explained in Chapter 7? We can use them to classify data, too. This is the **quantiles** method, and it consists on placing roughly the same number of cases (states, in the current example) inside each class. We have 51 observations in our data set, 50 states plus D.C., so we'd need to place roughly 51/6 = 8.5 states in each class. Some rounding and adjustment will be required. Notice that on **Figure 10.26**, there are classes with 10 states and others with 7 or 8.

Also, pay attention to the last class. It's 21.0 to 47.0, but the upper boundary of the class that precedes it is 18.0. There's a gap between 18.1 and 21.0 in our color scale because there are no observations in that region of the distribution. Gaps may puzzle readers, so it's advisable to add a little footnote explaining why they exist.

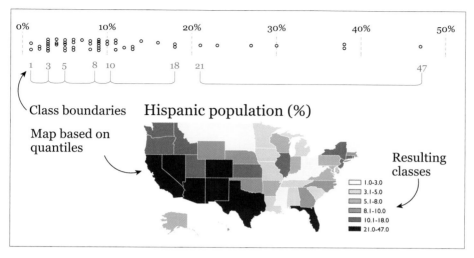

Figure 10.26 Choropleth map based on classes that contain roughly similar number of observations, between seven and ten each.

A third classification method is based on the mean and the standard deviation. This can be helpful to design **diverging color schemes**, as on **Figure 10.27**, which is the map that I like the best so far.

We know that 17 percent of people in the U.S. are Hispanic. That's our mean. The standard deviation of our data set is close to 10.0. We can use that as our class size. To calculate the class ranges, we begin with the mean, and we add and subtract the standard deviation as many times as needed to include the entire data set, like this:

Below the mean:

Class 1: 17.0 – 10.0 = **7.0**

Class 2: 17.0 – (2 × 10.0) = **-3.0**

There aren't negative values in our data set, so let's use the smallest figure (1.0) as the lowest boundary of this class.

Above the mean:

Class 3: 17.0 + 10.0 = **27.0**

Class 4: 17.0 + (2 × 10.0) = **37.0**

Class 5: 17.0 + (3 × 10.0) = **47.0**

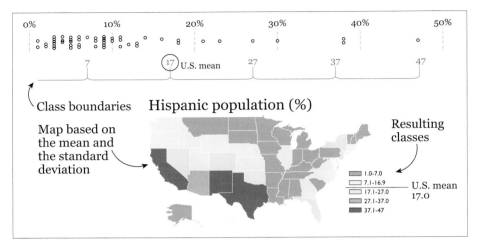

Figure 10.27 A divergent color scheme based on the mean and the standard deviation.

In our data set there isn't any state that matches the national mean of 17 percent. If that were the case, we could consider building a class just for it and use a neutral hue (perhaps light gray) to identify it.

There are many other ways of calculating class size available in GIS (Geographic Information System) and mapping software. A group of methods called **optimal** tries to find natural breaks between the intervals. One of the most popular among cartographers is the **Fisher-Jenks algorithm**, which is applied on **Figure 10.28**. The results are similar to Figure 10.25.

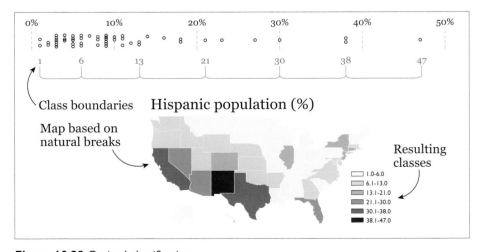

Figure 10.28 Optimal classification.

Software tools will also let you design non-classed choropleth maps, in which the color scale is a gradient, as on **Figure 10.29**.

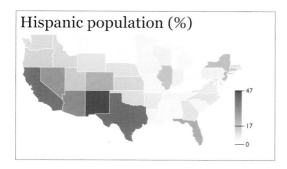

Hispanic population (%)

Figure 10.29: Unclassified choropleth map.

Using Choropleth Maps

A single choropleth map can be effective at revealing potential stories, but often the best approach when exploring data is to put several maps side by side. Compare **Figure 10.30** to **Figure 10.31** and **Figure 10.32**, and see if you notice promising patterns that are worth analyzing with the help of experts in public health statistics.

Maps should often be combined with linked charts or tables to achieve a richer understanding. **Figure 10.33** is an interactive visualization by the **Berliner Morgenpost** that includes a non-classed choropleth map of crime rates per 1,000 people in Berlin, a search box, and a sortable ranking and bar chart.

The Berliner Morgenpost has published many other fine data maps with elegant color schemes. **Figure 10.34** uses shades of blue and orange to identify neighborhoods in the city inhabited mainly by native Berliners or by people born in other places.

Figure 10.30 Map by the Pew Research Center. Notice the high proportion of seniors in areas like South and West Florida.

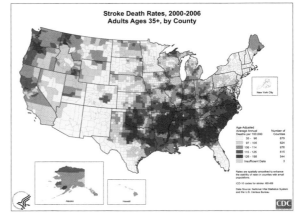

Figure 10.31 Map by Schieb L. "Stroke Death Rates, 2000-2006, Adults Ages 35+, by County." May 2011. Centers for Disease Control and Prevention. Notice that strokes are more common in the South, but not necessarily in the areas with a higher proportion of elderly people.

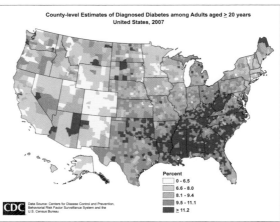

Figure 10.32 Map by Karen Kirtland. 2007 Estimates of the Percentage of Adults with Diagnosed Diabetes Division of Diabetes Translation, Centers for Disease Control and Prevention. Diabetes tends to concentrate in the same counties as stroke.

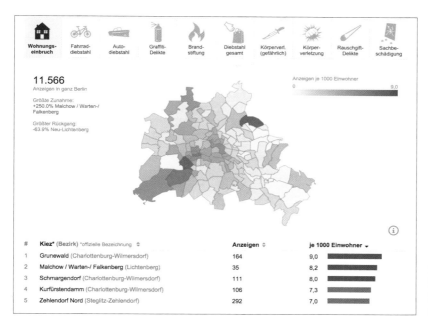

Figure 10.33 Crime in Berlin. Berliner Morgenpost: http://tinyurl.com/owuf6w6.

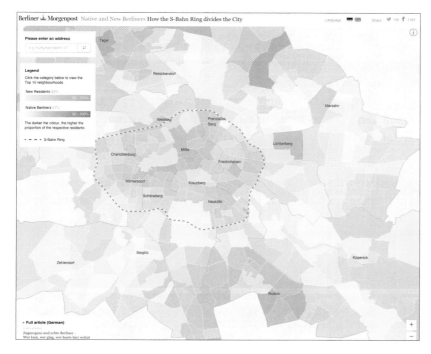

Figure 10.34 "Native and New Berliners." Berliner Morgenpost: http://tinyurl.com/p8upc94.

Figure 10.35 "Where the population of Europe is growing— and where it's declining." Berliner Morgenpost: http://tinyurl.com/nvq9b49.

The same colors are applied on the diverging color scheme on **Figure 10.35**: shades of blue for regions in Europe where population shrank between 2001 and 2011, and shades of orange for those that experienced growth. Gray identifies areas that remained unchanged.

Color schemes in choropleth maps can become quite complex. See **Figure 10.36** for an example. Here, analysts at the Centers for Disease Control and Prevention (CDC) categorized counties according to poverty rates and spatial concentration. The way classes on this map were calculated isn't disclosed, unfortunately, but the result is still persuasive.

A very well-known shortcoming of choropleth maps is that regions in the world vary wildly in size. Imagine that you do a world map of child mortality rates. Large countries such as Brazil, Russia, and the U.S. will stand out, while small countries with relatively large population densities (Israel, Switzerland) will be almost invisible. We face this same problem when designing maps of most countries. In the case of the U.S., large but sparsely populated states like Montana and the Dakotas will look more prominent than small but densely populated ones, like Massachusetts.

There are several strategies to overcome this challenge; most of them are based on disposing of geographical reality and designing very abstract diagrams like the one on **Figure 10.37**, by ProPublica, where all states are transformed into circles of identical size.

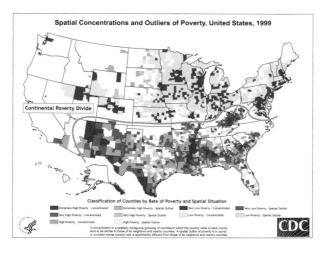

Figure 10.36 Spatial Concentrations and Outliers of Poverty, United States, 1999 James B. Holt, Centers for Disease Control and Prevention.

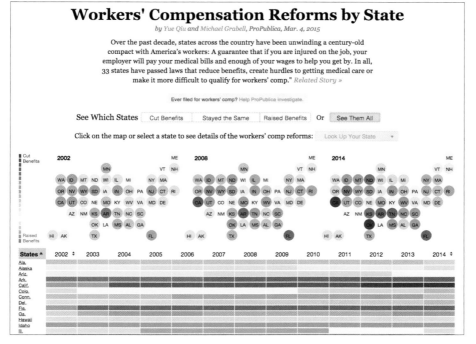

Figure 10.37 "Workers' Compensation Reforms by State." ProPublica: http://projects.propublica.org/graphics/workers-comp-reform-by-state.

If circles on that visualization had been sized in proportion to population, we'd end up with a **cartogram**. A cartogram is a map in which areas are scaled up or down based on some magnitude. **Figure 10.38**, by Zeit Online, is both a cartogram and a choropleth map: each country is represented by a rectangle that expands or shrinks according to the total amount of Catholics. Shades of blue encode the percentage of the population that is Catholic.

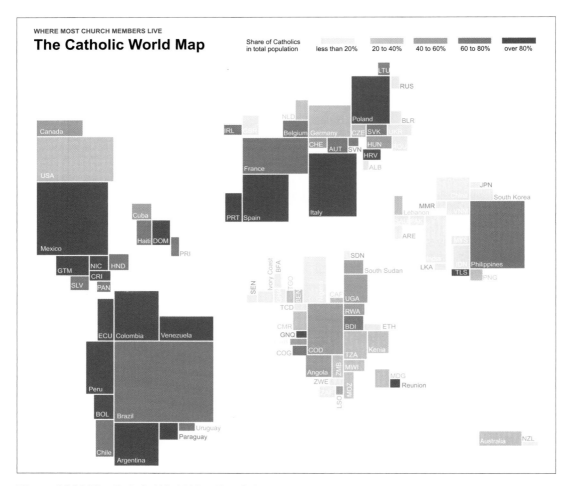

Figure 10.38 The Catholic World Map, Zeit Online.

Other Kinds of Data Maps

This chapter has covered the basics of proportional symbol maps and choropleth maps, but there are many other kinds of maps capable of displaying data.

Often, data can't be properly encased within neatly defined spatial units such as countries, provinces, or zip codes. Think of the weather and temperature maps you often see in the news. They are examples of **isarithmic maps**, or contour maps. **Figure 10.39** is a good example. Here, the boundaries of each color splotch are drawn by connecting points of equal value.[6] In this case, these points share the same density of deaths due to heart disease.

Shapes in isarithmic maps don't need to be curvy and smooth. The maps on **Figure 10.40** are divided into hexagons that don't really correspond to any German administrative units.

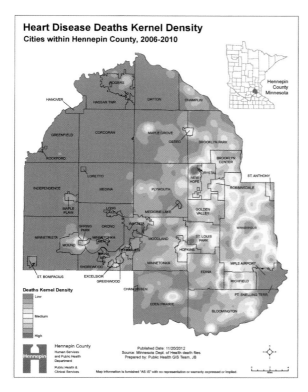

Figure 10.39 Map by Brondum J. "Heart Disease Deaths Kernel Density, Hennepin County, Minnesota." November 2012. Hennepin County Human Services and Public Health Department.

---

6 The prefix "iso" means "same," as in "isomorphism," which means "having the same form."

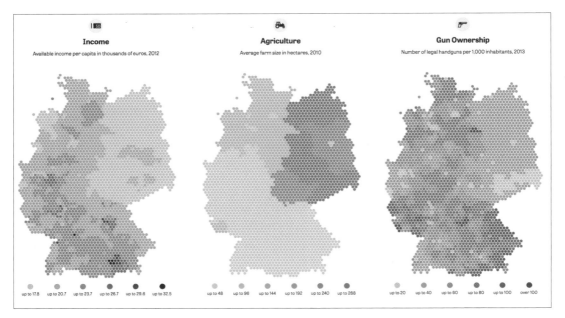

Figure 10.40 Maps from "A Nation Divided," Zeit Online:
http://zeit.de/feature/german-unification-a-nation-divided.
Notice the stark differences between West Germany and East Germany.

Cartographers, designers, and coders are constantly experimenting with unusual map varieties. To end this chapter, I'd like to point out **Figure 10.41**, an interactive map by Estado de São Paulo. Colors correspond to the party that won in each district in the 2010 Presidential election. Red is PT (Partido dos Trabalhadores) and blue is for PSDB (Partido da Social Democracia Brasileira.)

The height of each peak is proportional to the difference of votes in favor of the winning party. I am not a huge fan of 3D data displays, but this case is special, as readers can rotate the map at will to see it from different angles.

Figure 10.42, by Mike Bostock, and **Figure 10.43**, by Jason Davies, are **Voronoi maps** of distances to airports. In Voronoi maps and diagrams, surfaces are tesselated into polygons, each with a dot inside. Each polygon is drawn in a way that all points within it are closer to the central dot than to any other dot on the display. Interact with these maps. You'll be bewitched.

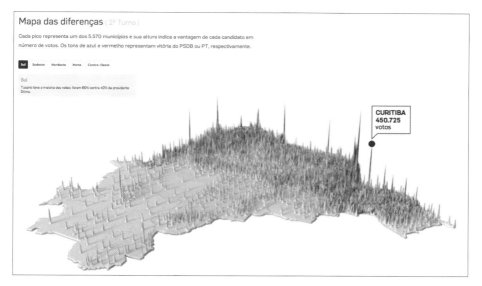

Figure 10.41 Estado de São Paulo. Presidential election results:
http://infograficos.estadao.com.br/politica/resultado-eleicoes-2014/.

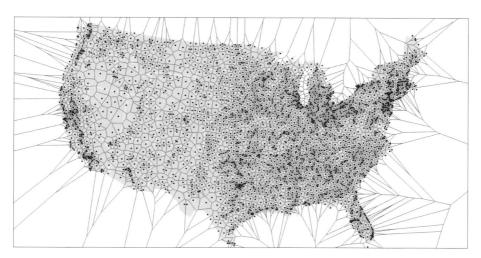

Figure 10.42 Voronoi map of U.S. airports, by Mike Bostock:
http://bl.ocks.org/mbostock/4360892.

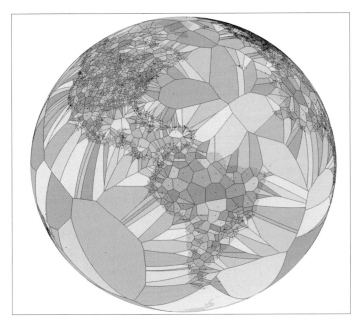

Figure 10.43 Interactive 3D Voronoi map of world airports, by Jason Davies: https://www.jasondavies.com/maps/voronoi/airports/.

To Learn More

- For a good introduction of how to design good color schemes for maps, read Rob Simmon's series of six articles titled "Subtleties of Color." You can find them here: http://earthobservatory.nasa.gov/blogs/elegantfigures/2013/08/05/subtleties-of-color-part-1-of-6/.

- ColorBrewer is an excellent follow-up to Simmon's articles. It lets you choose color schemes that are appropriate for colorblind people and are print-friendly, photocopy-safe, etc. See http://colorbrewer2.org/.

- Brewer, Cynthia. *Designing Better Maps: A Guide for GIS Users*. Redlands, CA: ESRI, 2005. Brewer is one of the people behind ColorBrewer. This book is an excellent introduction to the principles behind that tool.

- MacEachren, Alan M. *How Maps Work: Representation, Visualization, and Design*. New York: Guilford, 1995. Its title says it all.

- Monmonier, Mark S. *How to Lie with Maps*. Chicago: University of Chicago, 1991. This is the most concise primer on map design I've ever read. Its title should actually be "How NOT to Lie with Maps."

- Peterson, Gretchen N. *Cartographer's Toolkit: Colors, Typography, Patterns*. Fort Collins, CO: PetersonGIS, 2012. A good book to have by your side when choosing styles for your maps.

- Slocum, Terry A. *Thematic Cartography and Geovisualization* (3rd edition). Upper Saddle River, NJ: Pearson Prentice Hall, 2009. The bible of data mapping.

||

Uncertainty and Significance

Quantitative knowing is dependent on qualitative knowledge (…) In quantitative data analysis, numbers map onto aspects of reality. Numbers themselves are meaningless unless the data analyst understands the mapping process and the nexus of theory and categorization in which objects under study are conceptualized.

—John T. Behrens, "Principles and Procedures of Exploratory Data Analysis"

"Catalan public opinion swings toward 'no' for independence, says survey," read the December 19, 2014, headline of the Spanish newspaper *El País*.[1] Catalonia has always been a region where national sentiments run strong, but independentism hadn't been a critical issue for the Spanish government in Madrid until the last quarter of 2012. Catalonia's president, Artur Mas, said that the time had come for the region to be granted the right of self-determination.

Between 2012 and 2014, public opinion in Catalonia was divided between those who desired it to become an independent state and those who didn't. The former were more than the latter, particularly in 2012 and 2013, when mass demonstrations for the independence of that region were frequent.

---

1   The English version of the article, which—and this is decisive—doesn't include the charts or the margin of error of the survey:
http://elpais.com/elpais/2014/12/19/inenglish/1419000488_941616.html.

El País's story was based on data from the Catalan government's survey institute, the Centre d'Estudis d'Opinió (CEO). As the first chart on **Figure 11.1** shows, the situation in Catalonia had reversed: there were now more people against independence than in favor of it.

Or were there?

There was a crucial data point buried in the story: the margin of error of the survey was 2.95 percentage points. *El País* commented that this was "a relevant fact, considering how close the yes and the no to independence are." Indeed. This should have rung some serious alarms. Let's plot the same data with that margin of error (second chart in Figure 11.1) around them.

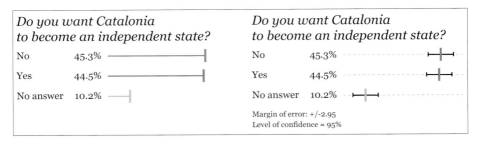

Figure 11.1 Displaying the margin of error can change your view of the data.

The margin of error is just another name for the upper and lower boundaries of a **confidence interval**, a concept we'll learn about soon. If you visit *El País's* source,[2] you'll see that they disclosed the technical specifications of the survey: a sample of 1,100 people—which I assume is random—and an error of +/-2.95 around the point estimates (45.3 percent, 44.5 percent, etc.) with a level of confidence of 95 percent.

Here's what the researchers mean, translated to proper English: "If we were able to conduct this exact same survey—same methods, same sample size, and a completely different random set of respondents—100 times, we estimate that in 95 of them, the confidence interval will contain the actual percentages for 'yes' and 'no'." We can't say the same of the other five samples."

The margin of error hints at a challenge to *El País's* story: the 45.3 percent and the 44.5 percent figures are much closer to each other than they are from the

---

2   English summary of the survey: http://tinyurl.com/qxfnm44.

boundaries of the confidence interval. Based on this, it seems risky to me to write a four-column headline affirming that one is truly greater than the other. This tiny difference could be the product of a glitch in the survey or of simple random noise in the data.

When two scores have non-overlapping confidence intervals, you may assume that they are indeed different. However, the opposite isn't true: the fact that confidence intervals do overlap on a chart, as it happens in this survey, isn't proof that there isn't a difference between them. What to do in this case?

Let's begin with a guess. We're going to play the devil's advocate and assume there *isn't* a difference, that the real split among the citizens of Catalonia is even: 50 percent want Catalonia to become independent, and 50 percent don't. So our assumption is that the real difference between "yes" and "no" is zero percentage points. This assumption of no difference is called a **null hypothesis**.

After we have posed this hypothesis, we receive the results of an appropriately sized survey, based on solid polling methods, and it tells us that it has measured a difference of 0.8 points (45.3 percent minus 44.5 percent). What is the probability that this result, which is not that far from a zero difference, is the product of mere chance?

The answer is more than 80 percent.[3] A statistician would say that the difference isn't statistically significant,[4] which simply means that it's so tiny that it's

---

3   I didn't do anything by hand, but relied on software, as usual. There are many pretty good, free tools for this kind of calculation online. See this one, by Vassar College: http://faculty.vassar.edu/lowry/polls/calcs.html. You just need to input the two proportions you wish to compare and the sample size. The website http://newsurveyshows.com also has a lot of useful tools. The math behind all those websites is related to what is explained in this chapter, but it lies beyond my purposes in this book.

4   My friend Jerzy Wieczorek (http://www.civilstat.com), a PhD candidate in statistics at Carnegie Mellon University at the moment of this writing, reminds me that statistical significance, a concept we'll explore later, isn't so much about what the "true" values are so much as about how precisely we measure things. When I asked him about El País's story, Jerzy suggested the following analogy:

"Imagine a literal horse race, where the judges chose inexpensive stopwatches which are accurate to within +/- 1 second 95 percent of the time. The watches' readouts display an extra decimal place, but you can't trust it.

"In this race, the top two horses' stopwatches put Horse A at 45.3 seconds and Horse B at 44.5 seconds. It looks like Horse B was faster. But given the precision of your stopwatches, Horse A could plausibly have been (say) 44.8 seconds while Horse B could plausibly have been (say) 45.1 seconds. Maybe Horse A was actually faster.

Now you wish you'd bought the other (really expensive) stopwatches which are accurate to within +/- 0.1 seconds 95 percent of the time. But you didn't, so all you can honestly say with this data is that the race was too close to call."

indistinguishable from noise. If I were the editor in charge of the first page of *El País* that day, I wouldn't have written that headline. We cannot claim that the "yes" is greater than the "no," or vice versa. The data doesn't let us affirm that with aplomb.

In case *El País* wanted to find an alternative headline, another figure lurking in the story sounds promising to me: the percentage of people who favor independence in Catalonia has dropped from nearly 50 percent in 2013 to the current 44.5 percent. Assuming that those figures come from polls with identical sample sizes and methods, the difference (5.5 points) is well beyond the margin of error. The probability of getting such a drop due to mere chance is less than 0.001 percent. That's significant.

Where did all these numbers come from? To begin to understand it, I need to give you a sweeping tour through the mysterious world of standard errors, confidence intervals, and how to plot them. To follow the rest of this chapter, you need to remember some previous material:

- Chapter 4, which is an elementary introduction to the methods of science.

- From Chapter 6: the mean.

- From Chapter 7: the standard deviation, standard scores (also called z-scores), and the properties of the normal distribution.

Back to Distributions

Suppose you wish to get an idea of the heights of 12-year-old girls in your town. You know little of what this population looks like—you don't have a budget to measure hundreds or thousands of girls—but its unknown shape is represented in the top histogram of **Figure 11.2**.[5] Even if I designed a normal-looking curve, remember that the distribution may not be normal.

---

5   Statisticians have come up with some jokes about distribution shapes. See Matthew Freeman's "A visual comparison of normal and paranormal distributions," http://www.ncbi.nlm.nih.gov/pmc/articles/PMC2465539/.

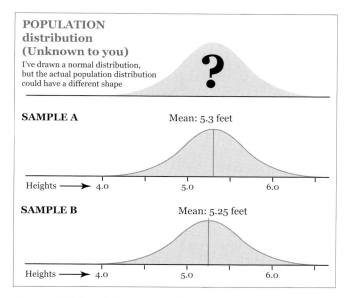

Figure 11.2 Population and samples.

Remember that a histogram is a frequency curve: the X-axis represents the score ranges, and the height of the curve is proportional to the amount of scores. The higher the curve, the more girls there are of that particular height.

You randomly choose a sample (A) of 40 girls, measure them and get a distribution like the second histogram. Its mean is 5.3 feet—a bit more than 5 feet and 3 inches—with a standard deviation of 0.5.

A different researcher draws a similar sample (B) using the same methods and gets a mean of 5.25 feet (exactly 5 feet and 3 inches) and the same standard deviation. The means of samples A and B are very close to each other. That's a promising clue that they are good approximations to the population mean.

However, if we draw tons of random samples of the same size from the population, it is also possible to obtain a few sample means that look far-fetched, such as the ones of C and D, on **Figure 11.3**.

These are possible, but not as likely as A and B if the true mean of the population is close to 5.3 feet (something we don't know, but let's assume for a moment that we do). Why? Here comes a critical idea: **think of the histogram not just as a distribution of the number of girls of each height, but as a *probability* chart**.

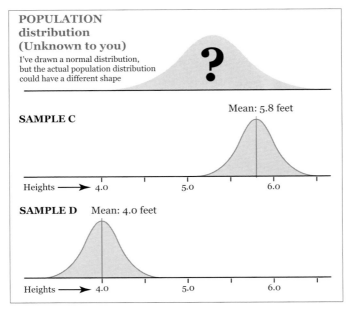

Figure 11.3 When drawing many samples from a population, it is possible to obtain a few with means that greatly differ from the population mean.

This is what I mean: our population histogram curve is very high in the middle section. A lot of scores lie in that part of the distribution. It is very low on the tails, so just a few girls can be found at either extreme of the chart. Imagine that you pick just one girl at random from the population and measure her height. Which would be more likely: that her height is between 4.8 and 5.8 feet (that's the mean of sample A plus/minus one standard deviation of 0.5) or that it is equal or higher than, say, 6.8 (the mean of sample A plus three standard deviations)?

If the distribution of heights in the population is roughly normal (and, again, *we don't know this*), your answer can be inspired by a chart we saw in Chapter 7 (**Figure 11.4**), which displays the percentage of scores that lie in between a certain number of standard deviations from the mean. We see that 68.2 percent of scores lie between –1 and 1 standard deviations from the mean, and just 0.1 percent of scores are above three standard deviations.

(Remember that the number of standard deviations away from the mean are called **standard scores, or z-scores**. If a specific value in your sample is 1.5 standard deviations away from the sample mean, its z-score is 1.5.)

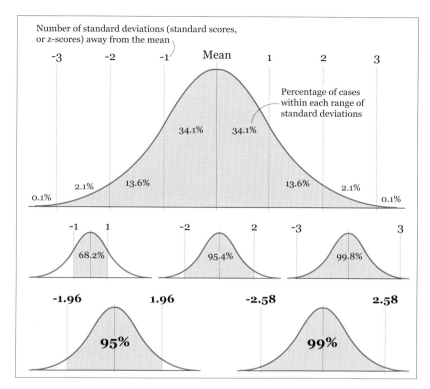

Figure 11.4 A reminder of the standard normal distribution.

I have made a couple of additions to the chart. They will become relevant in the next section:

- In a standard normal distribution, **95 percent of the scores lie between z-scores –1.96 and 1.96** (that is, between –1.96 and 1.96 standard deviations from the mean).

- Also in a standard normal distribution, **99 percent of the scores lie between z-scores –2.58 and 2.58** (they are between –2.58 and 2.58 standard deviations from the mean).

The Standard Error

I am asking a lot from your imagination, but I'll need you to make some extra effort. Bear with me for a few more pages. Use **Figure 11.5** to understand the following lines.

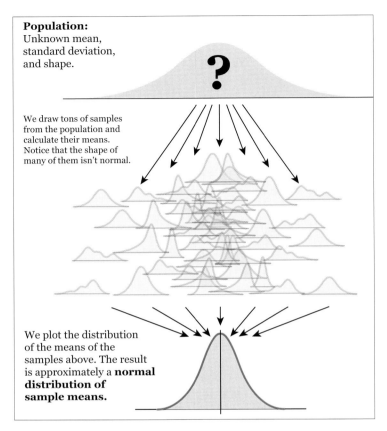

Population:
Unknown mean,
standard deviation,
and shape.

We draw tons of samples
from the population and
calculate their means.
Notice that the shape of
many of them isn't normal.

We plot the distribution
of the means of the
samples above. The result
is approximately a **normal
distribution of
sample means.**

Figure 11.5 The distribution of (imaginary) sample means.

Imagine that instead of drawing just a few samples from our population, we are able to get dozens of random samples of 40 girls each and that we calculate the mean of each of them. There's no need to draw them in reality. Just imagine that we can.

Next, imagine that we discard all scores from all samples, and that **we just keep their means**. Then, we draw a histogram of *just of these means*. This imaginary histogram is called **a distribution of sample means**.

As any other distribution, it will have a mean of its own (*a mean of sample means*) and a standard deviation. This standard deviation of many imaginary sample means is called **the standard error of the mean.**

The histogram of the distribution of our imaginary samples will have an approximately normal shape.[6] To understand why, remember what I said about the samples in Figure 11.3: every time we draw a sample, its mean can be equal, greater, or smaller than the mean of the population. If we take thousands and thousands of samples, most of them will have means that are a bit above or below the mean of the population, and just a few samples will have means that are very far from the population mean. In other words, samples with means that are close to the population mean are more probable than samples with means that are far from the population mean.

If you plot the means of all those imaginary samples, and then you calculate the standard deviation of that distribution of means, what you get is an estimate of error—**how much the mean of a sample of that specific size** (40 girls in our example) **might deviate, on average, from the population mean, measured in number of standard scores. This is what the standard error of the mean is.**

Here's how to compute the standard error of the mean (SE):

SE = Standard deviation of our sample / √Sample size.

Our sample has a size of 40 and a standard deviation of 0.5. Therefore:

SE = 0.5 / √40 = 0.5/6.32 = **0.08**

The size of the standard error is inversely proportional to the square root of the sample size. Here's the proof:

For a sample with a size of just 10 girls:

SE = 0.5 / √10 = 0.5/3.16 = **0.16**

For a sample with a size of 500 girls:

SE = 0.5 / √500 = 0.5/22.36 = **0.02**

So the larger the sample, the smaller the standard error will be. Bringing the standard error down is costly, though, because the relationship between sample size and standard errors follows a law of diminishing returns. For instance,

---

6   This is the Central Limit Theorem, a cornerstone in mathematics: with few exceptions (like distributions with very extreme scores), regardless of what the real shape of the population distribution is, if you calculate the means of a very large amount of large samples with the same size, and then you plot those means in a histogram, the resulting distribution will be normal.

multiplying your sample size by four will only cut the standard error in *half*, not make it a quarter of what it was before.

For a sample with a size of 20 girls:

SE = 0.5 / $\sqrt{20}$ = 0.5/4.47 = **0.11**

For a sample with a size of 80 girls (20 × 4):

SE = 0.5 / $\sqrt{80}$ = 0.5/8.94 = **0.056**

Moreover, it's impossible to reach a standard error of 0. Imagine that we could draw a sample of 1,000,000 girls. We'd still have some error, dammit!

SE = 0.5 / $\sqrt{1,000,000}$ = 0.5/1,000 = **0.0005**

Finally, as you've probably noticed, the standard error can be computed even if we don't know the size of the population that our sample is intended to represent. What really matters to reduce the amount of uncertainty isn't the size of the population per se, but the size of our samples and if they have been drawn following the strict rules of random sampling.

Building Confidence Intervals

A confidence interval is an expression of the uncertainty around any statistic you wish to report. It's based on the standard error, and it's usually communicated this way:

"With a 95 percent level of confidence, we estimate that the average height of 12-year-old girls is 5.3 feet +/-(margin of error here.)"

Remember that this also means, "If we could draw 100 samples of the same size, we estimate that in 95 of them the actual value we're analyzing would lie within their confidence intervals. We cannot say the same of the remaining five samples!"

To compute a confidence interval first, you need to decide on a **confidence level**. The most common ones are 95 percent and 99 percent, although you could really pick any figure you wish. What we need to remember is that **the greater the confidence level we choose, the greater the margin of error becomes**.

You can calculate confidence intervals of any statistic: means, correlation coefficients, proportions, etc. I'm going to give you just a few simple examples and refer you to the recommended readings if your brain tickles with excitement afterward.

Let's begin with the confidence interval for the mean of a sample. The average height of girls in our sample was 5.3 feet, and the standard deviation was 0.5. The 5.3 score is a **point estimate**. Reporting it on its own isn't correct. We must also disclose the uncertainty that surrounds it. The formulas for the confidence interval of the mean of a large sample and how to apply them are in **Figure 11.6**.

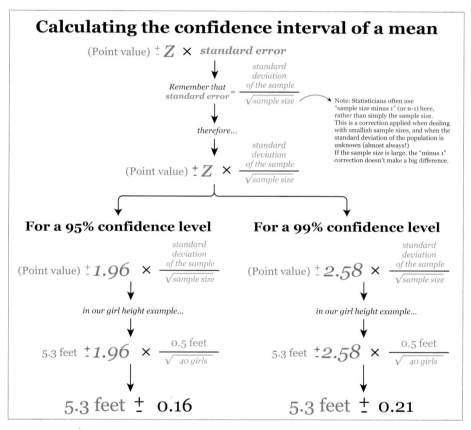

Figure 11.6 Calculating the confidence interval of a large sample mean.

The z in red is called the **critical value**, and it's closely related to the confidence level and to z-scores. A few pages ago we saw that in a standard normal distribution, 95 percent of the scores lie between –1.96 and 1.96 standard deviations, and 99 percent lie between –2.58 and 2.58. Therefore, we use a 1.96 critical value in our formula when we wish to build a 95 percent confidence interval and 2.58 when our preference is a 99 percent confidence interval.

Things get trickier if your sample is small, say 12 or 15 girls. In a case like this, statisticians have shown that the distribution of sample means isn't necessarily normal. Therefore, using a z-score as critical value isn't an option.

When a sample is small and the standard deviation of the population is unknown, the distribution of the sample means may adopt the shape of a t distribution, whose tails are fatter than those of a normal distribution. Don't worry about the details of t distributions. Just remember this simple formula: small sample size = not normal.

So how to decide which critical value to use in our confidence interval formula instead of 1.96 or 2.58?

First, get your sample size. Let's suppose just 15 girls were measured. Subtract 1 from the sample size, so you get 14 (to understand why, refer to the bibliography and look for "degrees of freedom"). After that, decide on the confidence level you wish, 95 or 99 percent. With all that, go to the table on **Figure 11.7** and follow its instructions.

As you can see on that table, for a sample size of 15, we need to go to the 14th row (15 – 1 = 14). Then we need to take a look at the two other columns: for a confidence level of 95 percent, our critical value is 2.145, and for 99 percent, it is 2.977. The resulting formulas are on **Figure 11.8**.

Read the table again and notice that the larger our sample size gets, the closer the t critical values get to 1.96 (if you chose a 95 percent confidence level) and 2.58 (when it's 99 percent). The reason is that the larger a sample size is, the more similar the shape of the t-distribution becomes like our lovely normal distribution. This is why some statisticians say that, when your sample size is truly large, even if the standard deviation of the population is unknown, you can use z-critical values, as I explained on Figure 11.6. **Other statisticians recommend to *always* use t-critical values, regardless of sample size**.

For smaller samples, the t-critical values are larger than z-critical values. You can think of this as an extra fudge factor: with a small sample, your results are less precise, and the t values help to make the confidence interval wider so that you don't overstate your certainty.

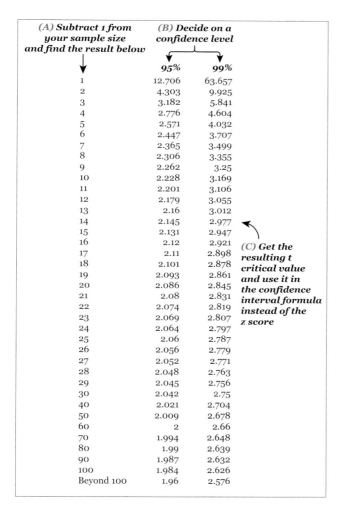

(A) Subtract 1 from your sample size and find the result below	(B) Decide on a confidence level	
	95%	99%
1	12.706	63.657
2	4.303	9.925
3	3.182	5.841
4	2.776	4.604
5	2.571	4.032
6	2.447	3.707
7	2.365	3.499
8	2.306	3.355
9	2.262	3.25
10	2.228	3.169
11	2.201	3.106
12	2.179	3.055
13	2.16	3.012
14	2.145	2.977
15	2.131	2.947
16	2.12	2.921
17	2.11	2.898
18	2.101	2.878
19	2.093	2.861
20	2.086	2.845
21	2.08	2.831
22	2.074	2.819
23	2.069	2.807
24	2.064	2.797
25	2.06	2.787
26	2.056	2.779
27	2.052	2.771
28	2.048	2.763
29	2.045	2.756
30	2.042	2.75
40	2.021	2.704
50	2.009	2.678
60	2	2.66
70	1.994	2.648
80	1.99	2.639
90	1.987	2.632
100	1.984	2.626
Beyond 100	1.96	2.576

(C) Get the resulting t critical value and use it in the confidence interval formula instead of the z score

Figure 11.7 How to obtain the t critical value to use in your confidence interval formula when your sample is small.

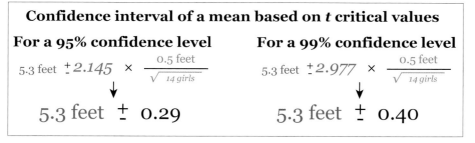

Confidence interval of a mean based on t critical values

For a 95% confidence level

$$5.3 \text{ feet } \pm 2.145 \times \frac{0.5 \text{ feet}}{\sqrt{14 \text{ girls}}}$$

$$5.3 \text{ feet } \pm 0.29$$

For a 99% confidence level

$$5.3 \text{ feet } \pm 2.977 \times \frac{0.5 \text{ feet}}{\sqrt{14 \text{ girls}}}$$

$$5.3 \text{ feet } \pm 0.40$$

Figure 11.8 Updating our confidence interval formula, using a small sample size and t critical values rather than z critical values.

A few final notes:

- Many papers report confidence intervals (CI) following a format similar to this: Mean = 23.3, 95 percent CI 20.3–26.3 (the lower limit of the confidence level is 20.3, and 26.3 is the upper limit). Doing some arithmetic, we can see that the margin of error here is +/- 3.0, for a 95 percent confidence level.

- Just to give you another quick example of how to compute confidence intervals, follow the instructions and example on **Figure 11.9**, if you're dealing with percentages.

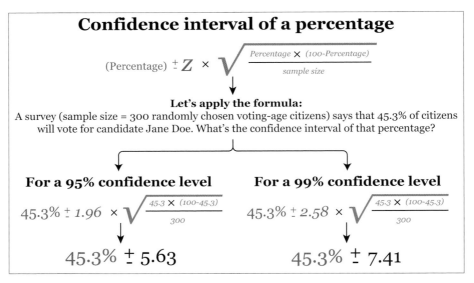

Figure 11.9 Confidence intervals for a percentage. Sometimes researchers add a correction to this formula based on ratio between the sample size and the underlying population.

Disclosing Uncertainty

Confidence intervals are a means to envision the uncertainty in our data. This uncertainty is crucial information, as visualizations or stories that mention only point estimates, without the padding that surrounds them—and these include the graphics in this book so far, and many that I have produced in my career as a journalist and designer—convey an unjustified feeling of strict accuracy.

The most straightforward way of communicating the uncertainty in a visualization is as a note in your graphic. However, if it's feasible, **work to find a way**

to display it on the visualization itself in a manner that doesn't clutter it.[7] In **Figure 11.10**, you have three elementary methods, two of them based on error bars. These and their many variations have been in use for decades, but they have come under criticism in the past few years due to their shortcomings.

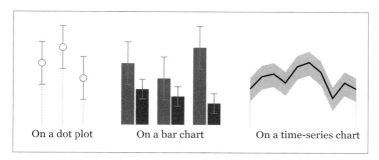

On a dot plot On a bar chart On a time-series chart

Figure 11.10 Elementary methods for visualizing uncertainty, based on error bars.

The most obvious one is that error bars have an all-or-nothing quality, which can lead to misleading inferences. Roughly speaking, a confidence interval works as a probability distribution: scores closer to its upper and lower boundaries are less likely, in theory, than scores close to the point estimate we are reporting. This feature is hidden in error bars.

To address this problem, in a paper presented at the 2015 IEEE (Institute of Electrical and Electronics Engineers) VIS conference in Paris,[8] University of Madison-Wisconsin computer scientists **Michael Correll** and **Michael Gleicher** discussed alternative classic methods of showing uncertainty: the gradient plot, the violin plot, and a modified box plot not based on the median or quartiles, as the classic one invented by John Tukey, seen in Chapter 7 (**Figure 11.11**).

Gradient plots and fuzzy error bars or backgrounds are design strategies that have been pursued by other designers, like **Alex Krusz**, who developed a fun web tool to visualize data sets with different variances (**Figure 11.12**).[9] Vienna

---

7 Here are a couple of good introductions to uncertainty in visualization: "A Review of Uncertainty in Data Visualization," by Ken Brodlie, Rodolfo Allendes Osorio, and Adriano Lopes (http://tinyurl.com/nwbkm6f) and a blog post by Andy Kirk at http://tinyurl.com/kqjnh94.

8 Michael Correll and Michael Gleicher: "Error Bars Considered Harmful: Exploring Alternate Encodings for Mean and Error," https://graphics.cs.wisc.edu/Papers/2014/CG14/.

9 The tool is at http://krusz.net/uncertainty/; its source code is at https://github.com/akrusz/dragon-letters and Krusz's article explaining it all is at http://tinyurl.com/q2fj23f.

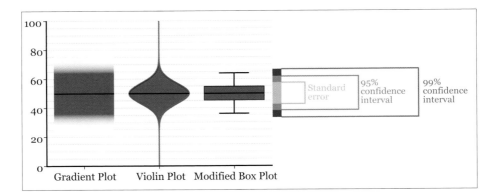

Figure 11.11 Alternative ways of displaying a point estimate (a mean, for instance) and confidence intervals. The gradient blue box serves as a comparison.

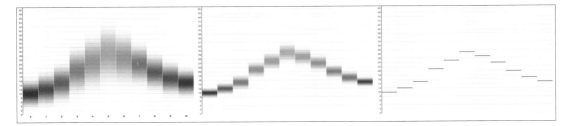

Figure 11.12 Charts displaying data with decreasing variances, by Alex Krusz.

Institute of Demography's statistician **Guy Abel** has even created a package for the R programming language, called "fanplot," which creates charts emulating the plots that the Bank of England has used in its forecasts since 1997 (**Figure 11.13**).

Uncertainty can also be revealed on maps. Living in Florida, one faces uncertainty almost every year during hurricane season. In **Figure 11.14**, a map from the National Oceanic and Atmospheric Administration (NOAA) shows the probable path of Hurricane Charley in 2004. As this is a forecast, the error area gets wider the more the line moves away from the latest current location, 5 p.m., Friday on the map.[10]

---

10 Visualizing uncertainty on maps has concerned cartographers for ages. Read Igor Drecki's "Representing Geographical Information Uncertainty: Cartographic Solutions and Challenges" for an overview of techniques and relevant literature: http://tinyurl.com/pawvyty, and Alan MacEachren, et al., "Visualizing Geospatial Information Uncertainty: What We Know and What We Need to Know," http://tinyurl.com/o6tpsuj. Also by MacEachren is "Visualizing Uncertain Information," http://tinyurl.com/oxmfk88.

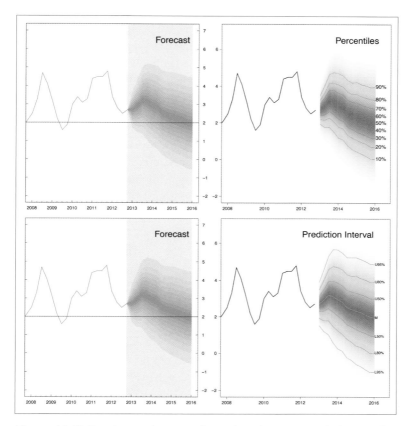

Figure 11.13 Fan chart with percentiles and prediction intervals (not confidence intervals.) (By Guy Abel. Source: http://journal.r-project.org/archive/2015-1/abel.pdf).

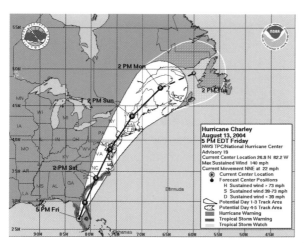

Figure 11.14 A hurricane forecast map (NOAA).

The Best Advice You'll Ever Get: Ask

Journalists and designers usually don't generate their own data, but instead obtain it from sources such as government agencies, non-profit organizations, corporations, scientists, and so on. Many of those sources have a strong presence online, and they provide troves of information unthinkable just a decade ago.

Today, any aficionado with access to a computer, an Internet connection, and some popular (and free!) software tools can explore distributions, run a simple linear regression, estimate uncertainty, and then publish a story or visualization, all on her own. That's a recipe for disaster, as what she won't be able to do by herself is to assess if any of those findings are truly meaningful. For that, she'd need deep domain-specific knowledge.

So here's the most important piece of advice you'll ever get if you want to do visualization and infographics either as an amateur or a professional (I hinted at it in previous chapters): **the secret behind any successful data project is asking people who know a lot about the data at hand and its shortcomings, about how it was garnered, processed, and tested**.

If you have downloaded some data from public sources and explored it using the techniques explained in this book, **don't publish anything: take your hunches to experts**. Three are always better than two. Here's what **Scott Klein**, head of the news applications department at ProPublica, has to say about this:

> What differentiates journalism from other disciplines is that we always rely on the wisdom of smarter people. It is crucial that we talk to somebody even if we think that we perfectly understand a data set or the math we've done with it. Whenever we're working on a project at ProPublica, we always call people who can tell us we're wrong. We show them what we've done, how we've done it, what our assumptions are, the code we generated. All this is crucial to our ability to get things right.[11]

Any journalist will tell you that a key component of her job is to create, cultivate, and then extend a network of sources to consult when the time comes. Let me suggest a few germane questions to ask before *and* after you play with that inviting data set in the Downloads folder of your computer.

---

11   In "What Google's News Lab Means for Reporters, Editors, and Readers,"
http://contently.net/2015/07/02/resources/googles-news-lab-means-reporters-editors-readers/

How Has Stuff Been Measured?

Physicist **Werner Heisenberg** once said that what we observe is not nature itself but nature exposed to our method of questioning. The way we look at the world influences how we categorize and record our observations.

Statistician **Andrew Gelman** considers measurement "the number one neglected topic in statistics" and adds that it's a puzzling situation because measurement constitutes "the connection between the data you gather and the underlying object of your study."[12]

This is a big challenge for everyone, as there's an all-too-human temptation to take data at face value, oblivious to the famous dictum **"garbage in, garbage out."** If you begin with poor data, you will end up with poor conclusions. Fact-checking large data sets is beyond my skills, and I guess that most of you are in a similar situation. But there's still plenty we can do to begin assessing the quality of the sources we use.

Next time you download a spreadsheet from the United Nations or the International Monetary Fund—just to name two popular sources of country-level data—don't just look at its rows and columns. Read the documentation that usually accompanies spreadsheets. This is part of the **metadata**, or *data about the data*.[13] If no documentation is available, or if it is unclear or spotty, you'll need expert advice. Well, really, you'll need expert advice *regardless*.

Data from sources that are widely considered reliable shouldn't be free from scrutiny and skepticism. After studying the way African development figures are computed, **Morten Jerven**, an economist at Simon Fraser University (Canada) concluded:

> More than half of the rankings of African economies up to 2009 may be pure guesswork [and] about half of the underlying data for continent-wide growth statistics are actually missing and have been created by the World Bank through unclear procedures. The prevailing sentiment is that data availability is more important than the quality of the data that are supplied.[14]

---

12 "What's the most important thing in statistics that's not in the textbooks?" http://tinyurl.com/ntlkofa.

13 Similarly, if you publish a visualization or story based on any kind of data, you should disclose the methods you've used. This is becoming common practice in journalism, and I really hope that it will continue that way.

14 From *Poor Numbers: How We Are Misled By African Development Statistics and What to Do About It* (2013).

Similar dismaying messages are common in other books, like **Zachary Karabell's** *The Leading Indicators* (2014). Does all this mean that we should raise our hands up in the air and pray to Tlaloc, the rain god?[15] No. It just means that we need to be extra careful when dealing with data we haven't generated ourselves, even when numbers come from the most trusted sources.

Dispatches from the Data Jungle

Heather Krause is the founder of Datassist, a statistical consulting firm that specializes in visualization design and that also aids journalists and non-profit organizations in making sense of data. While I was working on this chapter, Heather shared with me several recent experiences that illustrate the amount of work that is often necessary to ascertain that the information you're planning to present is sound.

During a project about rural milk production in Bangladesh, Heather saw that one of the variables in the data sets she was analyzing was called "group gender composition" with possibilities of male, female, and mixed.

One day, while working in the field, Heather looked up from her laptop at some people fetching milk and noticed that there were only men in it. That didn't make a lot of sense. According to the data, that group had a female gender composition. Her field facilitator explained that the variable labeled "group gender composition" did not mean the actual gender makeup of all the members of the group. It meant *who the data collector thought was doing the actual work at home.*

Heather's conclusion is, "Never rely on a variable's name or your assumptions about the data to tell you what the numbers really represent." She then offered another example, even more illuminating:

> Understanding violence against women (intimate partner violence, or IPV) involves analyzing trends, exploring attitudes, and examining factors in its increase or decrease. It's complicated. Violence against women is a broad term with varying definitions and it often goes unreported. Who do you ask? All women? Married women? Women who have ever been in a relationship?

---

15   I wrote that line right after coming back from Mexico. Incidentally, I brought a Tlaloc stuffed doll for my 4-year-old daughter. In spite of Tlaloc being an ugly and menacing toothy beast, she loved it. The doll now occupies a place of honor in her bed, next to the teddy bear she's owned since she was born.

I often download datasets on IPV from various websites. During one project, I found data of the prevalence rate of IPV in Cameroon. The figures from different sources were anywhere from 9, 11, 14, 20, 29, 33, 39, 42, 45, to 51 percent. And this isn't unique to Cameroon. Similar patterns of wide variation exist in most countries [**Figure 11.15**].

Why the discrepancies? All the data was collected within a three-year span, much of it in the same year. The difference is what the data is specifically measuring. Upon reading the detailed metadata, the way different organizations measure IPV [see a summary in **Figure 11.16**] boils down to three main dimensions:

1. What is being measured?

What definition of intimate partner violence are the data collectors using? IPV can be measured in many ways. If you are giving a prevalence rate for IPV, does that include the rate of only physical violence? Or does it also include sexual violence? Does it include emotional violence? Does it count physical AND sexual violence or physical AND/OR sexual violence?

The definition of IPV that your data is based on is going to have a big difference in the rate you get. For example, in Cameroon the rate of physical IPV is reported at 45 percent, the rate of sexual at 20 percent, physical and/or sexual 51 percent.

2. Who is the population being measured?

What ages of women are covered in the data you have? Surveys vary widely from including only traditional fertility-aged women to including women of all ages—and many variations in between. This is an especially important piece of metadata if you want to compare trends over time. For example, in Peru the rate of physical violence in the past 12 months ranges from 11 to 14 percent depending on what ages are being included.

In a situation like IPV, the marital status of the women included in the survey is quite important to understand when using this data. Are you working with data that estimates the rate of partner violence among all women? Or the rate among currently married women? Or the rate of all women who have ever been in a relationship?

3. What time period is being measured?

Prevalence data needs to say clearly what time period it's measuring. Some IPV data measures violence experienced in the woman's lifetime; others measure violence experienced in the past 12 months, and others measure experiences in the last 5 years. This makes a significant difference in the results. In the USA, the rates of IPV even range from 20 to 36 percent while the rate of IPV in the previous 12 months range from 1 to 6 percent.

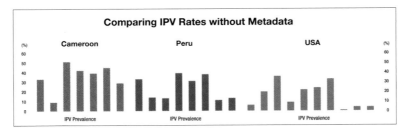

Figure 11.15 Bars represent the intimate partner violence rate (IPV) measured by several sources in these three countries. Notice the enormous differences. (Chart by Heather Krause, http://idatassist.com/.)

What is being counted by your number?

Select sources of data on IPV

		WHO	UN-HIV	NISVS	EU-VAW	WB	DHS	UN-POW	IVAWS
What's included?	Physical Violence	■	■	■	■	■	■	■	■
	Sexual Violence	■		■		■	■	■	
	Emotional Violence			■		■	■		
How old?	Age 15-49		■				■	■	
	Age 15-69	■				■			
	Age 18-69								■
	Age 18-74				■	■			
Who?	All Women			■		■			
	Ever Married Women	■			■	■	■		
	Marital Status Unspecified		■					■	■
When?	Lifetime			■	■	■	■	■	■
	Last Twelve Months		■			■	■	■	■

Figure 11.16 What is being measured when studying intimate partner violence rate (IPV)? (Chart by Heather Krause, http://idatassist.com/.)

Remember these tales next time you're tempted to write a story or design a visualization without doing some checking, asking sources, and then including footnotes, caveats, and explainers so readers understand the limitations and biases in the data.

Significance, Size, and Power

Much research is based on comparing statistics from different groups and estimating if discrepancies between them are likely to be due to chance or not. In many cases, scientists report *p* values, a term you've probably found (and dreaded) in the past.

Here's a definition by statistician **Alex Reinhart**: "A *p* value is the probability, under the assumption that there is no true effect or no true difference, of collecting data that shows a difference equal to or more extreme than what you actually observed."[16]

This is very confusing for someone with just a pedestrian understanding of statistics—me—so let's imagine that a team of social scientists wants to test if a particular learning technique has any effect on the reading skills of first-graders. We'll call the technique the "treatment" and the possible changes in student performance the "effect."

Ideally, they would proceed this way:

1. Researchers begin with the assumption that the new technique won't have any effect whatsoever on students' reading skills. This assumption is called a **null hypothesis**, as we learned before.

2. They draw a large random sample of students. Let's say 60.

3. They test those students' reading skills.

4. Students are randomly divided into two groups of 30. One of them is called the **experimental group** and will be taught using the novel technique for, say, a month. The other 30 students will keep receiving the same reading lessons they did before. They are the **control group**.

5. After a month, all students are tested again.

6. Researchers analyze the data and see if students in the experimental group have improved or not. The scientists compute the before and after performances of the experimental and control groups, and then they calculate if those differences (if they detect any, of course) might be the product of chance.

---

16 *Statistics Done Wrong* (2015). See the end of this chapter.

7. If researchers estimate that differences would be unlikely if they were the result of chance, they say that they got a statistically significant result. They will "reject the null," as the null is the hypothesis that said that there wouldn't be any differences between the experimental group and the control group after the treatment was applied to the former.

8. Researchers will express all this by writing something like "differences were such and such, and were statistically significant p<0.05 (or p<0.01)." That's the p-value. You can read 5 percent instead of 0.05 and 1 percent instead of 0.01 if it's easier for you.

The *p* value is the probability of measuring such differences (or larger ones) if there weren't really any differences between the experimental and the control group after the experimental group received the treatment. In other words, the *p* value is simply an estimation of how likely it is to measure such an effect by mere chance. It is the probability (again, 5 percent or 1 percent) of obtaining the data we obtained if the null hypothesis were true, if the difference between experimental group and the control group were zero.

It's important to understand what a *p* value is not: a p value is *not* the probability of the effect being *real*. It is *not* the probability of the scientist having found a relevant effect. And it doesn't imply that the researchers are 95 percent certain that our novel teaching technique is effective.

I can't stress these points enough, as they are the source of many bad news stories. They are also among the reasons why, even if p values are widely spread in science, it's extremely risky to read too much in them.[17]

Here's another reason: a **statistically significant effect can be *insignificant in logical or practical terms***, and a non-significant result obtained in an experiment can still be significant in the colloquial sense of the word. No statistical test can be a substitute to common sense and qualitative knowledge on the part of whoever is analyzing the data.

---

17 The literature criticizing the perfunctory use of p values in research is large, and it has merit, as p values are easily manipulated. For a summary, read "The Extent and Consequences of P-Hacking in Science" (http://tinyurl.com/np8jpef) and "Statistics: P values are just the tip of the iceberg" (http://tinyurl.com/nrpnh4a). Some experts in statistics argue that we should dispose of p values outright. Others say that p values are just one tool among many others, and that they are still valid if not used on their own.

Statistician **Jerzy Wieczorek** explained it well: "Statistics is not just a set of arbitrary yes/no hoops to jump through in the process of publishing a paper; it's a kind of applied epistemology," or of systematic reasoning.[18]

As a consequence, **a single research paper reporting a statistically significant result doesn't mean much**. It needs to be weighed against a solid prior understanding of the phenomena the data describes. **Replication is a cornerstone in science:**[19] the more studies show statistical significant effects, the more our uncertainty will shrink. As Carl Sagan used to repeat, "Extraordinary claims require extraordinary evidence." Beware of press reports about experiments or papers that claim to have found results that defy common knowledge. They will be likely just the result of chance.

Another feature to pay attention to when reading scientific papers is the **effect size**. Suppose that you're testing if a medicine is effective against the common cold. Getting a statistically significant result after testing it with people isn't enough because the p value tells you nothing about how large the effect of the medicine is.

It might be that tons of people in the experimental group felt better sooner after having the medicine than people in the control group who didn't get the treatment. That may be a statistically significant result, but perhaps not an important one. It may be that "sooner" means just "one hour less," so the medicine is not really worth much. The number of minutes is the effect size in this case, which we could actually call *practical significance*.

Effect sizes are connected to the **power** of the tests that researchers conduct. The statistical power of a test is the probability that the experiment will detect an effect of a particular size. Power is connected to sample size: a small sample may not be enough to detect tiny—but perhaps extremely relevant—effects, in which case we'd say that the test is **underpowered**.

On the other hand, an **overpowered** test, one in which the sample chosen is very large, may detect statistical significant effects that are irrelevant for practical purposes, maybe because the effect size is minimal. **Papers that don't report**

---

18 Epistemology is the study of what distinguishes justified belief from opinion. The article this quote came from is at http://tinyurl.com/obxcn8j.

19 Read Jeffrey T. Leek and Roger D. Peng's "Reproducible research can still be wrong: Adopting a prevention approach" at http://www.pnas.org/content/112/6/1645.

significance, effect sizes, and power together deserve extra skepticism, as a general rule.

The following example, from **Alex Reinhart**'s *Statistics Done Wrong*, illustrates the relationship between these properties. It also shows how crucial it is that citizens understand them, at least at a conceptual, non-mathematical level:[20]

> In the 1970s, many parts of the United States began allowing drivers to turn right at a red light. For many years prior, road designers and civil engineers argued that allowing right turns on a red light would be a safety hazard, causing many additional crashes and pedestrian deaths. But the 1973 oil crisis and its fallout spurred traffic agencies to consider allowing right turns on red to save fuel wasted by commuters waiting at red lights, and eventually Congress required states to allow right turns on red, treating it as an energy conservation measure just like building insulation standards and more efficient lighting.
>
> Several studies were conducted to consider the safety impact of the change. In one, a consultant for the Virginia Department of Highways and Transportation conducted a before-and-after study of 20 intersections that had begun to allow right turns on red. Before the change, there were 308 accidents at the intersections; after, there were 337 in a similar length of time. But this difference was not statistically significant, which the consultant indicated in his report. When the report was forwarded to the governor, the commissioner of the Department of Highways and Transportation wrote that "we can discern no significant hazard to motorists or pedestrians from implementation" of right turns on red. In other words, **he turned *statistical* insignificance into *practical* insignificance**.
>
> Several subsequent studies had similar findings: small increases in the number of crashes, but not enough data to conclude these increases were significant.
>
> Of course, these studies were underpowered. But more cities and states began to allow right turns on red, and the practice became widespread across the entire United States. Apparently, no one attempted to aggregate these many small studies to produce a more useful dataset. Meanwhile, more pedestrians were being run over, and more cars were involved in collisions. Nobody collected enough data to show this conclusively until several years later, when studies finally showed that among incidents involving right turns, collisions were occurring roughly 20 percent more

20 Reinhart's example is inspired by Ezra Hauer's "The harm done by tests of significance" at http://tinyurl.com/pevpye8.

frequently, 60 percent more pedestrians were being run over, and twice as many bicyclists were being struck.

Alas, the world of traffic safety has learned little from this example. A 2002 study, for example, considered the impact of paved shoulders on the accident rates of traffic on rural roads. Unsurprisingly, a paved shoulder reduced the risk of accident—but there was insufficient data to declare this reduction statistically significant, so the authors stated that the cost of paved shoulders was not justified. They performed no cost-benefit analysis because they treated the insignificant difference as meaning there was no difference at all, despite the fact that they had collected data suggesting that paved shoulders improved safety! **The evidence was not strong enough to meet their desired *p* value threshold**. A better analysis would have admitted that while it is plausible that shoulders have no benefit at all, the data is also consistent with them having substantial benefits. That means looking at confidence intervals.

To Learn More

- Field, Andy, Jeremy Miles, and Zoë Field. *Discovering Statistics Using R* (5th edition). Thousand Oaks, CA: SAGE. Don't be scared if you ever see this 1,000-page brick of a book in front of you. It's fun to read, and it comes in handy when you need a refresher about any statistics-related topic. Besides, Field, the main author, is an Iron Maiden fan. I guess that this makes the book more appealing just to me and other old-fashioned metalheads.

- Karabell, Zachary. *The Leading Indicators: A Short History of the Numbers That Rule Our World*. New York, NY: Simon & Schuster, 2014. After reading it, you'll never look at GDP figures the same way you did before.

- Reinhard, Alex T. *Statistics Done Wrong: The Woefully Complete Guide*. San Francisco, CA: No Starch Press, 2015. After studying a few intro to statistics textbooks, this little gem will tell you why many of your intuitions are flat wrong. Don't feel discouraged, though. You will learn a lot from it.

- Ziliak, Stephen T., and Deirdre N. McCloskey. *The Cult of Statistical Significance: How the Standard Error Costs Us Jobs, Justice, and Lives*. Ann Harbor, MI, The University of Michigan Press. The fiery title of its book can give you an idea of its style. Read it only after you've gotten a good grasp of elementary statistics.

PART IV

practice

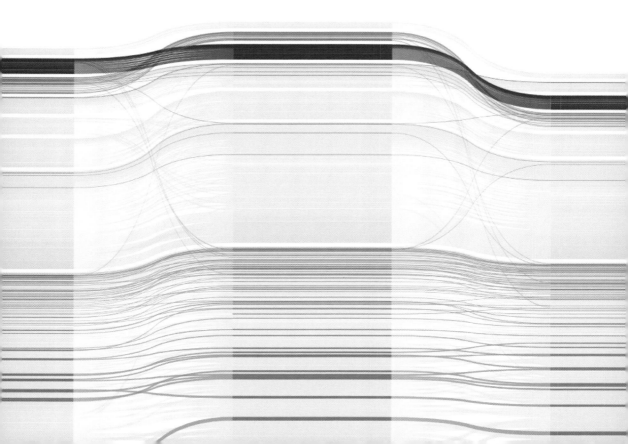

12

On Creativity and Innovation

Progress is not possible without deviation. It is important that people be aware of some of the creative ways in which some of their fellow men are deviating from the norm. In some instances, they might find these deviations inspiring and might suggest further deviations which might cause progress.

—Frank Zappa, http://tinyurl.com/ot37azm

Everything is "edgy" today; everyone's creative or an innovator or an innovative creator who thinks outside the box.

—William Deresiewicz, "Excellent Sheep"

In December 2014, I visited my University of Miami colleague **Dr. Vance Lemmon**, a distinguished professor in developmental neuroscience. Vance works at The Miami Project to Cure Paralysis,[1] one of the most important centers studying spinal cord injuries in the world. Vance also happens to be a visualization enthusiast and a friend.

---

1   Its website is: http://www.themiamiproject.org.

While we had lunch, Vance showed me several slides from one of his talks. He stopped on **Figure 12.1** and explained the image on the top left. It's a side view of the spinal cord of a rat. The left (green) portion is the side connected to the brain.

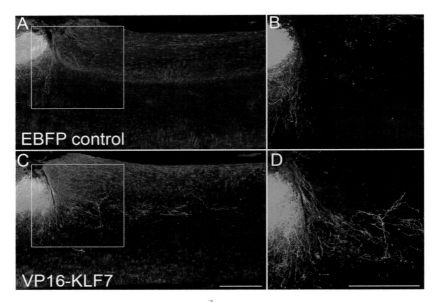

Figure 12.1 Visualizations of the spinal cord of a rat by The Miami Project to Cure Paralysis, from a paper published in PNAS: http://tinyurl.com/qa4yj94.

The spinal cord's main function is to serve as a two-way information conduit between the brain and the rest of the body. The nervous system is made up of many different kinds of cells, but the main ones are neurons, tree-like cells that communicate with each other through branches that protrude from their cell bodies. There are two kind of branches, axons and dendrites. If you damage or sever the axons—the green lines on Figure 12.1—that run through the spinal cord, you provoke paralysis.

Vance's lab uses gene therapy to stimulate axon regeneration. They insert viruses inside the brains of rats and mice whose spinal cords have been cut. These viruses are modified to carry different kinds of genetic materials and to target nerve cells.

When a virus attaches to a neuron, it inserts its genes into the cell's genome. Researchers at Vance's lab have tested different combinations of genes and discovered that some of them seem to trigger axon regeneration. Neurons stimulated in this way could potentially restore the connection between the brain and the rest of the body.

Images A and B in Figure 12.1 show the connections before gene therapy. Images C and D show them after the therapy. When I compared them, I exclaimed, "Whoa, that's a lot of new connections!"

Vance replied (and I'm not quoting him verbatim): "It looks impressive, doesn't it? The problem is that there aren't really a lot of new axons. It just looks like that because axons and dendrites aren't perfectly straight. They fold and twist, so to an untrained eye it seems that the therapy has unleashed an enormous growth. Results of these experiments are very promising, but not as promising as the images may suggest to you.

"To the untrained eye." Let's keep that in mind.

||||█|█|██■|||

On September 18, 2015, the Pew Research Center published the results of a survey about the knowledge that Americans have about science. The center asked questions on physics, chemistry, earth sciences, and so on. One included a scatter plot comparing the sugar consumption per capita with the number of decayed teeth per person in several countries. The chart shows that the more sugar people put in their mouths, the more likely they are to get cavities.

Among the respondents, 63 percent got the message of the chart right. Results were better for people with a college education (more than eight out of ten interpreted the plot correctly) and much worse for people with a high school diploma or less (half of them were able to understand the chart). See **Figure 12.2**.[2]

Is this bad news? I don't think so. It's excellent news. Had this same survey been conducted a couple of decades ago, my guess is that the percentage of people reading the scatter plot correctly would have been much smaller, particularly among those without advanced degrees. Why has this progress happened? I'd blame the media.

I took a course on data journalism and statistics in college. It covered basic correlation and regression, so it exposed me to scatter plots when I was in my twenties. Had that not been the case, where else could I have learned how to read a scatter plot? Perhaps in the newspaper.

---

2   "The art and science of the scatterplot," http://tinyurl.com/ogeaz3k.

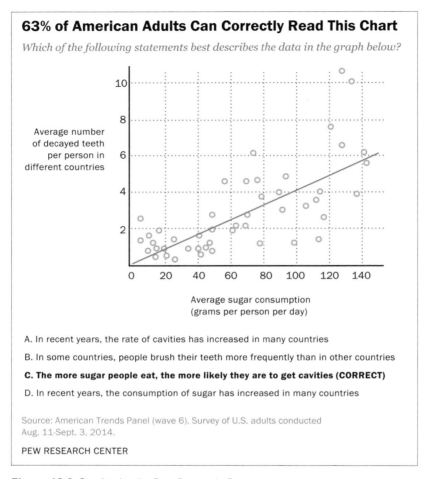

Figure 12.2 Graphic by the Pew Research Center.

I've been a newspaper reader since I was 8 years old. Up until the late 1990s, I don't remember seeing a single scatter plot in the publications I read on a regular basis. The situation was similar in online media. News designers and journalists stuck to graphic forms most of us learn in elementary school, such as the bar chart, the time-series chart, and the pie chart. That was about it.

But at some point, and I don't really know when, designers in news media took the scatter plot out of the realms of science and statistics and began using it, showing it to the general public. The first time, they probably left a huge portion of their readership puzzled. The second time, this portion would have been smaller. **Some readers' eyes would have been trained already**.

Many journalists and designers believe that any visualization should be understood in the blink of an eye. That's a mistake. Visualization has a grammar and a vocabulary.[3] Visualization is not meant just to be *seen*, as I've already pointed out in this book, but to be *read*, like written text.

It is true that you may confuse part of your audience the first time you show them an unusual chart. But if that chart is really needed, you should not refrain from using it just because of that.

We journalists and designers tend to believe that our readers are sillier than we are, and the opposite is normally the case. Moreover, if we think that many readers won't understand a specific graphic, we can always do what the *New-York Daily Tribune*, a 19th-century newspaper, did in 1849 (**Figure 12.3**): offer an explanation. The *Tribune* editors needed a time-series chart to show cases of cholera week by week, but they guessed that many of their readers hadn't seen a line chart before. So they added a caption that explains how to read the chart. Go ahead, take a look at it. It only looks childish to you because you've seen line charts since you were a kid.

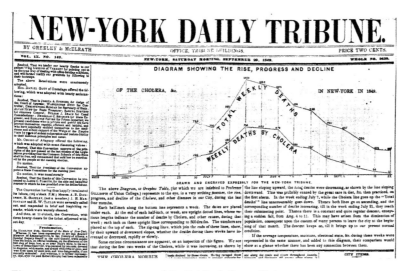

Figure 12.3 Image courtesy of ProPublica's Scott Klein.

---

3   It is not a coincidence that one of the best books about visualization is titled *The Grammar of Graphics* (Leland Wilkinson, 1999).

A good visualization isn't just a good choice of visual forms to display the data. The words you write to accompany it matter too. The folks at *The New York Times* graphics desk call this the **annotation layer**. Some annotation would have been really helpful for me when seeing Vance Lemmon's visualization of axons and dendrites. The words would have made up for my lack of pre-existing knowledge about what I was seeing.

Perhaps you're thinking that verbalizing how to read a simple chart is patronizing. It isn't. Assuming that your readers won't ever understand a scatter plot is. The same is true about many other graphic forms that are underused in news media, such as the histogram, the dot-and-whisker plot, and the ones that we'll still need to invent to tell compelling stories in the future.

The Popularizers

The purpose of this chapter is to pay tribute to the work of many people who I believe are popularizing, improving, and in some cases, trying to expand the vocabulary and grammar of graphics. We invent new words to refer to new phenomena. Why wouldn't we invent novel visual strategies to express ideas we couldn't fathom otherwise, or gently educate the public on how to read existing visualization forms?

An example of the latter is the work of the Pew Research Center itself, particularly its Fact Tank blog. Its designers aren't afraid of publishing scatter plots on a regular basis (**Figure 12.4** and **Figure 12.5**) or of asking their readers to stop for a few seconds to figure out a chart (**Figure 12.6**). Needless to say, if you request effort from your audience, you ought to be ready to deliver some worthwhile insight. I believe that these charts succeed in that respect.

Stephen Few, the person who has written most authoritatively about how to use visualization to analyze business data, is also well known for imagining new kinds of charts. My favorite is his **bullet graph**, invented in 2005.[4] You can see it on **Figure 12.7**.

---

4   You can read more about the bullet graph at Few's website, http://perceptualedge.com/. Here's an article about this kind of graphic: http://tinyurl.com/psacvvw.

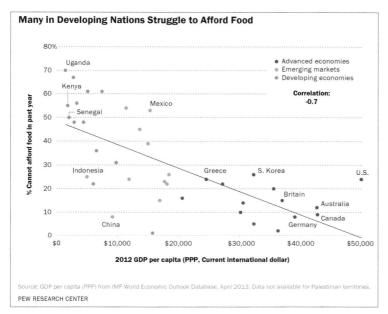

Figure 12.4 Graphic by the Pew Research Center: http://tinyurl.com/pp3bskp.

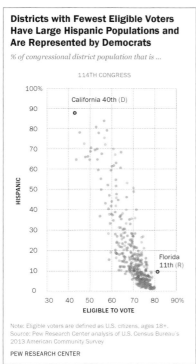

Figure 12.5 Graphic by the Pew Research Center: http://tinyurl.com/p36laaj.

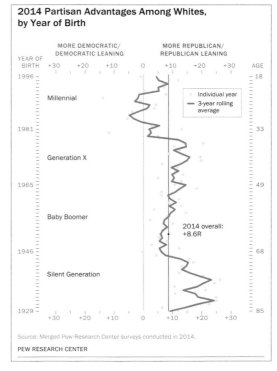

Figure 12.6 Graphic by the Pew Research Center: http://tinyurl.com/nbs8php.

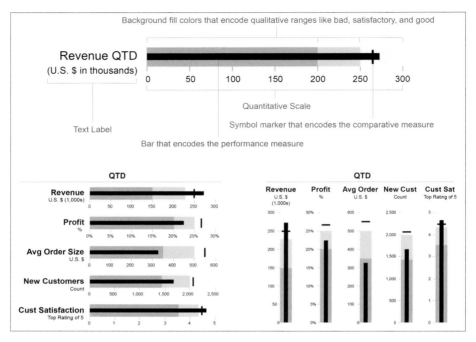

Figure 12.7 How to use bullet graphs. Graphic by Stephen Few: https://www.perceptualedge.com/articles/misc/Bullet_Graph_Design_Spec.pdf.

A bullet graph compares a metric—the black bar—to some sort of target or other measure, such as previous performance; that's the thin black line. Both objects are placed over background colors that represent ranges such as "bad," "average," and "excellent." The bullet graph condenses a large amount of data into a tiny space. Imagine trying to display all this information with a traditional bar chart. It'd be a cluttered mess.

If you're interested in expanding your horizons, the world of statistics can be a bottomless source of joy. As you've seen in this book, statisticians like William Cleveland, Naomi Robbins, Edward Tufte, John Tukey, Leland Wilkinson, and others have been tireless popularizers and innovators. Among my favorite charts coming from this realm is the **funnel plot**. We saw an example in Chapter 7, when we discovered that cancer rates are both highest and lowest in sparsely populated areas.

The funnel plot is a way to visualize the relationship between a variable and the population or sample size you're studying. The one on **Figure 12.8** was done by **Xan Gregg**, a computer engineer at SAS-JMP.

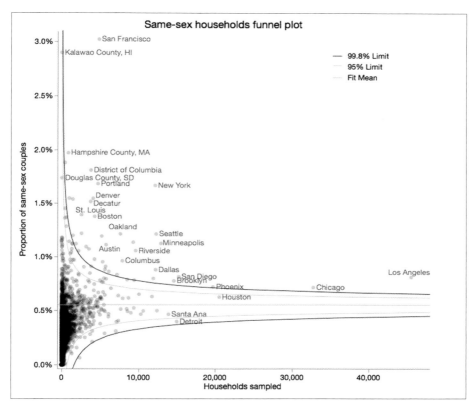

Figure 12.8 Chart by Xan Gregg. http://tinyurl.com/nb5uzpp.

In the article where this chart was published, Xan discusses a county-level map of same-sex couples by *The New York Times*.[5] The map showed the rates of same-sex couples per 1,000 people, and it was based on data adjusted by Gary Gates, a researcher at the University of California-Los Angeles' Charles R. Williams Institute on Sexual Orientation Law and Public Policy.

Xan was aware that population size was an important factor to explain the variation observed. Here's why:

> Douglas County, South Dakota, has one of the highest proportions of same-sex couples in the country at 17.4 per 1,000, while nearby Hanson County has the minimum of 0. Each of these counties has fewer than 1,500 households, and given the sampling rate of the American Community

5 "Graph Makeover: Where same-sex couples live in the U.S.": http://tinyurl.com/nb5uzpp.

Surve for South Dakota, we can estimate that fewer than 30 households were sampled in each county. So one same-sex couple in 30 respondents for Douglas County looks like a relatively large proportion even after Gates' adjustments. Meanwhile 0 same-sex couples in 30 looks like none for all of Hanson County.

In Xan's chart, the Y-axis is the percentage of same-sex couples, and the X-axis is the number of households sampled. As you can see, the smaller the sample, the larger the variation of the percentage is. It is quite obvious why this happens: if you sample just ten couples, and only one of them is a same-sex couple, you'll get a rate of 10 percent.

I bet that you're tempted to claim that "my readers will never understand a chart like the funnel plot!"—to which I'd reply that you better hold your judgment. Many at the *New-York Daily Tribune* probably thought the same about time-series charts in 1849, and they still published one with an explanatory caption.

News Applications

When I began my career back in 1997, news graphics desks were made mostly of people coming from journalism, graphic design, and fine arts. Nowadays, some graphics desks don't even call themselves "graphics" desks anymore. They are "news applications" or "visuals" departments; they have computer scientists, statisticians, hackers, web designers and developers in their ranks; and they don't just produce charts, maps, and diagrams, but software tools as well. The world has changed for the better.

A good example is **NPR's Visuals team**.[6] Led by Brian Boyer, whom we met in Chapter 2, the team's output is consistently engrossing. NPR is also a pioneer of **responsive design** applied to visualization: its graphics automatically adapt to the size of the screen the reader is using. This is a common feature in many other organizations' work nowadays, but it wasn't when NPR started building visualizations this way, years ago.

The charts on **Figure 12.9** belong to a story about how automatization changes the job market, killing some professions and bringing up new ones. They were done by Quoctrung Bui, who works for NPR's "Planet Money" program in close collaboration with Brian's team.

---

6   Its blog is at http://blog.apps.npr.org.

Menus in this visualization let readers switch between percentages and total scores, or select a specific job and see how the Y-scale of the corresponding chart changes. Transitions are animated: when you navigate through jobs, the Y-scale adapts to the maximum and minimum scores displayed. **Animated transitions are preferable to abrupt ones**.

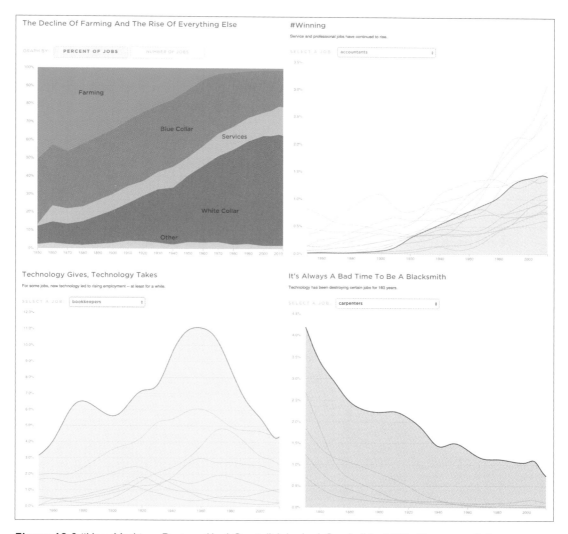

Figure 12.9 "How Machines Destroy (And Create!) Jobs, In 4 Graphs," by NPR's Quoctrung Bui; http://tinyurl.com/l4psdxj.

⁍

In the summer of 2014, I spent more than a month working with **ProPublica's News Applications team**. My goal was to collect data for a PhD dissertation that I'll need to write sooner or later (keep me in your prayers). In my notebook, I wrote that ProPublica's News Applications desk "is not a graphics desk with an interest in technology, but a technology team with an interest in graphics— among many more things." The team doesn't just make visualizations. They are not a service desk. They report stories, and do the writing, besides building searchable databases and interactive visualizations.

ProPublica's graphics are often deceptively simple, like **Figure 12.10**, by Eric Sagara and Charles Ornstein. This small, interactive array can get sorted from highest to lowest (click on "Last year") or alphabetically ("State"). As in the NPR graphic above, transitions are animated. The chart of the national average always remains on the upper-left corner, to make comparisons easier. The visualization is responsive too. Depending on the size of your device, a different number of charts will be placed on each row.

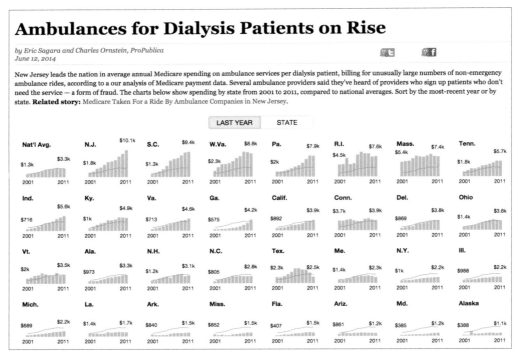

Figure 12.10 Visualization by ProPublica; https://projects.propublica.org/graphics/ambulances.

Figure 12.11, by Lena Groeger and Michael Grabell, is the result of an investigation about compensation for body damages suffered on the job. Each state in the United States has its own rules to decide how much money a worker would receive if she gets injured. Losing a pinky finger, for instance, would get you nearly $80,000 in Oregon, but just $2,000 in Massachusetts. I confess that I felt uneasy the first time I saw this visualization. I first thought that the decision of scaling the limbs in proportion to money was a risky one, as it makes the illustrations look creepy. But that may be appropriate. It's a creepy topic, after all.

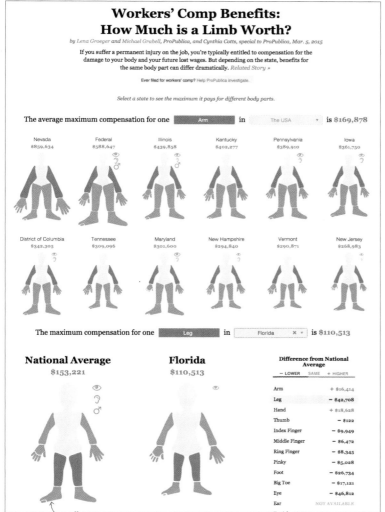

Figure 12.11
Visualization by ProPublica; https://projects.propublica.org/graphics/workers-compensation-benefits-by-limb.

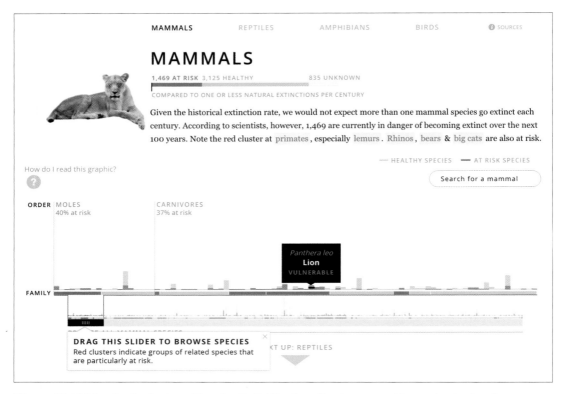

Figure 12.12 Visualization by Anna Flagg for ProPublica; http://projects.propublica.org/extinctions/.

ProPublica regularly collaborates with scientists and designers to develop their projects. **Figure 12.12**, a database of endangered species, was designed by Anna Flagg, a data journalist now working for Al Jazeera.[7] Notice how certain words in the intro copy are used as buttons, how elegantly arranged all elements are, and how carefully colors and fonts were chosen. Also, see the "how to read this graphic" question mark on the top left; when you hover over it, a window with a small explanation diagram pops up.

ProPublica has also experimented with what my University of Miami colleague and mentor **Rich Beckman** calls **interactive multimedia storytelling**.[8] In the

---

7   Her portfolio is at http://www.annaflagg.com.

8   Before coming to Miami, Rich was a professor at the School of Media and Journalism at the University of North Carolina-Chapel Hill (he hired me there in 2005; I stayed until the end of 2009.) Rich created the first coding and programming specialization ever offered in any U.S. journalism school.

past, news organizations used to publish all text on one side of the page (or of the screen) and videos, photos, and graphics on another side. But that hardly makes any sense. Isn't it much better to seamlessly integrate all elements of the story and make them refer to each other?

That's what **Figure 12.13** does. "Losing Ground," by Brian Jacobs and Al Shaw, is a project about how Louisiana's coast is changing due to rising sea levels. As the intro to the project says, "The state is losing a football field of land every 48 minutes—16 square miles a year."

Figure 12.13 Multimedia project by ProPublica; http://projects.propublica.org/louisiana/.

⫿⫿⫿⫿⫿⫿⫿⫿

I am going to ask you something. I want you to quickly say what comes to your mind without giving the question any conscious thinking. OK, here it comes: What is the news organization that produces the best visualizations and infographics in the world? I bet that many of you chose *The New York Times*.

That's not surprising. In the past couple of decades, the *Times* graphics desk, first under the leadership of **Charles Blow** (until 2004) and then with **Steve Duenes**, has become the main inspiration for visualization designers worldwide, and not just those interested in journalism. It's a very large department that produces lots of excellent projects.

Most *Times'* visualizations strike the balance between being engaging, readable, and deep. See **Figure 12.14**, by Mike Bostock, Matt Ericson, and Robert Gebeloff. A series of small multiple lattices are arranged as a linear narrative. Chart titles highlight relevant data points ("…While payroll taxes have risen for all—but not as much for the affluent") helping readers grasp the gist of the story. In a news publication, this kind of title is preferable to the more aseptic style researchers favor, something like "Payroll tax variation between 1980 and 2010."

Figure 12.15, by Ford Fessenden and Mike Bostock, is also a data-driven story. Here, charts and maps fit naturally in between paragraphs of copy that comment on them and anticipate what readers will see. This project is richly layered: clicking on the maps of certain New York neighborhoods takes readers to a detailed explorable map of the entire city.

The *Times* also produces visualizations that put you, the reader, at the center of the stage. The first thing that you'll see when visiting **Figure 12.16**, by Josh Katz and Wilson Andrews, is a series of questions about how *you* pronounce various words, or about which terms *you* use to refer to different objects. The visualization then estimates where *you* were born. The predictive model behind this project is based on the Harvard Dialect Survey, by professors Bert Vaux and Scott Golder.

When you visit this visualization, notice that you don't need to answer the 25 questions to get results. Each time you make a choice, a little map on the left side of the screen gets updated. That kind of instant feedback is critical if you want to maintain your readers' attention.

(Incidentally, I replied to all questions, and the graphic told me that I am probably from Texas. I obviously wasn't born in the United States. I guess that this is close enough—I'm from A Coruña, Spain.)

How the Tax Burden Has Changed

Most Americans paid less in taxes in 2010 than people with the same inflation-adjusted incomes paid in 1980, because of cuts in federal income taxes. At lower income levels, however, much of the savings was offset by increases in federal payroll taxes, state sales taxes and local property taxes. About half of households making less than $25,000 saved nothing at all. About the Data » | Related Article »

$0-25k $25-50k $50-75k $75-100k $100-125k $125-150k $150-200k $200-350k $350k+

Tax rates have fallen for most Americans, especially high earners.
Share of yearly income paid in federal, state and local taxes, by income bracket.

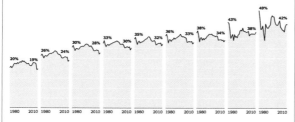

Average tax rates were lower for every income group in 2010 compared with 1980, but rates fluctuated during the intervening decades. Savings from federal income tax cuts in 1981 and 1986, under President Ronald Reagan, eroded as other taxes increased. New federal cuts in 2001 and 2003, under President George W. Bush, again reduced the total tax burden. Tax revenues rose in 2010 as the economy recovered from the recession.

What's driven the changes? Federal income tax rates have declined ...
Share of income paid in federal income taxes.

Federal income tax rates fell in the 1980s after decades of relative stability. The cuts were partly reversed in 1993 under President Bill Clinton, before rates fell again in the early 2000s. For households earning less than $25,000, the tax rate in recent years has been negative because the expansion of government payments like the earned income tax credit exceeded the amount of taxes paid.

... while payroll taxes have risen for all — but not as much for the affluent.
Share of income paid in federal payroll taxes.

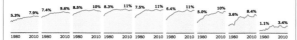

Payroll taxes finance Social Security and provide some financing for Medicare. The Medicare tax applies to all earnings at the same rate. But the Social Security tax applies only to earnings below a threshold, which stood at $106,800 in 2010. And neither tax applies to investment income. As a result, upper-income households pay a smaller share of income in payroll taxes.

State and local taxes have risen, most of all for the lowest income groups.
Share of income paid in property, sales and state income taxes.

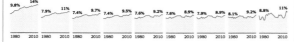

State and local governments impose the same property and sales tax rates on everyone without regard to income. Even after the housing crash, the rise in housing prices since 1980 has outpaced income growth for most households, increasing the burden of property taxes. And lower-income households spend a larger share of income than other households, incurring sales taxes.

And corporate taxes — ultimately paid by people — have declined.
Federal and state corporate tax burden, as a share of income.

Figure 12.14 Graphic by *The New York Times*, http://tinyurl.com/cxdgacu.

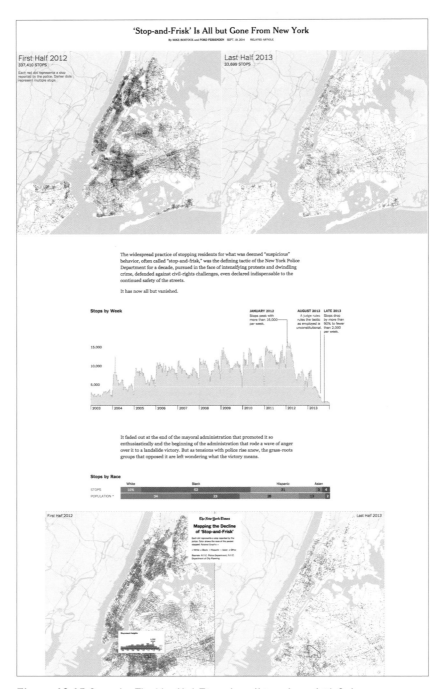

Figure 12.15 Story by *The New York Times*, http://tinyurl.com/qj4q2ol.

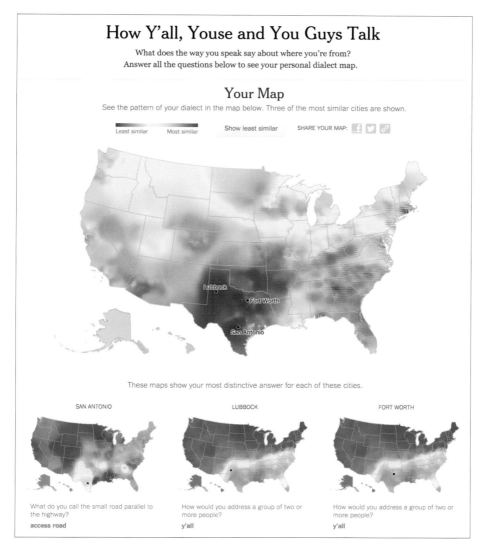

Figure 12.16 Interactive quiz by *The New York Times*, http://tinyurl.com/pke94a2.

The *Times* is keen on experimenting with charts and maps. **Figure 12.17** is a good example. It was designed by Amanda Cox, Mike Bostock, Derek Watkins, and Shan Carter, and it shows the results of the 2014 midterm elections on maps that look like watercolor paintings.

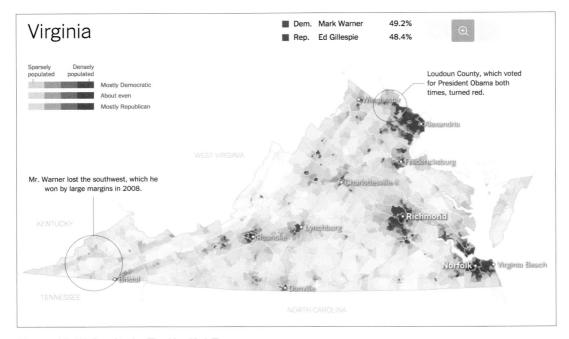

Figure 12.17 Graphic by *The New York Times*,
http://www.nytimes.com/interactive/2014/11/04/upshot/senate-maps.html.

What makes this project so different to many other choropleth maps is that the color scheme doesn't represent a single variable (political orientation) but two (political orientation and population density.) Bivariate scales aren't common in news publications right now, but they can come in handy.

‖‖▌▐█▌█▌‖‖‖

The New York Times' popularity sometimes eclipses astonishing work by other U.S. news organizations, such as *The Washington Post*, the *Boston Globe*, *National Geographic* magazine, or *The Wall Street Journal* (WSJ). This is unfortunate, as much can be learned from projects like **Figure 12.18**. This *WSJ* multi-chart display by Andrew Van Dam and Renee Lightner is an overview of trends in U.S. unemployment rates.

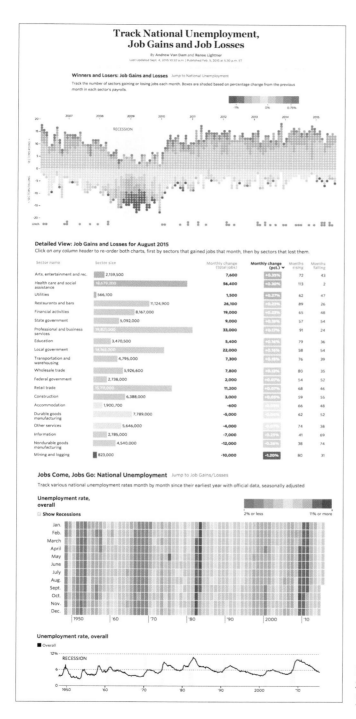

Figure 12.18 Visualization by *The Wall Street Journal*, http://graphics.wsj.com/job-market-tracker/.

Each dot on the top chart represents a sector in the economy. Notice that during the most recent recession, between 2008 and the middle of 2009, most sectors destroyed jobs. How many? Hues and shades represent percentage change from the previous month in each sector's payrolls. Underneath, a bar chart, a heat map, a time-series chart, and several filters add detail to the display.

The *Journal* is very fond of heat maps. **Figure 12.19**, by Tynan DeBold and Dov Friedman, is one that won deserved praise when it was published, as it persuasively reveals that vaccines work. The black line going across each chart, which corresponds to the moment when each vaccine was introduced, works as a sharp boundary. Before it, colors are intense and ominous, indicating a large incidence of each disease; after the line, diseases vanish.

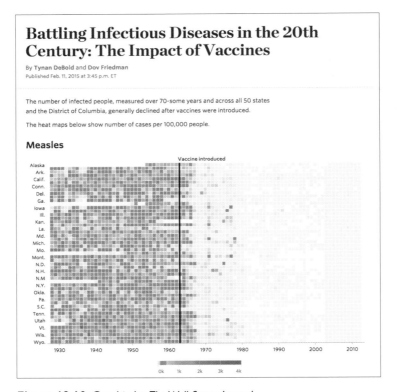

Figure 12.19: Graphic by *The Wall Street Journal*, http://graphics.wsj.com/infectious-diseases-and-vaccines/.

No visualization is ever perfect, and sometimes attentive readers will make time to propose improvements. **Valentine Svensson**, a mathematician at the European Bioinformatics Institute, argued that a time-series chart may be more appropriate to present the data, so he designed several charts like **Figure 12.20**.[9] I must confess that I felt torn when I compared the original *WSJ* chart with Svensson's. I like them both, and I'm not sure which one I'd choose if I were doing this project myself.

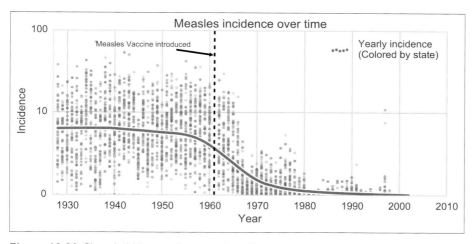

Figure 12.20 Chart by Valentine Svensson, http://tinyurl.com/qgpajgp.

Svensson's reaction is an expression of a trend that I hope will strengthen in the future. We're witnessing the rise of a culture of experimentation and innovation in visualization. That's great, but not enough. **A culture of experimentation needs to be accompanied by a culture of constructive criticism**. That's the point of a wonderful essay titled "Design and Redesign in Data Visualization," by **Fernanda Viégas** and **Martin Wattenberg**, visualization designers at Google, who wrote:

> Design is not a science. But "not a science" isn't the same as "completely subjective." In fact, the critique process has brought discipline to design for centuries. For visualizations which are based on an underlying shared data

---

9   Svensson wrote an entire article about this: "Modeling Measles in 20th Century US," http://tinyurl.com/qgpajgp.

set, there's an opportunity for an additional level of rigor: to demonstrate the value of a critique through a redesign based on the same data (...) Criticism through redesign may be one of the most powerful tools we have for moving the field of visualization forward. At the same time, it's not easy, and there are many pitfalls, intellectual, practical, and social.[10]

Fernanda and Martin happen to be two of the most innovative individuals out there. Their famous Wind Map (**Figure 12.21**) shows wind direction and strength in real time. **Figure 12.22** reveals the amounts of different colors in photos of the Boston Common park posted on Flickr. Whites and grays dominate during the fall and winter, and bright hues become common in the spring and summer. There's little very surprising about this, but how often have you seen the evidence for something you already guessed so beautifully expressed?

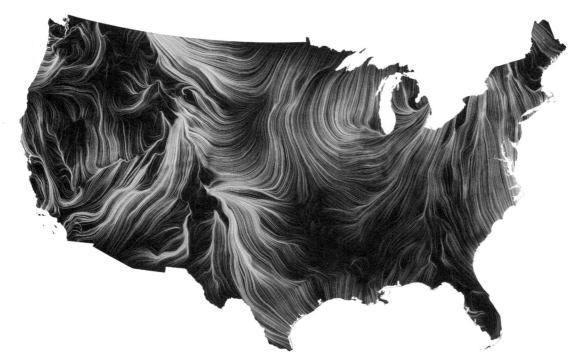

Figure 12.21 Fernanda Viégas and Martin Wattenberg's Wind Map, http://hint.fm/wind/.

10 The essay has appeared in multiple online publications. Here's one link: http://tinyurl.com/ozhpcjm.

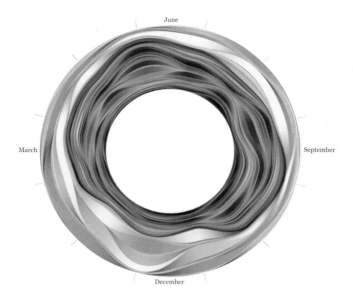

Figure 12.22 Flickr Flow, by Fernanda Viégas and Martin Wattenberg (annotations by Alberto Cairo), http://hint.fm/projects/flickr/.

In the past five years, several online-only news publications that heavily use infographics and data visualization have been launched. Among them, I'd like to single out **FiveThirtyEight.com**. FiveThirtyEight is led by Nate Silver, who became famous while writing about politics and sports at publications like Daily Kos, *Esquire*, and *The New York Times*.[11] Trained as a statistician, Silver predicted the outcomes of several elections with an accuracy rarely seen before in news media.

Figure 12.23 and **Figure 12.24** will give you an idea of the kind of visualizations FiveThirtyEight produces. The first one, by Allison McCann, is an example of the slightly edgy and geeky style that the publication favors. FiveThirtyEight's priority is clarity, but that doesn't make its designers refrain from having fun.

---

11   Before becoming a writer, Silver was already famous for PECOTA (Player Empirical Comparison and Optimization Test Algorithm), a system to predict baseball players' performance. He's also the author of a fine and popular book about statistics and data analysis, *The Signal and the Noise* (2012).

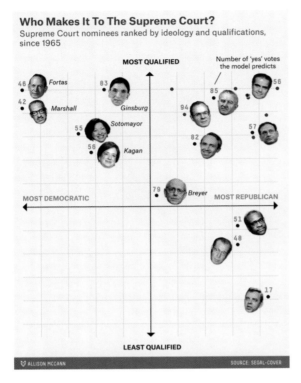

Who Makes It To The Supreme Court?
Supreme Court nominees ranked by ideology and qualifications, since 1965

Figure 12.23 Graphic
by FiveThirtyEight;
http://tinyurl.com/kryl27c.
Copyright © ESPN. Reprinted
with permission from ESPN.

Figure 12.24, by Aaron Bycoffe, is a very detailed story of the endorsements received by candidates to the Democratic and Republican presidential primaries since 1980. The Y-axis corresponds to the cumulative endorsement points each candidate received from one year before the Iowa caucuses until the party conventions.

These points are calculated based on the kind of endorsements each candidate receives. Here's the explanation provided in the story: "Not all endorsements are equally valuable. We use a simple weighting system: ten points for governors, five points for U.S. senators, and one point for U.S. representatives (there are roughly five times as many representatives as senators and ten times as many representatives as governors.)"

Hillary Clinton is the Democratic candidate who, historically, began with a larger amount of endorsements. One year before the Iowa caucuses, she already had almost 200 endorsement points. On the Republican side, most candidates began with almost no support at all.

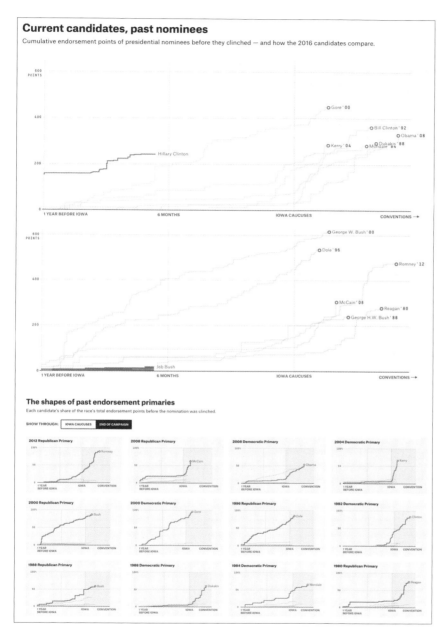

Figure 12.24 Graphic by FiveThirtyEight; http://tinyurl.com/nbzmqyc.
Copyright © ESPN. Reprinted with permission from ESPN.

Those Enchanting Europeans

In preceding chapters, I tried to include as many non-U.S. visualizations as possible. This one won't be an exception. We've already seen some work by **Zeit Online**. I'd like to show you another of their projects, **Figure 12.25**, which displays the opinion disparities that still exist between Germans living in the western part of the country, and those on the eastern regions who were under Soviet influence until the reunification of Germany in October 1990.

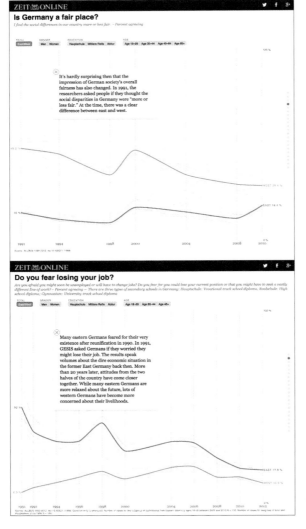

Figure 12.25 "Charting Germany," Christian Bangel, Julian Stahnke, Kim Albrecht, Paul Blickle, Sascha Venohr, Adrian Pohr. Zeit Online. http://zeit.de/charting-germany

The multiple time-series charts in this project reveal that Germans tend to think more alike than they did 25 years ago, but cultural differences persist, even when filtering by age and gender, something that readers can do using the menus on top.

Figure 12.26, by the **Berliner Morgenpost**, is another graceful example of the enduring power of traditional graphic forms, like the time-series line chart. It shows the increase in rent prices in Berlin. Each line is a zip code. Prices are in euros per square meter. The visualization can be navigated with the arrow keys on your keyboard, by hovering over the lines, or by searching for a zip code. In any case, whenever a line is highlighted, a little locator map shows where the zip code is.

The Morgenpost likes to experiment with combinations of various graphic forms. In **Figure 12.27**, a time-series chart serves as the slider to control a large heat map of measles cases per district in Berlin. Vaccination against measles isn't

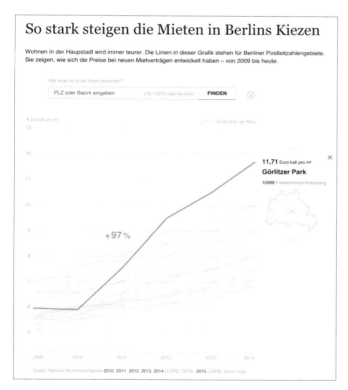

Figure 12.26 The stark increase of rental prices in Berlin.
Berliner Morgenpost: http://tinyurl.com/osfbefu.

compulsory in Germany, and the amount of parents who ignore all relevant science, and therefore refuse to have their children vaccinated, has increased in the past decade. Those factors have led to hundreds of new cases in 2015, and even the death of a baby.[12]

Figure 12.27 The spread of measles in Berlin's districts. Berliner Morgenpost: http://tinyurl.com/oejb4q7.

Maarten Lambrechts, a visualization designer and journalist from Diest, Belgium,[13] embodies a trend I've observed in the past decade: an increasing number of people with backgrounds in technical and scientific fields (Maarten is an engineer) have finally understood that journalism isn't just what newspapers or news magazines or broadcast TV do. Marteen became interested in visualization while working in Bolivia as an agricultural economist. Later on, almost by happenstance, he landed several jobs in journalism.

---

12 Deutsche Welle has a good summary of the 2015 epidemic, the worst in a decade: http://tinyurl.com/pvcm9fn.

13 http://www.maartenlambrechts.be

Maarten's most interesting projects focus on climate and weather patterns. The Y-axis on **Figure 12.28** is average monthly temperatures. Each line is a year between 1833 and 2014. There's much to explore on this chart, but the main take-away is that all years between 2005 and 2014 are way above the historical average.

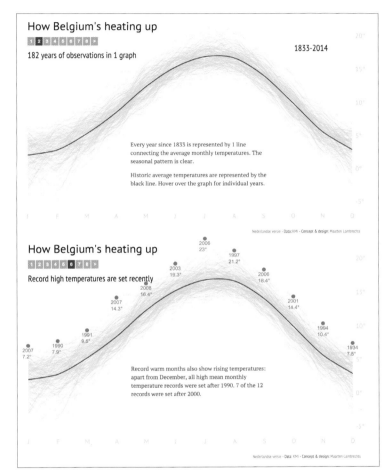

Figure 12.28 "How Belgium's Heating Up," by Maarten Lambrechts; http://www.maartenlambrechts.be/vis/warm2014/warm2014.html.

Figure 12.29 is an experimental visualization of weather data from Cairo and Singapore. You choose a date, and the graphic will show you temperature, rainfall, wind speed and direction, and cloud cover. Circular plots always make me feel nervous, but I'm fine with these. The one showing wind direction and strength makes a lot of sense; as for the others, I prefer plots based on straight axes—you can estimate proportions more efficiently—but I understand the design choice here, as the data is cyclical.

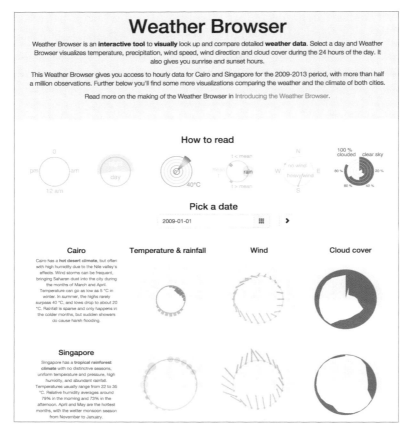

Figure 12.29 "The Weather Browser," by Maarten Lambrechts; http://www.maartenlambrechts.be/vis/weatherbrowser/. Read an explanation of how this project was done at http://www.maartenlambrechts.be/introducing-the-weather-browser/.

Making Science Visual

Many science magazines, both popular and specialized, produce wonderful graphics. Recently, *Science* magazine hired Alberto Cuadra, an experienced infographics designer from Spain,[14] and every issue of *Popular Science* contains at least one large display of data and visual explanation. *Scientific American* is also in that group.

---

14 http://www.acuadra.com

Scientific American's head of graphics is **Jen Christiansen**.[15] Trained as a natural science illustrator and art director, Jen has established collaborations with many of the most renowned infographics and data visualization designers in the field. **Figure 12.30**, done in collaboration with **Jan Willem Tulp**,[16] plots the confirmed exoplanets, as of September 2012.

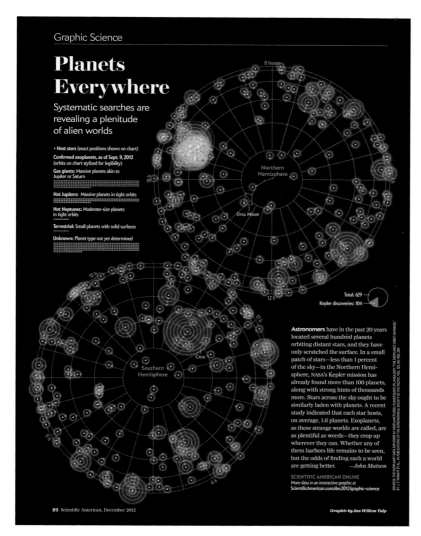

Figure 12.30 Graphic by Jan Willem Tulp for *Scientific American* magazine.

15 http://jenchristiansen.com
16 http://tulpinteractive.com

Moritz Stefaner[17] authored the intricate diagram on **Figure 12.31**, on the inter-actions between species of bees and plants. This is one of those graphics that requires a lot of effort on the part of the reader in exchange for a significant payoff (if you're into bees!).[18]

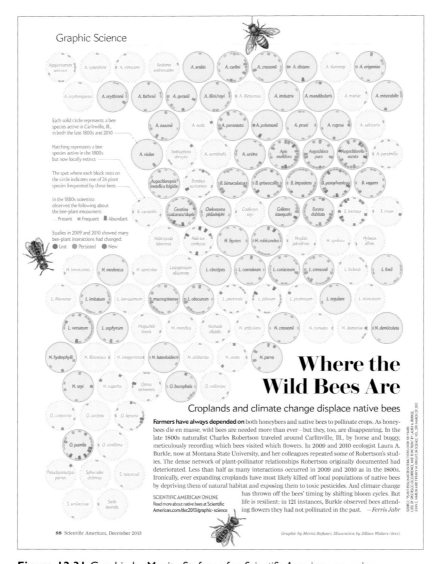

Figure 12.31 Graphic by Moritz Stefaner for *Scientific American* magazine.

---

17 http://truth-and-beauty.net
18 Moritz documented the bees project in this article: http://tinyurl.com/lot5l2e.

Scientific American has also partnered up with **Periscopic**,[19] a visualization firm based in Portland, Oregon. **Figure 12.32** is a part of a special issue about diversity in science. The graphic compares the percentage of PhDs awarded to men and women in more than 50 countries. It begins by showing you all PhDs aggregated; then you can use the menus and buttons above and below the graphic to sort the data in multiple ways and to see just specific PhD categories. For instance, compare "Math & Computer Science" to "Social & Behavioral." The disparity is glaring.

Figure 12.32 Visualization by Periscopic for *Scientific American*; http://tinyurl.com/qd4qvev.

19 http://www.periscopic.com

Culture Data

Visualization can also be used to explore realms that aren't usually thought of as amenable to quantification, such as literature or movies. Take **Figure 12.33**, which is part of a large interactive project titled Culturegraphy, by information designer **Kim Albrecht**.[20]

The project uses data from the Internet Movie Database (IMDB) to explore cross-movie references, when each movie is mentioned in another movie. Culture-graphy doesn't show all existing movies, just the 3,000 most connected ones. These references don't need to be explicit, by the way. If a movie borrows a line from another one, that's considered a reference, even without mentioning the movie title. "May the force be with you," a saying made famous in *Star Wars: A New Hope* (1977), also appears in movies like *Beverly Hills Cop II* (1987).

Jeff Clark, a data visualization designer who runs a company called Neoformix,[21] is the author of many graphics about cultural data. My favorites belong to a series called Novel Views (**Figure 12.34**), which visualizes Victor Hugo's *Les Miserables*.

One of the plots presents the characters by order of appearance and then shows the number of times their name is mentioned with bars of varying lengths. The mood of each chapter is represented through color: blue indicates the presence of words like "love" and "good," and red corresponds to a prevalence of words with negative connotations. Other diagrams in the series let Victor Hugo's fans see thematic connections between chapters.

---

20 http://www.kimalbrecht.com
21 http://neoformix.com

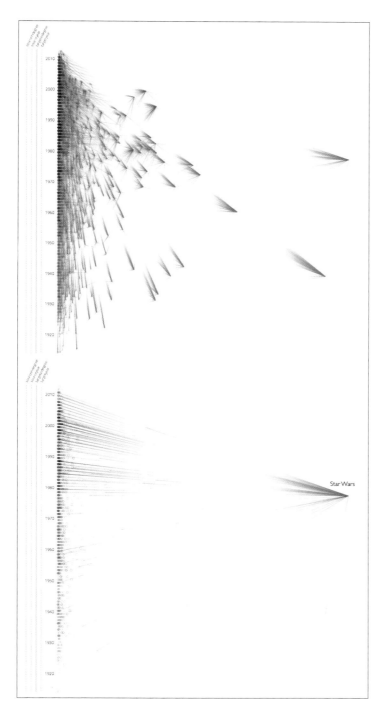

Figure 12.33 Culturegraphy:
http://www.culturegraphy.com/.

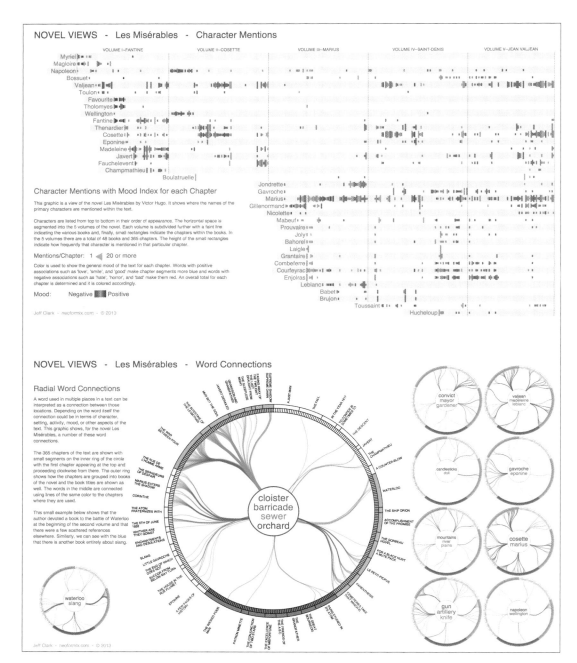

Figure 12.34 Novel Views, visualizing Victor Hugo's *Les Miserables*, by Jeff Clark; http://neoformix.com/2013/NovelViews.html.

The Artistic Fringes

The designers in this last section operate at the fringes between traditional data visualization—ruled by the capacities and constraints of human visual perception and cognition—and artistic expression. After reading so much in this book about appropriate and not-so-appropriate practices when presenting information visually, it may be a refreshing experience to visit a realm where those rules are stretched, bent, and sometimes broken.

Broken, yes, but rarely in a random manner. Creativity and innovation are hard work in all disciplines. Consider painters like Picasso or Jackson Pollock. Their most famous pieces, the ones that shattered conventions, came after they had spent decades mastering their craft, being inspired by those who preceded them, copying them, and following canonical rules. If you allow me the cliché, **you cannot think "out of the box" if you don't know really well what the inside of the box looks like.**

This said, there are people out there like **Giorgia Lupi**. Giorgia is the main driving force behind the visualization firm **Accurat** (www.accurat.it), which has won worldwide recognition for works like **Figure 12.35**.

This graphic compares the number of pages each atlas of world history devotes to each time period (upper timeline of each section) with an actual timeline in which centuries are equally spaced. The *De Agostini Atlas of World History* devotes half of its pages to modern and contemporary history (from 1500 onward), while the *Garzanti Atlas of World History* uses two-thirds of its pages for the same purpose. Vertical color bars indicate space allocated to different topics.

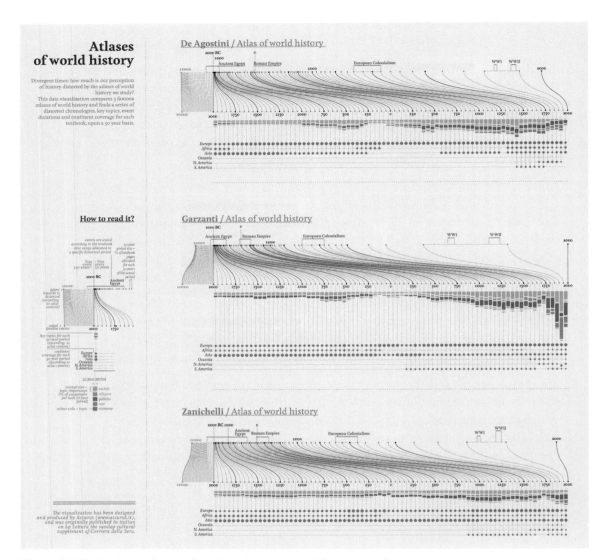

Figure 12.35 Graphic by Accurat; http://visual.ly/atlases-world-history-english.

Giorgia is an accomplished artist, as her delicate sketches (**Figure 12.36**) prove. Many of her most personal visualizations are devoted to the study of art, history, and literature. **Figure 12.37** chronicles the lives of 90 famous painters. Don't feel overwhelmed by the amount of information included. Spend some time reading the key and then enjoy the experience. Remember: these graphics are not intended to be understood in just one quick glance.

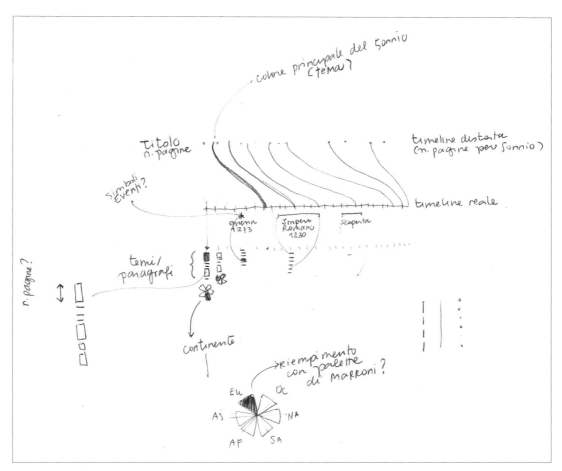

Figure 12.36 Sketches by Accurat's Giorgia Lupi.

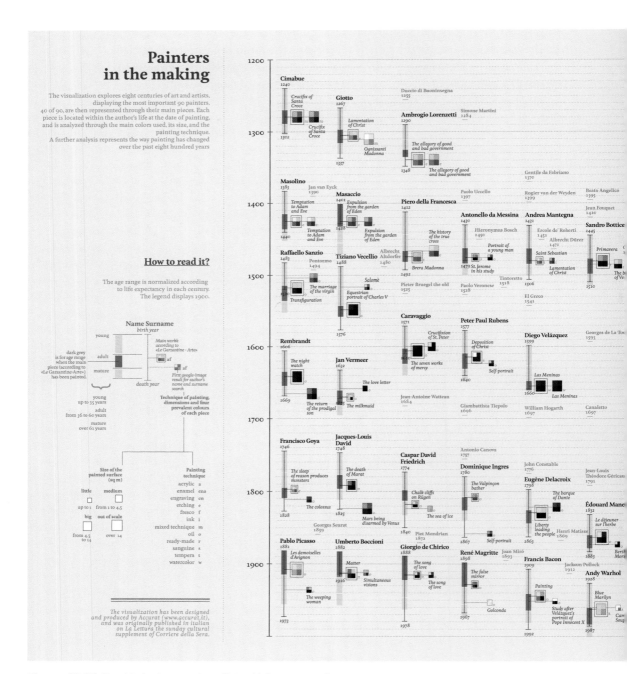

Figure 12.37 Graphic by Accurat; http://visual.ly/painters-making.

How does the way of painting change over the centuries?

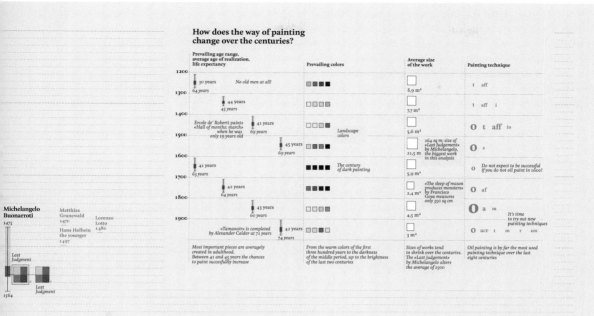

Prevailing age range, average age of realization, life expectancy	Prevailing colors	Average size of the work	Painting technique
1200 — 30 years *No old men at all!* 64 years		8.9 m²	t aff
1300 — 44 years 45 years		7.7 m²	t aff i
1400 — *Ercole de' Roberti paints «Hall of months: march» when he was only 19 years old* — 41 years 69 years	*Landscape colors*	5.6 m²	O t aff in
1500 — 45 years 69 years		21.5 m² *164 sq m: size of «Last Judgement» by Michelangelo, the biggest work in this analysis*	O s
1600 — 41 years 63 years	*The century of dark painting*	5.9 m²	o *Do not expect to be successful if you do not oil paint in 1600!*
1700 — 42 years 64 years		2.4 m² *«The sleep of reason produces monsters» by Francisco Goya measures only 350 sq cm*	O af
1800 — 43 years 60 years		4.5 m²	O a m *It's time to try out new painting techniques*
1900 — *«Tamanoir» is completed by Alexander Calder at 71 years* — 42 years 74 years		3 m²	O acr r sm

Most important pieces are averagely created in adulthood. Between 41 and 45 years the chances to paint successfully increase

From the warm colors of the first three hundred years to the darkness of the middle period, up to the brightness of the last two centuries

Sizes of works tend to shrink over the centuries. The «Last Judgement» by Michelangelo alters the average of 1500

Oil painting is by far the most used painting technique over the last eight centuries

Michelangelo Buonarroti
1475

Last Judgment

1564

Matthias Grunewald 1470

Hans Holbein the younger 1497

Lorenzo Lotto 1480

Last Judgment

800 years, 90 painters,
360 shades of color,
660 sq m of painted surface,
12 types of painting techniques

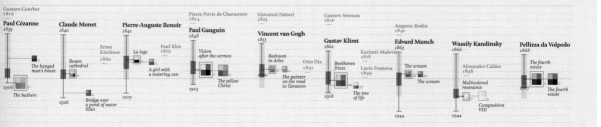

Gustave Courbet 1819

Paul Cézanne 1839

The hanged man's house

1906

The bathers

Claude Monet 1840

Rouen cathedral

1926

Ernst Kirchner 1880

Bridge over a pond of water lilies

Pierre-Auguste Renoir 1841

La loge

1919

Paul Klee 1879

A girl with a watering can

Pierre Puvis de Chavannes 1824

Paul Gauguin 1848

Vision after the sermon

1903

The yellow Christ

Giovanni Fattori 1825

Vincent van Gogh 1853

Bedroom in Arles

1890

The painter on the road to Tarascon

Otto Dix 1891

Gustave Moreau 1826

Gustav Klimt 1862

Beethoven frieze

1918

The tree of life

Kazimir Malevic 1878

Lucio Fontana 1899

Auguste Rodin 1840

Edvard Munch 1863

The scream

The scream

1944

Alexander Calder 1898

Multicolored resonance

1944

Composition VIII

Wassily Kandinsky 1866

Pellizza da Volpedo 1868

The fourth estate

1907

The fourth estate

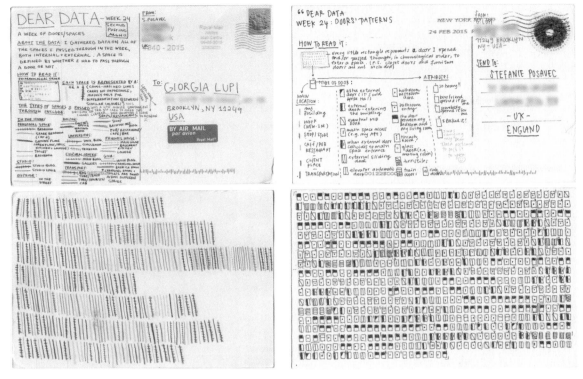

Figure 12.38 Postcards from the "Dear Data" project, by Stefanie Posavec and Giorgia Lupi; http://www.dear-data.com/.

During 2014 and 2015, Giorgia partnered up with another data artist, **Stefanie Posavec**,[22] to launch **Dear Data**,[23] a project described by both authors as "Two women who switched continents to get to know each other through the data they draw and send across the pond."

This lovely initiative began with two ladies who have only met twice in person—Giorgia lives in New York and Stefanie lives in London—and who share an interest in doing art with numbers. Each began collecting data about their daily lives. Based on that personal research, they drew a weekly postcard-sized, hand-drawn visualization like **Figure 12.38** for 52 weeks.

---

22 Stefanie's website is http://www.stefanieposavec.co.uk. I interviewed her for my previous book, *The Functional Art*.

23 The project's website is http://www.dear-data.com/.

Mathematician, designer, and coder **Santiago Ortiz** is one of the most forward-thinking minds in visualization. The projects in his portfolio are sometimes genial, sometimes bizarre and crazy, but always suggestive[24]. Something similar can be said of New York-based artist **Jer Thorp**[25], who has been hailed as "the man who makes data beautiful."[26]

To an orthodox journalist and graphics designer like me, Santiago's (**Figure 12.39**) and Jer's (**Figure 12.40**) visualizations often look perplexing, risky, and even incomprehensible, but I also believe that it is in those features that their true value resides. They are experiments. Many of their experiments will fail, but a handful of them will inevitably stick.

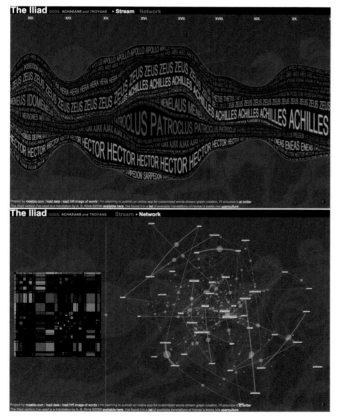

Figure 12.39 *The Iliad*, visualized by Santiago Ortiz; http://moebio.com/iliad/.

24 http://moebio.com
25 http://blog.blprnt.com
26 "This Man Makes Data Look Beautiful," http://tinyurl.com/nmeb4cj.

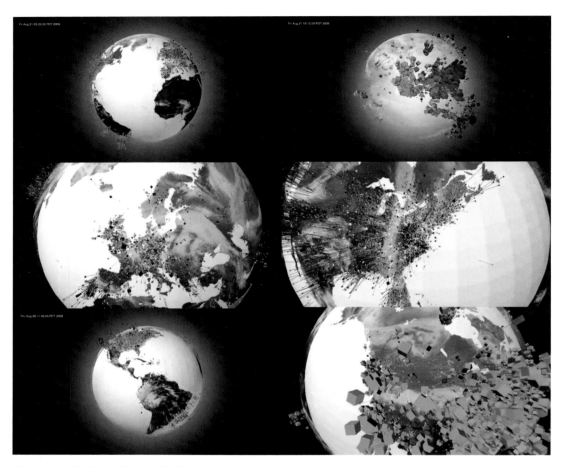

Figure 12.40 "GoodMorning!" a Twitter visualization that shows about 11,000 "good morning" tweets over a 24-hour period, by Jer Thorp; http://blog.blprnt.com/blog/blprnt/goodmorning.

It is a common pattern in history to see the scandalous become routine, and, as J. R. R. Tolkien wrote in *The Lord of the Rings*, "not all those who wander are lost." In this world, I am willing to argue, we need both sedentary dwellers and nomadic wanderers. The former keep our collective Island of Knowledge safe and dry. The latter strive to expand its shorelines, always looking at a horizon of promise far away, beyond the perilous Sea of Mystery.

Epilogue

What Lies Ahead

That's it. I've run out of pages! I am sorry to end *The Truthful Art* in a cliffhanger—if that's even possible in a book about communication, journalism, data, and visualization. I owe you an explanation.

Whenever I write and teach, the audience I have in mind is myself a decade ago. I like to write and teach in a way that would have helped my past self avoid years of mistakes, detours, dead ends, sweat, and headaches. I write books I wish I could have read then. Unfortunately, the amount of things I was ignorant about in my thirties was too large to fit inside a single volume. Therefore, I decided to split it up into two. *The Truthful Art* outlines some fundamentals of visualization for exploration and presentation. The following one, *The Insightful Art*, which I'll begin writing right away with the goal of publishing it in 2019, will cover topics I hinted at in Chapter 12. For instance:

1. Visual design: type, color, composition, interaction, etc.

2. Writing effective copy.

3. Narrative and storytelling.

4. Visualization for mobile platforms.

5. Animated visualization and motion infographics.

I hope you'll bear with me until then. I'll do my best to make the wait worth it.

Index